GOODBYE TO RUSSIA

GOODBYE TO RUSSIA

A Personal Reckoning from the Ruins of War

Sarah Rainsford

BLOOMSBURY PUBLISHING
LONDON · OXFORD · NEW YORK · NEW DELHI · SYDNEY

BLOOMSBURY PUBLISHING
Bloomsbury Publishing Plc
50 Bedford Square, London, WC1B 3DP, UK
29 Earlsfort Terrace, Dublin 2, Ireland

BLOOMSBURY, BLOOMSBURY PUBLISHING and the Diana logo are
trademarks of Bloomsbury Publishing Plc

First published in Great Britain 2024

Copyright © Sarah Rainsford, 2024

Sarah Rainsford is identified as the author of this work in accordance
with the Copyright, Designs and Patents Act 1988.

Some names and details of individuals have been changed to preserve their anonymity.
All rights reserved. No part of this publication may be reproduced or transmitted
in any form or by any means, electronic or mechanical, including photocopying,
recording, or any information storage or retrieval system, without prior
permission in writing from the publishers

Bloomsbury Publishing Plc does not have any control over, or responsibility for,
any third-party websites referred to in this book. All internet addresses given in this
book were correct at the time of going to press. The author and publisher regret any
inconvenience caused if addresses have changed or sites have ceased to exist,
but can accept no responsibility for any such changes

A catalogue record for this book is available from the British Library

ISBN: HB: 978-1-5266-7036-6; TPB: 978-1-5266-7035-9; EBOOK: 978-1-5266-7034-2;
EPDF: 978-1-5266-7033-5

2 4 6 8 10 9 7 5 3 1

Typeset by Newgen KnowledgeWorks Pvt. Ltd., Chennai, India
Printed and bound in Great Britain by CPI Group (UK) Ltd, Croydon CR0 4YY

To find out more about our authors and books visit www.bloomsbury.com
and sign up for our newsletters

For my parents

Contents

We Are at War ... 1

PART I
A Killing by the Kremlin ... 13
Bucha ... 27

PART II
Security Threat ... 35
Moscow, January–June 1992
A Russian Education ... 43
Protest ... 53
Slava ... 57
The Moskva ... 61
Delayed Expulsion ... 63

PART III
'V' ... 73
Fallen Statues ... 79
Poisoned ... 83
Enemy of the People ... 93
Vera Golubeva ... 97
We Can't Stop or They Win ... 99
The Railway Station ... 107

PART IV

I'm Not the Enemy	113
St Petersburg, 1994–1995	
Window on the West	121
The Shamrock	125
Royal *Britannia*	131
Russia Obsessive, Unemployed	135
Expelled	137

PART V

Bodies	145
Russia 2000–2005	
The *Kursk*	153
A Reporter	161
School No. 1	169
Please Don't Judge	179
Journalists Should Die Old	185

PART VI

Tarusa	195
Under Surveillance	199
A Spy Story	205
Journalism is Not a Crime	219
Tarusa	221

PART VII

Ukraine's Missing Children	229
The Undesirable Activist	235
The Summer of Protest	247
Blame the Russian Federation for my Death	253
Stay Human, Please	261
War Criminal	265
Mugs	269

PART VIII

Last Days — 275
The Final Battle — 283
Goodbye to Anna — 291
Swan Lake — 295
When the Crab Whistles on the Hill — 301

PART IX

Truth on Trial — 307
Liquidating Memory — 315
Hostages — 321
Freedom Costs Dearly — 325

Epilogue: The Ruins — 335

Bibliography — 347
Acknowledgements — 349
Index — 353

'It is really tragic ... that it took a large-scale war in the middle of Europe ... for most Western leaders to finally open their eyes to the true nature of this regime.'

Vladimir Kara-Murza, August 2022

We Are at War

KRAMATORSK, UKRAINE, 24 FEBRUARY 2022

On the day Russia invaded Ukraine I was woken just before 05:00 by the thud of explosions. For weeks I had believed that Vladimir Putin would not launch the all-out war I could now hear outside my window in Kramatorsk, eastern Ukraine, because nothing good could possibly come of it. I reasoned that his intelligence agents must surely be telling Putin what I had seen for myself: that Ukrainians would greet Russian troops with Molotov cocktails, not cheers and flowers. But either Putin didn't know that, or he didn't care, because his military were now bombing targets across Ukraine and his tanks were rolling towards Kyiv.

US intelligence had been warning for weeks that an invasion was imminent. Tens of thousands of Russian troops were amassed on Ukraine's border and, each day, newspapers across the world would print new maps with little arrows, showing where forces were being sent and how they might attack. Some dismissed the military build-up as coercive diplomacy: when Putin did the same the previous spring it got him a summit with Joe Biden. Even Volodymyr Zelensky was playing down the threat. In late January 2022 we were called to the presidential palace in Kyiv, where Zelensky lashed out at Western embassies for evacuating their diplomats. When we pressed him about the danger of an invasion, he was evasive. Russian aggression had been a daily reality for Ukraine for years, Zelensky stressed. There was no need for panic.

In Kyiv some were following instructions posted online and preparing grab bags in case they had to flee in a hurry, but there was no mass exodus. One day I watched hundreds of women learning wartime self-defence, with a whole session on what to do if Russian soldiers broke into their flats. One tip was to stuff a handkerchief full of coins and whack them. The very notion of enemy troops entering Ukraine's capital seemed so far-fetched then, there were lots of giggles. Another weekend, we headed for the woods outside Kyiv to film men and women, some quite elderly, training to join territorial defence units. A few were doing drills using guns cut out of plywood because there weren't enough real weapons to go around. Everyone was focused, giving their all, but the idea that Kyiv would need defending by these people still felt absurd.

Some sources had named 16 February as invasion day. That morning my team zig-zagged across Ukraine with Zelensky as he visited the troops on a morale-boosting tour. From military exercises near the Belarusian border we travelled to Mariupol, the port city that would soon be under siege. For two days we skirted low over the treetops on helicopters, sailed out into the Black Sea, then ran through trenches to front-line positions. There had been shelling that morning, but Zelensky defied his security advisers to go there anyway, and we followed.

It was 21 February when I began to believe that Putin would actually order an invasion. I was in the hotel gym in Kyiv as he convened his Security Council in Moscow, sitting behind a desk with his top officials arranged far away on chairs like schoolchildren. He was preparing to give formal recognition to Russia's two puppet states in eastern Ukraine, the Donetsk and Luhansk People's Republics, known by their Russian acronyms DNR and LNR. It was a move that he'd resisted for years. Now Putin called his team to the podium to voice public support for the landgrab, one by one.

Diary entry, Kyiv, 21 February 2022

I leave the gym and tell the man at reception, 'I'm going mad watching Moscow!' He looks blank. 'Putin,' I say. 'He's carving up your country!' He looks back at me. 'Have a nice evening, madam.' I scuttle off.

Perhaps the receptionist didn't realise it yet, but for Putin this was a critical move. The man who loves to say he's playing by the rules, even as he twists them grotesquely, was building up his justification for war. Right after that meeting the Kremlin clarified that the DNR and LNR 'republics' covered the entirety of the Donetsk and Luhansk regions of the eastern Donbas, not the much smaller occupied parts. It was a disturbing escalation. I began drawing up new *will-he, won't-he* columns in my notebook, only this time I wasn't calculating whether Putin would invade. It was to decide whether he'd stop at the Donbas or push further. Kramatorsk would be a prime spot to seize either way.

Our train east crossed a landscape that matched the stripes of Ukraine's flag, mile upon mile of pale yellow fields rising towards a blue sky. In Kramatorsk, bridges and lampposts were daubed with the same colours, a reminder of where loyalties lay. That evening a choir in national costume performed patriotic songs in the central square. Many who gathered to watch, families and children, wrapped themselves in the flag as they sang the Ukrainian anthem. In a radio interview that night I described the defiant mood, including the man who told me he would 'stay until the shells fly'. He and his friends were Russian speakers but they did not want to join Russia. I told the *Newshour* presenter that people were mostly staying put. 'Until they see the danger face to face I don't think they're quite prepared to leave.' Streets were busy, restaurants full and flower shops open. But people were scared. 'We don't know where Putin will stop.'

It was just before midnight when I saw an announcement from the Kremlin. The newly recognised DNR and LNR had now written to Putin requesting help to 'repel Ukrainian aggression'. Alone and sleepless in my hotel room, I felt sick. *I think this is it. Every step is in place*, I messaged a colleague, who called me back with calming words and reassurance. I then pulled my flak jacket out of its bag and went back to scouring the internet. The theatrical decor of my room in the Comfort Park Hotel, with pictures of necking swans and a draped sateen canopy over the bed, added to my sense of unreality as I lay contemplating what Putin was about to unleash. Five months later, the hotel would be destroyed in a Russian missile strike.

When Zelensky posted a video on Facebook appealing directly to the Russian people to stop the war, he must have known it was hopeless. It was the last speech he would make in a suit and tie, as a peacetime president. He revealed that he had made a phone call to Putin in the Kremlin. 'The result was silence.' Switching to Russian, the language he'd spoken all his life, Zelensky told Russians not to believe the lies they were fed by their own leader. 'The Ukrainian people want peace,' he insisted. 'But if you attack us and try to take our country, our freedom … we will defend ourselves. You will see our faces, not our backs.'

Diary entry, Kramatorsk, 24 February 2022

00:38: I'm lying in my jeans. I have a bag next to the door with random stuff crammed in, in case I have to run. All my kit is charging. Flak jacket propped against the door. I can't sleep. My phone is full of tweets and WhatsApp messages declaring that: 'War will start at 04:00 local.' One said 01:00, but that came and went. Someone from the *Today* prog in Kyiv thought he could hear distant thuds and asked on the group chat. No one answered.

Just as I was drifting off to sleep, Russia fired its first missiles across the border. I fumbled to find a livestream of Russian state TV on my phone, my fingers suddenly useless. Then Putin appeared on the screen declaring what he was calling a 'Special Military Operation' to liberate Ukraine. With the sound of explosions in the distance, I tried to balance the phone on the side of the sink, convinced for some reason that I needed to brush my teeth before covering any war. But my hands were shaking and Putin's snarling face kept sliding to the bathroom floor. I wasn't so much scared of the bombs at that point. I was more shocked that Russia had really done it and because I knew that the war Putin never needed to launch would be bloody and terrible.

I also felt the beginnings of a sense of shame that's harder to explain. Russia was not my country but I'd spent almost a third of my life there, on and off, since arriving as a student-teacher just after the USSR fell apart. I'd developed deep affection for the country, its language and people. Now Russia had launched an unprovoked invasion that would leave tens of thousands dead, force millions from their homes, and people I knew well would go on to justify that. Reporting on this war was like covering no other conflict for me. My shame was mixed with revulsion.

It wasn't like I didn't know what Putin was capable of. As a BBC journalist, I'd covered his rule from the very start in 2000: the rise of the 'grey man' from the FSB intelligence service. I'd seen him chip away at every last institution of democracy, every vestige of freedom. He had steadily removed all the checks on his power, silencing the free press, crushing political opponents and outlawing protest. I'd seen him take control of TV channels so that they now pumped propaganda into Russian homes about a 'hostile' West and 'Nazi' Ukraine. I'd also watched Putin convince Russians that he'd raised their country 'from its knees' to make it a force to reckon with again on the global stage. It was a narrative of recovery that became one of aggression. Perhaps such talk was born out of Putin's own sense of hurt and humiliation at the Soviet collapse, but it triggered something deep within many Russians and they approved.

Then, in August 2021, six months before Russia went to war, I was expelled as a 'threat to national security'. I was being forced out of my adopted home and barred from returning indefinitely, singled out as hostile, like so many of the Russians I'd reported on who had dared to challenge or criticise. My expulsion was a signal to the Western press pack in Moscow that we were no longer off-limits. A year into the war, Russia drove that point home far more forcefully when it arrested Evan Gershkovich, a *Wall Street Journal* correspondent, on a patently false charge of espionage. There was an exodus of foreign journalists who suddenly realised that any one of them could be next.

I began this book before the war, in my enforced exile. It started as the story of Russia's slide from democracy told through the lives of those I'd met along the way. I saw it as a lament for a Russia lost, and a warning of where the crushing of liberties could lead. But by ordering the full-scale invasion of Ukraine, Putin moved faster than my worst fears.

Vladimir Putin's war on Ukraine began long before 24 February 2022. It was launched in 2014 when he annexed Crimea illegally, using covert Russian troops with the markings removed from their uniform. Russia then kindled unrest in the east of the country, determined to thwart Ukraine's aspirations of joining the EU and NATO, to stop it slipping from Moscow's grasp. Back then, Russia claimed the fighting in the Donbas region was internal – a civil war. When Russian troops were captured by Ukrainian forces, officials in Moscow would smirk that they were there as volunteers, 'on holiday'. But in 2022 Putin was hiding nothing. He openly ordered Russian forces across the border, claiming that 'Nazi' Ukrainians were committing genocide and Russian speakers needed protection. It was a lie delivered with such conviction, perhaps he even believed it.

In 2014 it was the start of war in Ukraine that had returned me to Moscow after postings to Istanbul, Madrid and Havana. That February I'd had to watch on TV from thousands of miles away in Cuba as protesters on Kyiv's Independence Square were shot by riot police. The biggest news in Havana then was that Tom Jones would appear at the next cigar festival. I emailed my husband that I was 'horrified' and felt 'a total fraud' stuck in Cuba. By the end of the month I was reporting from Kyiv, then from the Donbas on the outbreak of open war.

I found a country of sharp divisions, where many in the Russian-speaking east looked more naturally to Moscow than Europe.

That didn't mean they wanted to break away, but Russia had been exploiting and exacerbating the tensions for years. In addition to Crimea, it eventually controlled two territories, the DNR and LNR, run by Russian placemen after 'referenda' held against Ukrainian law and in polling stations full of armed men.

Posted back to Russia full time a few months later, I found divisions there, too. The annexation of Crimea that so shocked the world had been welcomed by many Russians and Putin's approval rating had soared. People who'd given barely a moment's thought to the status of the peninsula, transferred to Ukraine in 1954 under the Soviet leader Nikita Khrushchev, were now hailing its audacious 'return' to Russia as the righting of a great historical wrong. Their slogan was *Krym Nash*, Crimea is Ours, and anyone who disagreed openly was slammed as a traitor.

Russia was wealthier, and life easier for many, than it had been for years. I found many cities transformed, with clean streets, smiling service, attractive parks. But the political climate was growing uglier. Officials and state media painted Western countries as hostile and subversive, and critics of the Kremlin were described as 'the enemy within' and collaborators with foreign powers. I began to spend much of my time reporting from courtrooms, charting increasing efforts to stamp out all kinds of dissent. It was a dark period that opened with the shooting of one opposition politician, Boris Nemtsov, and covered the attempted assassination of another, Alexei Navalny, with a military-grade nerve agent. Navalny would die suddenly three years later, locked up in an Arctic prison camp for his politics.

When Putin openly ordered his troops into Ukraine in 2022, any lingering nostalgia I had for Russia, and regret at being expelled, were extinguished in an instant. I reported from across Ukraine on the torture and execution of civilians, often by young Russian soldiers who'd expected to breeze into Kyiv in a couple of days but who ended up pinned down by Ukrainian fire. In places like Bucha some took out their fear and fury on the locals with rape and murder. Soldiers defecated on the floors of people's homes and they looted, not only stealing fridges, car tyres and electrical goods, but women's underwear that they then posted back to Russia as presents for their wives. Documenting what was happening first hand felt even more urgent as it became a crime within Russia even to call the invasion a war. Those who persisted in telling the truth there would end up in prison, some serving longer sentences than the men hired to murder Nemtsov beside the Kremlin.

For a time, as I travelled through Ukraine witnessing the impact of Russia's war, it was hard to contemplate the lives being upturned across the border: the Russian opposition figures fleeing into exile or being locked up for condemning their country's aggression. Their suffering was intense, but it paled next to the fight of Ukrainians to survive each night under Russian bombs. Many I met then had no sympathy at all for any Russians. They blamed them all for failing to stop Putin sooner; for being weak and passive for too long.

One night shortly before the invasion, I was at a small gathering in Kyiv whose host had fought in the Donbas in 2014. Dmytro's old uniform was hanging ready in his wardrobe, but he'd been to see his therapist because he was stressed at the idea of returning to the front. The group in his kitchen were all educated, intelligent Ukrainians, but I was taken aback by how harshly they spoke of Russians. I tried talking about some of the people I'd reported on, those fiercely opposed to Putin who had suffered because of that, but they didn't want to know. Putin could refer to Ukrainian 'brothers' all he liked, but for that crowd there was no longer any such thing as a good Russian.

And yet many Russians who have stood up to Putin have paid dearly, some with their lives, like Nemtsov and Navalny. Activists like Vladimir Kara-Murza, sentenced to twenty-five years in prison just for talking of Russian war crimes, are the persecuted conscience of their country. Many others are now in exile, watching what Russia is doing in Ukraine with disgust. Their feelings of guilt are intensified by a sense of their own powerlessness and the knowledge that this moment had been building for many years. As I follow the long road to war on these pages, these Russians are my guide. The exceptional characters who see themselves as patriots, but who are damned as traitors by Putin and his cheerleaders.

My goodbye to Russia is not intended as an exhaustive story of the Ukraine war or a complete history of Putin's rule. The moments I share from Ukraine are a few stark snapshots of what I witnessed in the opening months of the invasion, scenes I will never forget. The moments from Russia are also fragments. But pieced together, they reveal how Putin's invasion became possible. Above all, perhaps, this is my own, personal reckoning with the Russia I first encountered thirty years ago, a place of hope changed so deeply under Vladimir Putin that it could launch the biggest conflict in Europe since the Second World War, lauded by a propaganda machine that has been fashioned into a powerful weapon and with no opposition left to stand in the way.

PART I

'Putin's task is not to make Russia prosper and its people successful. It is to keep power. That's his only aim.'

Boris Nemtsov, April 2014

A Killing by the Kremlin

MOSCOW, 27 FEBRUARY 2015

The manager had saved the best table in the café for Boris Nemtsov and his Ukrainian model girlfriend, next to the large windows that looked out across Red Square towards the Kremlin, brightly lit up on the other side. It was a dank February night, drizzling lightly, but the scene through the glass would have been pretty. The ice rink had already closed but there was an old-fashioned merry-go-round covered in fairy lights and stalls selling pancakes and *pelmeni*, Russian dumplings. Cosy inside the Bosco café, Nemtsov and Anna Durytska shared a meal of oysters and Chardonnay.

The opposition politician had come from Ekho Moskvy radio station, where he'd been calling Russians to a big protest he had planned for that week. Alexei Navalny, the anti-corruption activist, should have been organising it with him, but he'd been arrested for handing out flyers on the metro and sentenced to fifteen days in custody. Like all strident critics of Putin, Nemtsov was banned from state media. But Ekho was editorially independent, and on air there he was as direct and passionate as ever. The protest rally was against everything from Putin's economic policy to the war in Ukraine that had begun the previous year with Russia's covert takeover of Crimea, and then spread to the Donbas in the country's east. Nemtsov denounced a 'mad, aggressive and deadly policy' and called Putin a pathological liar for claiming he had nothing to do with it. He accused the president of sending Russian soldiers to their deaths, then denying they were even fighting. On air that night he sounded tired, describing the immense pressure on opposition figures like himself. 'It's hard but we need to tolerate it, because our truth is stronger than all of the lies that pour out of them.'

At 21:53 the politician's driver dropped him off close to GUM, the grand nineteenth-century arcade that runs along one side of Red Square. His girlfriend had already been browsing the designer stores in its passages for over an hour. She'd flown in from Kyiv that day and the couple had spent the afternoon at Nemtsov's flat before he set off on foot to the radio studio and she headed for a massage. They'd agreed to meet at GUM for dinner afterwards and, when they did, Nemtsov dismissed his driver, saying he and Anna would walk the short distance home across the bridge. The politician had told a friend he'd felt 'more watched' recently. But as the couple settled into their seats at the expensive café, neither noticed the two men hovering in the shadows outside.

The CCTV cameras at GUM showed 23:25 when Nemtsov and Anna stepped out into the cold night to cross the slippery cobblestones and head down the slope next to St Basil's Cathedral. A passing car captured the pair on its dash cam, a slight woman in a white fur coat arm in arm with an older man in jacket and loose jeans. The driver didn't spot anyone tailing them, and the couple themselves didn't hear a man make a phone call to give notice that they were on the move. Moments later, they stepped onto the bridge that sweeps across the Moskva river from St Basil's with its psychedelic onion domes. Just as the couple drew level with the corner tower of the Kremlin, a man pulled out a pistol and fired six times at Nemtsov's back. The killer then leapt over the high kerb to jump into a silver-grey getaway car with tinted windows and flee the scene. Anna looked to her feet, at first thinking the pistol sound was firecrackers. Then she saw her lover falling to the floor beside her and she began screaming.

It was 23:31 and Boris Nemtsov had been murdered. Above his body, lying on its back on the wet tarmac, strings of festive lights stretched all the way down to the Kremlin in the red, white and blue of the Russian flag.

Two weeks before he was shot, Nemtsov told an interviewer that his 87-year-old mother was nervous about him being so outspoken. 'When are you going to stop criticising Putin? He'll kill you!' he recalled her saying whenever he phoned her. The interviewer asked whether Nemtsov himself was worried that Putin could kill him soon, 'either personally or through an intermediary'.

Interview with Boris Nemtsov, *Sobesednik*, 10 February 2015

> NEMTSOV: Yes, a little. Not as worried as my mum, but still ... But I'm not that afraid of him. If I was really afraid, I probably wouldn't head up an opposition party, or do what I do.
> INTERVIEWER: I hope that common sense will prevail after all and Putin won't kill you.
> NEMTSOV: Please God. Me too.

I heard the news of Nemtsov's death on Ekho Moskvy, the radio station he had visited just a few hours earlier. It was a huge shock. High-profile assassinations were not unknown in Russia, but shooting a serving politician just metres from the seat of power was unprecedented. Nemtsov was handsome and engaging and he'd been in politics since the days I'd learned my first words of Russian, three decades earlier. A journalist friend messaged me. 'What are they doing? I feel so sick and scared for Russia. It's devastating.' For me, Russia became a darker place from that moment.

A few months before he was murdered, I'd seen Nemtsov leading thousands of people through Moscow on a march against Russia's military intervention in Ukraine. It was the biggest protest in the city for years. Some in the crowd carried Ukrainian flags and others held photographs of Russian soldiers with the caption 'Killed in Ukraine'. They told me the official denials of involvement in the war were nonsense. There were rows of graves in cities like Pskov that proved the Kremlin's deceit beyond doubt, but Russian journalists had been beaten up for trying to film them. So as the protesters surged through central Moscow demanding an end to the war, they were also shouting at their politicians to 'Stop lying!'

Through the police lines that day my producer spotted Nemtsov behind a large banner that read 'For Russia and Ukraine without Putin'. When Emma suggested we interview him, I was dismissive. I'd just returned to report from Russia after almost a decade posted to other countries and I thought there must be new voices among the opposition to hear, so we walked on. I still regret that.

Under Putin, Nemtsov had been pushed out of parliament to the margins of political life. But his political career had been born along with democracy itself in Russia. As a schoolchild in the Soviet seventies, his head teacher nearly scuppered his chances of a university place by describing him as 'politically unstable', meaning not a loyal communist. By 1990 Nemtsov was running for election in Russia's first free vote and in 1991, aged thirty-two, he was catapulted up the career ladder by Boris Yeltsin, Russia's first president, to became governor of Nizhny Novgorod. The city of military factories and a mini kremlin didn't feature in the guidebooks to the USSR I got for my first trip to Russia the following year: it had been closed to foreigners for much of the Soviet period. But Nemtsov was soon welcoming high-profile visitors there like Margaret Thatcher, who was charmed. The Nemtsov allure was legendary: he was divorced by his wife of many years after she took a call from his lover, who announced down the phone that the couple were expecting their second child.

Yeltsin eventually transferred his protégé to Moscow as deputy prime minister, where he continued to single him out, introducing him to world leaders as 'the future president of Russia'. Nemtsov was fond of Yeltsin but fiercely critical of the war he unleashed in 1994 to crush separatists in Chechnya, and by 1999 Yeltsin had changed his mind about the succession. Instead of staking Russia's future on a young liberal reformer, he switched his favour to a former officer of the Soviet KGB named Vladimir Putin.

In power, Putin went on to cast Russia's democratic awakening of the 1990s as an era exclusively of economic hardship and national humiliation. It was his way of positioning himself as the saviour from all that, and it worked. Many Russians linked Nemtsov to those tainted times, which is partly why I was so shocked when he was killed. The man who might have ruled Russia was further from the national spotlight than ever and posed no obvious political threat. Blocked from the federal parliament, in 2013 Nemtsov had been elected to the regional parliament of Yaroslavl, some 170 miles outside Moscow. His eldest daughter, Zhanna, remembers this as an especially low period. 'In his last years, I think he felt almost no support. It was partly due to people's euphoria over Crimea shifting to Russian control, which my father opposed. But it was also the general attitude towards him as a politician of the past.'

Nemtsov remained a serious irritant to the Kremlin nonetheless. Back in 2004, ahead of the presidential election, he'd written a newspaper op-ed warning voters against continuing the 'authoritarian regime of personal power' built by Putin and his henchmen from the security service. A decade later, he told a political chat show in Kyiv that the danger of authoritarianism had become reality. 'Putin's task is not to make Russia prosper and its people successful. It is to keep power. That's his only aim.'

The first time Nemtsov was arrested was on New Year's Eve 2010 at a demonstration defending the constitutional right to protest. He was sentenced to fifteen days in custody and spent the first two in a windowless cell that measured 1.5 metres by 2, sleeping on the floor without a mattress. Imprisoning such well-known political figures was unusual at that point, but that would soon change. The following winter brought a major wave of rallies against Putin's return to the presidency. He had vacated the Kremlin for a few years, swapping seats with Prime Minister Dmitry Medvedev to swerve a constitutional limit on terms in office, and the men's cynical move made people angry. Giant protests on Bolotnaya Square, in the heart of Moscow, ended in violent clashes with police and another fifteen days in custody for Nemtsov.

Perhaps more threatening for the political elite than the street protests, though, was Nemtsov's lobbying of the United States

Congress for sanctions. He was pushing hard for legislation that would allow senior Russian figures to face asset freezes and visa bans in the US for human rights violations. It was known as the Magnitsky Act and was initiated by the American-born investment manager Bill Browder whose lawyer, Sergei Magnitsky, had died in prison after exposing major fraud by the tax authorities and police. The legislation was passed by Congress in 2012 and the campaign would make Nemtsov plenty of high-placed enemies back home.

When he denounced the annexation of Crimea two years later, he was openly cast as a traitor. In a big speech of March 2014, Putin claimed that Russia had returned its 'inseparable' land. Amid angry jibes at the West, he referred to a 'fifth column' within Russia and 'national traitors'. After that, a giant banner appeared draped over the side of Dom Knigi bookshop in central Moscow. Nemtsov's face was in the middle above a caption that echoed Putin's words: *Fifth Column. Aliens among us.* In an interview a few days later, Nemtsov admitted that the move felt threatening. 'There's been a huge number of provocations, threats and vile things done against me in recent years. But it's hard to get used to horrible things.' That summer the threats included one to 'bash your head in with a hammer'. Investigators refused to look into it.

The last time Nemtsov's daughter, Zhanna, saw her father was in Yaroslavl, a week before he was murdered. He was exhausted. 'It wasn't a physical tiredness so much as a moral one, because of the constant pressure on him. He was constantly fighting for the right to speak.' That same week, a bearded biker calling himself 'The Surgeon' led a column of self-proclaimed patriots down Moscow's central Tverskaya Street in an officially sanctioned procession. Marching towards the Kremlin beneath the national flag, they styled themselves the 'Anti-Maidan', protecting Russia against uprisings like the one in Ukraine that had overturned a pro-Russian government there the previous year. Their banners called for Russia's own liberals to be 'done away with'.

As news of Nemtsov's killing spread, his close friends gathered on the bridge by the Kremlin. Among them were Ilya Yashin and Vladimir Kara-Murza, younger activists who had looked up to Nemtsov as a father figure of Russian democracy. Now their mentor was sprawled on the pavement, the lights of the GUM arcade still bright in the background. A police report noted Nemtsov's 'bluish' face, eyes 'open and bloodshot'. There was 'dark red liquid' still seeping from several wounds. A forensics team found six bullet casings scattered around, some near the body and some a few metres away by the bridge steps, possibly where the killer had been waiting. The ambulance crew had arrived only in time to record the death. 'A man's body lies on the pavement. Skin pale and soft to the touch. No pulse detected.'

A female officer came forward to address the TV cameras and reporters huddled beyond the red-and-white police cordon. 'A criminal case has been opened … the best experts have been brought in.' Her full make-up and smart uniform were oddly out of sync with the dismal crime scene. Among the items recovered from Nemtsov's pockets were his opposition party ID card and an icon of the orthodox Saint Boris.

The murder spot should have been one of the most heavily monitored and guarded places in Moscow, but no security camera footage was ever produced from the scene. The only images to emerge were from a weather camera installed on a building a significant distance away. On that footage a street-cleaning truck pulls alongside Nemtsov at the exact moment of the shooting, obscuring the view. A figure, apparently the gunman, then runs out from behind the truck to jump in a car that's just pulled up. Another couple stop near the body before hurrying down the bridge steps. The only other clear figure is Anna Durytska, the white blob of her fur coat rushing back and forth from the dying body of her lover to the street cleaner, begging for help. A few hours later, when Nemtsov's body had been carried from the scene in a black bag, the same truck would return to wash away the pools of his blood.

The killers did a much poorer job of covering their tracks. Ten days later I was in court in Moscow as armed police dragged five men down a corridor into a custody hearing. The murder suspects were bowed, heads down and hands cuffed behind their backs.

An extra officer followed behind with an unmuzzled Rottweiler, perhaps for dramatic effect as much as extra security. The gang's abandoned getaway car had been found covered in the suspects' DNA. Video footage from near Nemtsov's flat showed the men using the same vehicle to keep surveillance. On the night of the killing, two of the group were captured on CCTV near the GUM shopping arcade, stalking the politician and his girlfriend. The murder weapon was never found.

In court the five suspects sat with their coats pulled over their heads to hide their faces as the judge decreed they should be remanded in custody until their trial. The only one to speak was Zaur Dadayev, who was accused of firing the gun that killed Nemtsov. Black-bearded and wild-eyed, at one point he turned towards the TV cameras, proclaimed that he loved the Prophet Muhammad, then turned back to face the wall. His words added to speculation that Nemtsov's killing might be linked to the murderous attack on staff at the *Charlie Hebdo* magazine in Paris a few weeks earlier. The Chechen leader, Ramzan Kadyrov, described Dadayev as a 'deep believer' who, 'like all Muslims', had been shocked by the magazine's caricatures of the Prophet. It was true that Nemtsov had made a few comments in support of the journalists, but it became clear that the politician's murder had nothing to do with religion. The hit squad had been tailing Nemtsov, keeping watch on his home, for months before the Paris attack.

With the suspects in prison awaiting trial, we went looking for their friends and relatives. All five were ethnic Chechens, but several had grown up in the neighbouring republic of Ingushetia, in a typical Caucasus village of a few potholed streets and low-rise brick houses, half-hidden behind high walls. Two of the accused, Anzor and Shahid Gubashev, were brothers and, through a Chechen contact, their mother Zulay had agreed to meet us. She covered the kitchen table with sweet pastries and soft meringues and kept pushing the plates towards us, insisting that her sons were not guilty. Through sobs she told me she'd be the first to turn them in to police if she thought they were killers. 'I'd say, *do what you want with them*. But how can they be guilty if they wouldn't hurt a fly?' At that point she hadn't seen any of the evidence.

Zulay told us her sons had left for Moscow in their twenties to find work and, as far as she knew, they'd spent the next decade doing casual jobs in the capital. The family had seen the news of Nemtsov's death on TV and remembered him as a prominent national figure from the past. Zulay had been 'sad as a human being' but her family were far removed from Moscow politics. It was in their large and pristine living room that I got my first proper look at the faces the suspects had hidden during the custody hearing. Their sister scrolled through her phone showing me pictures of Shahid and Anzor, who investigators say drove the getaway car. There was a photo from a winter holiday in Egypt and another one of the brothers in matching striped jumpers. In a third, Shahid was squatting on his heels at the entrance to a cave with his cousin, Zaur Dadayev, the suspected gunman. We tracked down Dadayev's relatives, too, and even managed to talk our way into the family flat. We then sat awkwardly in the kitchen, sipping tea, as they refused to tell us anything about the man, his movements or his politics.

By the time the trial began, twenty months later, the accused men weren't bothering to cover their faces anymore. They would grin broadly and shout greetings to their families as they were led along a narrow corridor into court and the bailiffs pressed us up against the wall to let them pass. One time, I found myself squeezed behind a stone statue of Femida, the blindfolded lady of justice whose image is on prominent display in every Russian courthouse, although the chances of acquittal in any one of them is extremely low.

Inside the courtroom the men were held in a glass cage guarded by police in full urban camouflage and balaclavas, Rottweiler by their side, though the judge urged the jury not to read anything into those security measures. 'It doesn't mean they are guilty or dangerous. It's just procedure.' The prosecutor was a confident platinum blonde in thick foundation, stiletto heels and elaborately painted nails who was escorted everywhere by two bodyguards. She addressed the jury demonstratively, like she'd seen too many

American TV dramas. By contrast, the accused men's lawyers made mostly rambling, stumbling speeches, an air of defeat hanging over them. The suspects themselves fidgeted throughout, demonstrably ignoring proceedings. One did Sudoku puzzles, the others read newspapers or took occasional notes, and they sniggered behind their hands to one another constantly. Whenever they were called on to speak, they would proclaim their innocence, mock the prosecutor or make wisecracks, like adolescents.

Two of the men had made detailed confessions. In one eerie video clip recorded by investigators and leaked to the Russian press, Anzor Gubashev – whose mother had protested his innocence to me – was filmed beside a large heap of flowers at the murder spot. He described tailing Nemtsov from Red Square onto the bridge, where Dadayev then shot him in the back. Though Dadayev would also confess, both men later claimed that they had been stripped, beaten and forced to incriminate themselves. An independent prison monitor confirmed that Dadayev had marks on his feet consistent with electric shock, but the confessions were played to the jury even so.

The investigators concluded that Nemtsov's murder was a contract killing, but they quickly gave up hunting for the person, or persons, who commissioned the crime. A key suspect, Ruslan Geremeev, was deputy commander of the Chechen Interior Ministry battalion where Dadayev had served. But he disappeared. Geremeev was a close ally of Ramzan Kadyrov, the former separatist fighter who'd switched sides to work with the Kremlin and then got free rein to run Chechnya as he chose. Days after Nemtsov's murder, Kadyrov defended the suspected gunman as a 'true patriot', insisting he could not have taken 'one step against Russia' after fighting for the country for years. A few days later, Kadyrov was handed a state award by Putin.

During the course of the nine-month trial, in conversations in the court and in a café across the road, Nemtsov's close friend and his family's lawyer, Vadim Prokhorov, shared his frustration. 'You're telling me Putin's entire secret service could not find the organisers and sponsors of this killing?' Prokhorov was sure that the men on trial were only the lowest links in a chain that would, if followed properly, lead to senior figures within the Chechen government. It might even reach Kadyrov. There was certainly enough substance to have the Chechen leader questioned, but the lawyer said that request was always refused. 'It seems Putin doesn't want his foot-soldier touched.' He told me the official investigation had been stopped as soon as it came close to Kadyrov.

Other allies of Nemtsov referred to the Chechen leader during questioning in court. The young activist Ilya Yashin said that Nemtsov had been 'seriously afraid' of only one person. He pointed to the politician's own testimony about a death threat from Kadyrov in his memoir, *Confessions of a Rebel*. Alexei Venediktov, a prominent journalist, testified that the politician had been getting threats recently from men close to the Chechen leader. He had advised Nemtsov to employ a bodyguard.

Kadyrov himself publicly denied any involvement, arguing that there was 'no point' in him having Nemtsov removed. 'Had he done anything to us? Had he hampered me in any way?' He said he hadn't seen the politician in years. Still speculation swirled around Moscow. Could the Chechen leader have delivered a 'gift' to Russia's president by removing one of his biggest critics? Or was this a warning shot to Putin himself, who had turned a blind eye to his placeman's tyrannical rule in the Caucasus: was Kadyrov now parading his own power with a murder committed on the Kremlin's doorstep?

Putin vanished for days soon after the killing, an absence that was never explained. When he spoke of Nemtsov's assassination he called it vile, but he also labelled it a 'provocation'. An early statement from the Investigative Committee, which answers directly to Putin, suggested the murder could have been a plot by external enemies of Russia using Nemtsov as their 'sacrificial lamb'. State TV propagandists then went to town, presenting the killing as an attempt to demonise the president. Those closest to Nemtsov called that absurd. A few days after his friend was shot, Ilya Yashin was clear. 'I believe that Nemtsov was killed in an act of terror to scare society.'

The investigators did eventually produce a chief suspect for commissioning the killing, but instead of the commander, Ruslan

Geremeev, they accused his driver. They offered no explanation for this man's supposed motive or any idea how a driver in his twenties would find the equivalent of about £160,000 to pay the hit squad. In January 2016, the question of who ordered Nemtsov's murder was hived off from the main case and quietly shelved.

Meanwhile, the alleged hit team on trial denied any role in the killing. One described himself as 'pure as an angel's tear'. Another used his final speech to declare that he'd read Nemtsov's political autobiography while in prison and been impressed. In a perverse twist, he then thanked the politician's family for raising 'a courageous son'.

In June 2017, after deliberating for twelve hours, the jury returned to find all five of the accused guilty. When the judge confirmed the verdict, the men in the cage smirked. Zaur Dadayev reached up with his handcuffed hands and wrote the word *LOZH*, lie, in capital letters in the steam on the glass. The men were sentenced to between eleven and nineteen years in prison, but as the bailiffs ushered the press out of court, I looked back and caught a last glimpse of the five, laughing and joking as usual.

The protest that Nemtsov had planned for 1 March 2015 became a giant march of mourning for his death. The city authorities had banished the 'spring rally' to a distant suburb, but tens of thousands of people flocked to central Moscow instead, to head for the spot where Nemtsov had been killed. They were led by his daughter, Zhanna, who would eventually have to leave Russia after receiving threats. *If you don't shut up, we will kill you on the same bridge.* When we met up in London some time later, Zhanna told me she blamed Russia's president directly for her father's death because he had created the system and the climate that made the murder possible. 'I don't think [my father] was killed because of one thing, one statement. But he was very critical of Putin personally. He was his most outspoken critic.' Zhanna was poised and careful in her analysis, but firm. When I asked whether she had feared for her father's life, she paused, then shook her head. 'I worried about imprisonment. But I could never have imagined murder.'

On the day of the march through Moscow, those who wanted a different Russia carried posters on wooden sticks with black-and-white images of Nemtsov's face looking pensive, or gently smiling. Most just had one word beneath: *Boris'!*, Fight!, a play on his first name in Russian. Towards the front of the crowd, I spotted the former opposition MP Dmitry Gudkov in fluffy big earmuffs against the cold. As he walked, we talked, and he reflected on how his friend had represented an era of free speech and openness that had passed. He told me Nemtsov's vision had been crushed by a country that labels its critics as enemies and makes them targets. 'I don't know who ordered this murder, but I do know that the Russian authorities are responsible because they create an atmosphere of hate.'

Ilya Yashin was there, too, and we talked about the risk of open opposition now. 'It's important not to become paranoid. We'll try to not be scared and one day I believe we will wake up in the country Nemtsov was fighting for.' As he walked on towards the murder spot, a stream of Russian tricolour flags closed around him, carried by opposition supporters who wanted to show that they were patriots, too, not the traitors they were painted by Putin and his propaganda. As the mourners surged up onto the bridge and past the Kremlin walls, they began aiming their chants directly at the president. *Down with the police state! Russia without Putin!*

Two days later, Nemtsov's body was laid out in an open coffin, dressed in a dark suit and white shirt, and placed in the middle of the Sakharov Human Rights Centre. Friends took turns to speak at the open microphone, many accusing Russian officials of stirring up hatred with their propaganda. Outside, as a light snow fell, a long queue of people curled around the grounds and up onto the main road, waiting quietly to file past the coffin, leave flowers and say their farewells. At some moments it was like a parade of the 1990s, the window of freedom which Nemtsov had helped hold open. It was a day for reflecting on how Russia might have been. Boris Yeltsin's widow, Naina, was there and even John

Major flew in from London to pay his respects. 'Now I think we can say goodbye to our hopes for democracy,' Karina Orlova, an independent journalist, told me, as she queued. 'They have killed democracy.'

As the pallbearers lifted Nemtsov's coffin from its stand and carried it to a waiting car, the crowd chanted gently. *Russia will be free*. But their voices were soft, sounding less sure that day than ever before.

Bucha

UKRAINE, APRIL — MAY 2022

Outside the morgue in Bucha, a white-haired man sat alone on a wooden chair, hunched over an iPad. He was searching the screen for a missing relative, scrolling slowly through images of the dead, his face blank. A few steps away, another elderly man stood in a small queue. I asked him, gently, who he was looking for, but Hryhoriy was almost deaf and ended up shouting his response. His son, Volodymyr, had been tortured, killed and then burned by the Russians. *Kak shashlik*, Hryhoriy said. Like a kebab.

When Russian troops retreated from Bucha after almost a month of occupation, the town services could not cope with the scale of the death and loss, so this father had searched for his son's remains himself. All Hryhoriy recovered was a charred backbone, abandoned in a field. 'The dogs had been gnawing him for weeks,' he shouted at me. The little that was left of Volodymyr had eventually been identified using DNA tests, and the day I met Hryhoriy he was queuing for the paperwork to bury this one remaining bone of his son.

At the town's main cemetery there were lines of freshly dug graves. Every so often, a pick-up truck piled high with coffins would pull up beside one of them and the men on the back would shout out a name, then unload a body, cigarettes hanging from their lips. Some may have been official gravediggers, but most were more likely locals drafted in to help. There was no time for commiseration or ceremony, or even to pause and smoke properly, they had to drop off each coffin then drive on with their load.

One day in late April, I saw these men deliver a coffin to Ludmila. The simple cloth-covered box contained the body of her husband, Valeriy. The couple had been married for forty-seven years until a Russian soldier shot Valeriy in the back of the head and left him lying in a pool of blood on his own doorstep. As Ludmila told me all this beside her husband's grave, she pulled a plastic bag from her handbag and thrust it towards me. Inside was a black woollen hat with a hole shot through, some hairs and a small fragment of bone stuck to the edges. 'It's the hat Valeriy was wearing when he was murdered: here's the entry hole and this is where the bullet came out,' Ludmila held out her evidence, unflinching. She had found it when she discovered her husband's lifeless body and wrapped it up in case it was needed as evidence. Now she had no idea what to do with something so gruesome but so significant.

When the Russians first rolled into Bucha in early March, Ludmila and Valeriy had tried to stay safe. They had a vegetable cellar in their garden, a dugout known as a *pogreb*, that you reached through a wooden door and down a short flight of steps. It was cold and damp, the snow on the ground above not long melted, but as Ukrainian and Russian forces exchanged deadly fire, the *pogreb* was the least dangerous place to be. The town had been taken over by Russian troops in tanks that had streamed south in a giant column from Belarus. Before that, the Russians had been hovering near the border for weeks, supposedly deployed for joint military exercises. Officials in Moscow kept insisting the soldiers would return home once 'Allied Resolve-2022' was complete. But in the early hours of 24 February they began moving across the border. Inside their tanks the troops themselves had little idea what was coming.

By the time I met Ludmila, the Russians had been forced to retreat, or 'regroup' as the Defence Ministry in Moscow termed it, glossing over its failure to take Kyiv. Those who'd always believed the invasion an act of impossible madness had been proved right and the burned-out tanks that testified to Putin's miscalculation were everywhere. But in Bucha so many people were killed during the Russian occupation that the morgue was overwhelmed. Four weeks after the town was liberated, bodies were still being discovered in shallow graves, dug in haste. There was a giant refrigerated lorry alongside the main morgue and a row of metal trolleys behind it, piled with white body bags. In some cases, they lay two- or three-deep, tagged with numbers but no names. The flap of a tent blew open for a second on the grass nearby, revealing a body on a metal table where a French forensics team was working to determine the exact cause of another death.

The Kyiv regional police chief told me that more than a thousand civilians had been killed in the Bucha region during the occupation. Most did not die from shrapnel or shelling: more than half were shot dead, like Ludmila's husband. Faced with stark evidence of crimes by its soldiers, Russian officials resorted to outright lies. They said that the bodies found lining the main road into Bucha, some with their hands tied, were actors. They said that the ghastly scene that Ukrainians and foreign journalists uncovered when Bucha was retaken was a giant fake. They claimed it was the work of British intelligence agencies. After years of state TV presenters screaming that Ukraine was ruled by a 'Nazi'-led government backed by the West, such outlandish assertions may have convinced some in Russia. But to the real world beyond, the claims were cynical and repugnant.

Ludmila knows exactly what happened to her husband. She was sitting in the cellar with him, in the dark, as two armies clashed above ground. Their house had been damaged by shrapnel and she remembers Valeriy telling her not to worry. He promised to fix it once everything was over. 'Who will I build things with now? Who will I live with?' Ludmila suddenly wailed, hit by a fresh wave of grief.

On the day he was killed, Valeriy had ventured up from their underground hole to make a phone call. Moments later Ludmila heard a shot. Then a Russian soldier yanked open the cellar door and demanded she come out, threatening to throw a grenade down the stairs. Once the soldier was certain Ludmila was alone, he ordered her back inside where she cowered in terror until dark, then crept out to hunt for her husband. Her torch beam found Valeriy lying face down, dead on their doorstep. 'It was dark, and I was all alone and it was so frightening,' Ludmila lowered her voice. 'So I covered him with a blanket, poured sand onto the blood, then went back down into the cellar.'

More Russians arrived in Bucha the next day, some crashing through the couple's fence to park an armoured personnel carrier on their drive. The soldiers made their headquarters in the house opposite. Ludmila had called her daughter to tell her that her father was dead, but it was another five days before Olha managed to talk her way into Bucha through multiple Russian checkpoints. She'd chosen 8 March because she hoped that the Russians wouldn't shoot her on International Women's Day. When she made it, she found her father's body still sprawled outside their home.

Some of the soldiers helped Ludmila dig a hole in the family vegetable patch so that she and Olha could bury Valeriy in a temporary grave. Were these the Russians who had killed him, or others who regretted it? What did they think as they lowered the pensioner into the ground? I don't know that, only that the women marked the mound of earth over Valeriy's body with a wooden cross and then fled Bucha to safety.

When I visited the scene a few weeks later, following Ludmila's directions, her one-storey house was a burned-out wreck. Beer cans and spirits bottles were strewn all around the yard, mixed with pots of apple puree and crackers from Russian military ration packs. The khaki boxes were the same brand you could buy in the Army of Russia stores that appeared in Moscow after Russia annexed Crimea. The shops stocked T-shirts of Putin in macho poses as well as military-branded food and clothing, in a push to popularise the army and the idea of Russia as a resurgent power. But the litter at Ludmila's house had not been left by heroes. It was the detritus of men who shoot elderly civilians in cold blood.

After Bucha was liberated it took Ludmila several agonising weeks to find her husband's body again. A team from the prosecutor's office had exhumed garden graves all over town and taken the remains to various morgues for formal identification. But Valeriy's body had been left outside, face down, for so long that he was unrecognisable. Ludmila had to identify him by the blanket that she and Olha had wrapped him in when they buried him.

Now Valeriy's family had gathered at Bucha cemetery to bury him again, this time with more dignity. The coffin was heavy, lurching on the thick canvas straps as the gravediggers lowered it into the ground. There was no priest and no prayers. The family got only a moment to throw soil on the coffin before a digger asked brusquely whether they were done and began shovelling the remaining earth into the hole. As the men worked, Ludmila turned to her son in panic. 'Zheniya, it is him, isn't it? You're sure?' she wanted to know. She then realised she was still holding Valeriy's blood-soaked hat with the bullet hole and rushed to the grave to throw it in. It landed with the soil hitting the wooden box with dull thuds.

'I thought we'd make it to our fiftieth wedding anniversary. Where is my golden anniversary?' Ludmila cried, as we watched the hole in the earth fill up. Valeriy had been twenty when they met, she told me, and the best-looking boy in Bucha. 'You mustn't think badly of us that there's no one here, no ceremony,' she fretted after the diggers had gone and she was arranging a framed photograph of her husband next to purple plastic flowers. 'He has lots of friends, but no one is here because of the war.'

Over and over again, Ludmila asked her husband's forgiveness for letting him go outside that day, not knowing the Russian soldiers were so close. But when her tears dried she was clear about who she blamed: she wanted Vladimir Putin to pay for what happened in Bucha, not to die peacefully in his bed. 'Maybe Russia will just close an iron curtain round itself again,' she said, beside a long line of new graves and heaped flowers. 'But I want Putin to answer for this evil. For all these victims.'

On our way out of town, we stopped at a petrol station. As the driver filled the tank with his daily fuel ration, I sat on the kerb and scribbled some notes. One of our local producers, Sofiya, spent weeks in Bucha interviewing people for a documentary.

We would meet most days over breakfast in Kyiv before she headed back out for more. She told me she had to scrub her hands whenever she left Bucha because she felt as if she'd been to a morgue. 'All the people are like ghosts. It's like you're speaking to the dead.' That day, I knew exactly how she felt.

My phone rang and it was an accountant in Moscow wanting to know why I wasn't answering emails and when I planned to pay my final Russian tax bill. Taxes that would fund her country's missiles and bullets. I hung up.

It was an unusually sunny day. On the edge of town there were woods and lakes all around. Bucha was a pretty spot where families used to come from Kyiv to relax on the weekends. Nothing could ever be the same. But on the fence next to the petrol station someone had scrawled one defiant line of graffiti. *Bucha is Ukraine. Russian soldier, Fuck Off.*

PART II

Security Threat

MOSCOW AIRPORT, 10 AUGUST 2021

'Sarah Elizabeth, you are banned from entering Russia as a threat to national security.' The border guard at Sheremetyevo airport was reading from a single sheet of paper with a solemn air that was almost theatrical, but the words coming out of his mouth made no sense. 'What do you mean, banned?' I asked, unable to take it in. 'I'm a journalist. Is that a threat?'

I had just flown back to Moscow from Minsk where I'd had a tough encounter with Alexander Lukashenko, the authoritarian leader of Belarus and a close ally of Vladimir Putin. He'd been hosting his 'Big Conversation', an annual event to which a handful of foreign journalists are usually invited. It was exactly a year since Lukashenko's rigged re-election as president for a sixth term had set off nationwide protests on a scale never seen. Some 40,000 peaceful demonstrators were arrested, there was clear evidence of detainees being tortured, and hundreds were still serving prison terms. In the year since the protests were crushed, tens of thousands of Belarusians had fled abroad for safety as the purge of opposition supporters continued, despite Western sanctions.

'How do you respond to the notion that you have lost legitimacy as president and that now, for sure, Belarus needs change?' I asked, live on Belarusian state television, after listing the reasons for my question. Lukashenko erupted. From behind his giant wooden desk, he pronounced the injuries inflicted to detainees – giant bruises seen and filmed by my BBC colleagues – as 'fake, dear girl, fake'. He claimed that the protesters had thrown themselves at riot police. He then barked that I was an American lapdog and told me the West could 'choke on its sanctions'. His acolytes in the gaudy hall of the Presidential Palace applauded gleefully before turning on me with a vitriolic tirade that lasted almost half an hour.

Back at our hotel late that evening we were editing some of the exchange into a TV report when a news flash on my phone announced that Russia had imposed new sanctions against British citizens 'deeply involved in anti-Russian activities'. It was retaliation for two previous rounds of UK sanctions against Russian officials, one for allegations of corruption and the other for human rights abuses in Chechnya, which included the disappearance and torture of gay men. Now Russia's Foreign Ministry had declared a number of unnamed British citizens to be hostile. 'Entry to Russia is closed to them.' The statement accused the UK of leading a global race to 'blacken' Russia and called for an end to an 'unfounded' policy of 'confrontation'. I joked to my team that I was probably on the new Russian blacklist and they laughed at my melodrama. The next morning in Moscow the two of them sailed through passport control and I was stopped.

The guard in the glass booth asked me to step to one side as she began scanning every page of my passport. 'It's just a technicality.' She was polite, even reassuring, so I allowed myself to hope it was a computer glitch or some act of mild intimidation. The border guards in Moscow had been scrutinising our passports more closely lately, peering through a magnifying glass and tugging at pages, asking questions about our work. 'So what do you report on?' I would always reply as breezily as possible. 'Just life in Russia.' That was uncomfortable, but this felt different. Several men in uniform approached the cabin. There were hushed conversations and glances in my direction. My heart began to beat faster. I messaged my producer.

07:56 Problem at border. Three men. Asking me what I am here for and told me to wait five mins. Hopefully a tech issue

Those five minutes passed and I was directed to one side and a broken row of chairs and told to wait some more.

There had been warning signs about my status in Moscow. The Foreign Ministry, MID, had recently stopped giving me one-year visas. My first short-term visa was issued for three months, expiring awkwardly on New Year's Eve, but the most recent was valid for just eight weeks. At one point our office assistant was told that MID was keeping special tabs on me. I tried to pretend I wasn't rattled, but it was unsettling.

In June 2021 a low-ranking MID official announced by phone that my latest visa would be the last, then called back, claiming she'd made a mistake. *They like to think of me sweating, I guess*, I messaged a friend. *Wonder what happens next?* The call came two days after the British Navy sailed the HMS *Defender* battleship close to Russian-annexed Crimea. Moscow saw the route as a provocation and the *Defender* drew warning shots from a nearby Russian ship.

By then it was clear that I'd been singled out for harassment, as my colleagues still had year-long visas and no problems. When pushed to explain, a senior Russian source described me as 'hostage' to the political situation. You are the ammunition, he said, we just haven't yet decided when to fire.

As I waited and worried in the airport, I realised I'd landed at the terminal where my Russia story had begun. It was built for the 1980 Moscow Olympics but by the time I arrived in 1992, anxious and excited at the prospect of living in Russia, it already smelled strongly of sweat and cheap cigarettes. These days the airport has multiple airy alternatives, but flights to Belarus often use the old terminal. It was a strange sense of symmetry.

Our bureau chief messaged that she hoped the guards were being courteous and I replied that my fingernails were still intact. I then sent a photograph from my lonely seat that lurched alarmingly to one side whenever I moved, captioning it *Free the Terminal F One*. Beneath my eyes, above a purple face mask,

I had dark bags from the late-night TV edit in Minsk and dawn drive to the airport.

At 08:24 I messaged my husband. *Having some odd problem at the border. I assume it's all part of the game but it's not good. I really hope they are just trying to make me sweat.* I had put off telling him, not wanting to worry him unless I had to. Now I said I had no idea what was happening and he should probably stay close to the phone.

At 08:50 I was anxious enough to contact the British Ambassador, although I was embarrassed about bothering her. *I don't know why I am telling you. Guess there is nothing the embassy can do in these cases*, I typed. By then I'd had enough of sitting patiently and started quizzing every passing official on my fate. At some point, a junior guard dashed up to ask for more documents: the rental contract for my flat, any kind of ID, even my office entry pass. He didn't know what, exactly. 'Just give me anything you have.' I then spotted an official heading towards me with the sure stride and rounder belly that suggested a higher rank. At 09:15 Lieutenant Colonel Vizchenko of Russia's Federal Security Service, the FSB, called me into his office.

Following him in, I switched on the recorder on my phone. Powerless to change what was happening, I wanted at least to be able to report it. As the guard tried to read out his official text, no more than a couple of paragraphs, I kept interrupting, trying to make him clarify and justify what was happening. 'You are refused entry to the Russian Federation. Indefinitely. The initiator is the FSB,' he told me solemnly. 'Do you understand?' he asked in Russian. 'I understand you very well. I just don't understand what's going on.' The lieutenant colonel attempted to explain. On the recording, he sounds flustered. My own voice is upset but insistent.

> GUARD: It's for the protection of the security of the Russian Federation.
> SARAH: You mean I'm a threat to Russia?
> GUARD: You can find out more from the initiator…
> SARAH: I'm a threat to the Russian Federation? Do I look like a threat? I'm a journalist.

GUARD: I know. We found all the information on you.
SARAH: This is outrageous ... I've been coming here since 1992. My whole life is here. How can you refuse me entry to a country that's like my own?

It was a while before I registered that the ban on entering Russia had no expiry date.

SARAH: You mean I can't come here ever again?
GUARD: Yes.
SARAH: Are you serious?
GUARD: Yes.
SARAH: What for?
GUARD: We don't have that information...
SARAH: You realise that this is politics? ... What did I do? What article did I write?
GUARD: I can't tell you. But I have warned you that you will be criminally responsible if you try to cross the border ... Sign here.

I looked at the FSB guard holding out a pen and I looked at the paper and felt my eyes welling up with tears that I wouldn't let fall. I didn't want my distress recorded. The paper on the counter confirmed that I had been refused entry to Russia to 'ensure the defensive capability and security of the state'. Where the form said *for the period until* someone had scrawled *Bessrochno*. Indefinitely. I took the pen and signed my name, in anger. Then a guard led me back to the broken row of seats and told me to wait there to be deported.

WARSAW, AUGUST 2023

Two years on, my phone keeps reminding me of that day. Social media throws up a copy of the last report I'd filed in Belarus, then photographs from Moscow airport the following morning, tearful on that lonely bench. My distress, then so raw, feels distant now. I'm uncomfortable even thinking about it, or of my old affection for Russia, as missiles keep hitting Ukraine. Two teenage buskers were killed this week in an airstrike on central Zaporizhzhia. The girls' names were Svitlana Siemieikina and Kristina Spitsyna. I heard their music on the radio here and my expulsion from Russia seemed stupidly unimportant. An insignificant moment. But the path to Putin's war is made up of moments. Silencing the press, crushing protests, killing critics: they were all steps on the way to today's brutality. And back then, in life before this war, what happened to me was a shock. I'd been labelled an enemy by a country I called home. Back then, that hurt.

Moscow

January–June 1992

A Russian Education

Two weeks after the Soviet Union collapsed, I landed in Moscow with a suitcase full of cheese sauce mix and chocolate and a guidebook to a country that had ceased to exist. It was January 1992, I was eighteen years old, and I'd signed up to spend five months teaching English in Moscow. I'd been saving for the trip for months, serving fried breakfasts at a motorway service station, dressed in peach polyester from top to toe. All the grease was worth it to get to Russia.

I was met by Anna, a young student who had visited me in England the previous year on her first trip outside the USSR. She had stepped off the train then into the gloom of Worcester station immediately exotic in a bright red woollen cape, to form a friendship that was the start of my long and intense engagement with her country.

By the time I made my own first journey to Moscow, Anna's city was suddenly the capital of a brand-new country and her husband was speeding us towards their flat in his Lada. Every so often he would reach across to scrape tiny view-holes in the ice that had formed on the inside of the windows to give me my first glimpse of the broad avenues flashing past outside. It was −23°C degrees and I'd never experienced anything like it.

Letter to parents, 22 January 1992

Privet (greetings) from Moscow! Everything here is pretty 'hunky dory'. The hostel is definitely the best in Moscow. The beds are comfy, the room's warm, there's plenty of hot water etc. and no cockroaches!

Phoning home from Russia meant booking calls in advance from a surly telephonist at the post office. So I would write instead, long letters that crawled towards England carrying detailed descriptions of my daily life and travels. I also kept a diary in a spiralbound notebook I'd bought at Detsky Mir, a children's world that in those days stocked barely any toys, right next to the old KGB headquarters.

When I was expelled from Russia, and began to examine my relationship to the country, I dug out that lilac notebook. I found a bundle of my old letters and postcards, too, and a little scrapbook filled with theatre tickets and labels from food. There was even a ticket from Russia's second-ever rave, Gagarin II, when we'd danced in a cavernous space-themed pavilion until the first metro home. Those pages and papers are crammed full of flashbacks to my earliest days in Moscow. Going through them took me back to when the country was just opening up, long before Putin and his war. Vast, still-mysterious Russia was at the start of a tumultuous journey and I was there to experience it, close-up.

I arrived in the newly independent Russian Federation, run by Boris Yeltsin. Five months earlier, hardline communists had tried to depose the Soviet leader, Mikhail Gorbachev, and put a stop to his liberalising reforms. Their attempted coup had only hastened the disintegration of the USSR. The plotters who detained Gorbachev at his summer house in Crimea failed to arrest Yeltsin, Russia's elected president for just a few weeks. He made it to the White House to clamber onto a tank and denounce the takeover as illegal. The sight of Yeltsin urging the soldiers not to open fire on parliament cemented the gruff politician in the eyes of many at home and abroad as a symbol of change and hope for democracy.

But for those emerging into a new Russia from the ruins of an empire there was also real pain and turmoil.

Yeltsin had warned as much from the start. 'Russia is gravely ill. The economy is sick,' the president announced in his televised address that New Year's Eve, informing the nation that times would be tough as Russia moved to a market economy. A day later, his economic team scrapped the price controls on goods and food that had existed for decades. A portion of chicken suddenly cost 7 per cent of the average monthly wage as the cost of everything went through the roof. Yeltsin's team called it shock therapy, and it was very harsh.

The impact of the reforms was clear all around. The shelves at the grocery shop nearest to our student hostel were almost always bare unless there was a delivery of one product, usually onions, when a queue would stretch right down the street. We soon discovered the *babushki* hawkers who stood three-thick on the road leading down to the Kremlin. These Gorky Street grannies, with no hope of retiring and every certainty in life gone, would huddle for hours in the cold holding out jars of home-made jam or pickles. Some would sell bric-a-brac from their flats as food prices soared beyond the reach of their pensions. In time, the women began offering Pepsi and bottles of *shampanskoye*, or Soviet fizz. They would scour the shops, then queue for hours to resell whatever they found to people with more cash and less time to spend. Gorky Street became our outdoor supermarket and we would squeeze our way up and down the human aisles that began forming as soon as you hit the steps up from the metro. We learned to carry a *just in case* bag at all times, because you never knew what you might find.

Diary entry, Spring 1992

In the past couple of months, April and May, the number of kiosks around the metro has increased. Now there are about six, selling a variety of Western goods: Snickers, Mars, cigarettes and alcohol including Martini and Johnny Walker. By Russian standards these goods are extremely expensive. There is also a music kiosk where you can buy dodgy-looking pop cassettes. Depeche Mode seem to be hugely popular over here along with KLF and Queen. Interesting taste.

I was one of a group of six student-teachers in Moscow from the UK and our hostel was on Komsomolsky Prospekt, beside a fairy-tale church painted bright white, green and gold and just up the road from the wooden house where Leo Tolstoy wrote some of his later works. In the not-so-distant days of the USSR, Western students had been allocated Soviet roommates who were supposed to file regular reports to the security services on their 'friends'. Now we lived with people from all over the world. There was an Afghan whose family had been killed in the Soviet invasion of his country, and a young man from Kazakhstan who had fought in Afghanistan for the Soviets and still had nightmares.

The set-up was relatively smart. Each unit had two bedrooms and a bathroom and no obvious infestations, unlike many Russian friends' flats, where golden cockroaches would scuttle up the kitchen wall as we squeezed around a table for dinner. For any extras, like a plank to place under the mattress and stop the springs hitting the floor, you had to sweet-talk the hostel *komendantka*. A stern-faced woman, she was said to release all sorts of treasures from her cupboards for the right gift, but it took us some time to pluck up the courage to visit with lipstick and packs of tights from our stash of bribes. We then nudged them across her desk, explaining awkwardly how nice it would be to have a table lamp and some bedcovers.

Letter to parents, 17 February 1992

Beanfeast, cheese sauce mix, pot noodles, chocolate, Vegemite Immodium (permanent diarrhoea all round)

Scanning my letters home, I see that we became obsessed with food. Anyone who visited from abroad was asked to bring supplies. In return, my parents would fill slim blue airmail letters with anxious enquiries about our diet. When my university director of studies sent a reading list for the year, he added a note hoping I didn't 'starve too severely'. It was true that several students had been hospitalised after eating in the hostel canteen, but there was little danger of starvation. By then Moscow had two Pizza Huts, identical apart from the prices – one charged in roubles, the other in dollars. We once queued outside the rouble branch for three hours watching people sail past us and through the door as our toes grew numb with cold. It was how we learned that anything in Russia was available for a bribe, even a seat at Pizza Hut.

The McDonald's on Pushkin Square was still pulling big crowds two years after opening, but the real godsend was a Georgian restaurant called Guria, tucked away in a yard across the street from our hostel. For the equivalent of about fifty pence you could get *khachapuri* pies oozing salty, buttery cheese. For a long time it was the only place in town we'd ever find fresh tomatoes. Failing that, there were always the *babushki* selling warm cabbage pies by the metro, handing them over in small rectangles of grey paper that soaked up just a little bit of the grease.

I'd like to say I was first drawn to Russia by a fascination with late Soviet politics under Gorbachev, or the great works of Russian literature. But for me the initial interest was the language itself, as taught by an eccentric but effective teacher called Mr Criddle. Short and bearded, even a little gnome-like, he usually dressed in sandals and socks and ran his classes at Worcester Sixth Form College with old-fashioned discipline. Before we started the course, he had handed out copies of the thirty-three character Cyrillic script at our college open day with instructions to learn it or not bother turning up for class.

Mr Criddle had learned his own Russian in the mid-sixties at the Liverpool College of Commerce, taught by a graduate of a Cold War creation known as the Joint Services School for Linguists (JSSL). The JSSL had taken around 5,000 conscripted men from military boot camps in the 1950s and produced a whole generation of Russianists. The *kadety,* as the students called themselves, were trained to be high-level interpreters, ready to interrogate Soviet prisoners, decipher classified documents and run counter-propaganda operations should the USSR ever invade. As it never did, many ended up teaching the language in UK universities and schools.

The JSSL method was fast, deep and tough, with heavy emphasis on repetition and rote-learning. Its students had a *skukometer,* a made-up word from the Russian for boredom, to measure how brain-numbing a class was, and I would come to know how they felt. Mr Criddle had picked up the JSSL military style from his own teacher. Ignoring any official syllabus, he had a giant library of homemade flash cards which he used to drill us relentlessly. He'd cut all the images out of magazines and glued them to one side of the cards, writing the correct adjective endings or verb declensions on the back. He kept them in recycled envelopes at the back of the room. It was the exact opposite of how I'd learned French and German, where we chose a 'foreign' name and then role-played trips to the bakery or camp-site shop. For Russian, Mr Criddle had us create our own carefully indexed grammar books and then he dictated every page. It was a whole year before we learned anything practical like how to introduce ourselves, perhaps partly because no one was planning a summer holiday in the Soviet Union, but we could soon form the genitive plural in our sleep.

Still, it was in that classroom that my appetite for Russian and Russia began to grow. As occasional light relief, Mr Criddle would play us 1960s Soviet films set in a hot and somnolent Moscow, with trams and vats of the fermented drink *kvas*. We struggled through a Turgenev play and stumbled over verses of Pushkin and his *The Bronze Horseman* read out loud. Mr Criddle would also invite one of his local Russian friends in to give us conversation practice, although that wasn't much use as we could barely say a word. Learning the language wasn't easy, but that made the successes sweeter. Just as with Russia itself, the struggle was part of life and somehow part of the allure.

Our class all sailed through A-level, but I wrote home from Moscow a few months later that my spoken Russian was still 'embarrassingly bad'. I had planned the trip in order to improve that, immersing myself in Moscow life before studying Russian at university, and the job teaching English was just a way of getting there. I'd been given a few days' training and a certificate that claimed I was qualified, but the schoolteacher I was assigned to help was paid so little, she would find any excuse not to show up for class. Many of the students she abandoned me with came from families of the suddenly former-Soviet elite: well-off, surprisingly well dressed but not very well behaved. Most were also only three or four years younger than me, making it impossible to keep control. The teenagers would chat non-stop through my attempts at lessons. One girl sat powdering her nose.

My roommate, Mishal, once had the bright idea of asking her female students what they'd like to see in an ideal husband. They chose wealth, hands down. When I tried a balloon debate with my own class, they quickly sacrificed Einstein and Pushkin, shoving both overboard to save Marilyn Monroe. On political questions, the teenagers were scathing about Gorbachev, presumably mirroring their parents' views, and approved of his recent resignation. When Mishal asked about the break-up of the USSR, one girl launched into a tirade about how Ukraine was 'taking' Crimea, her family's favourite holiday spot.

There was a shortage of everything, including paper. At one point I asked my parents to send supplies from England because there was none in the school or in the shops. There was also a lack of cash. We were supposed to be paid for our work but the university would regularly run out of funds before we reached the front of the pay queue, giving us a tiny taste of Russian reality. Workers across the country were going without wages, too, although they didn't have a little stash of hard currency like us to fall back on. Our official monthly stipend was 350 roubles, which was worth less than $3, but you could go ice skating in Gorky Park for 2 roubles and it was only 75 kopecks to visit St Basil's Cathedral on Red Square. In a letter home on 19 February 1992 I declared 'Basil' to be my 'favourite sight in the whole world'. Two decades later, its multicoloured onion domes would be forever linked in my mind with Boris Nemtsov and the image of his lifeless body, face-down on the nearby bridge.

The private tuition I gave went far better than the classroom teaching, and my students' parents would feed me in return for my efforts. I would arrive at Zhanna's flat every Thursday afternoon to find a huge spread laid on by her mother: soup, a hot dish, cheese, cakes and sweets. I had no idea where she found it all, but after our lesson Zhanna would stuff all the leftovers into a plastic bag, telling me her mother would be angry I hadn't eaten enough. When I finally met her mother, she thrust even greater quantities of food at me, overjoyed that her daughter was getting some language practice with a real-life English person. It was the same for all our group. We were often the first Westerners people had ever met and we were welcomed into their homes and overfed.

Roommate's diary, 15 April 1992

As an army officer, Igor never dreamed he would be able to entertain foreigners in his home. He had never really questioned the Communist Party until he read Solzhenitsyn's *Gulag Archipelago*, which changed his life. At the time he didn't want to believe what he was reading. Now he was a supporter of Yeltsin ... To him, the most important thing was that Yeltsin had not taken away any of their new freedom.

Through teaching, I began to learn the practicalities of family life in Moscow, led in boxy identical flats that had to be kept neat because so many people were squeezed inside them. The decor was replicated right across the now-former USSR: a thick red rug hanging on one wall of the living room opposite a glass-fronted cabinet that usually displayed Lenin's collected works, unopened, and maybe Jack London's *The Call of the Wild*. At night the couch would become someone's bed and in winter, when a mother said she was taking her baby out 'onto the street', it often meant she was wheeling the pram onto the balcony of her tower block and opening the window. The same space was ideal for chilling vodka. For me, the sheer harshness of Russian life, from its climate to its politics, was always countered by the warmth to be found on the inside, from the homes to the people.

I would escape from giving classes whenever I could to travel widely across Russia and the ex-USSR, catching flights over graveyards of crashed plane carcasses and taking trains that we had to bribe the conductor to board, even with valid tickets. We would stay with Russian friends wherever we made them. In St Petersburg, renamed from Leningrad the previous year, we visited one family at their *kommunalka*, a communal apartment in an eighteenth-century mansion just off the grand central sweep of Nevsky Prospekt. The building had been divided into flats by the Soviet authorities, with multiple households sharing one kitchen and bathroom, and in the 1990s many still lived that way. Our hosts were reeling from the abrupt downward shift in their lives. The mother, Lena, was an engineer who had been laid off and was now working as a night watchwoman, which she was embarrassed to admit. Prices were rising so fast that many things were now completely out of the family's reach, including their much-treasured annual holiday to the Black Sea. All they had left was a box of memories on slides and a projector.

Lena talked fondly of the past and had no faith in the future under Russia's new leaders. Her greatest ambition for her children was for them to find foreign partners, fall in love and leave the country. She seemed lost. But Russians tend to live for the moment and the family still knew how to have fun. Slava, the father, took us on a joyous car tour of the city, even though petrol was scarce and only available for coupons. Back at the flat he then opened the vodka and switched on the television and we all danced round their living room like crazy people to the music from the adverts.

Protest

Most of my diary entries are about people and places rather than politics. There's little in my notes as an eighteen-year-old to suggest a journalist-in-waiting. I even managed to miss the first time protesters in Moscow clashed with riot police because I'd arranged to meet a man who was selling a cheap piccolo. I emerged from the metro station that day with a friend to find police blocking the steps up onto the street and the underpass crammed full of people. We shoved our way through to head straight for our meeting, inadvertently swerving the most violent protest since the Soviet collapse.

The new Russia had experienced its first riot a few weeks earlier in Stavropol, when shoppers smashed windows in a rage over the price of sausage. The protest in Moscow came on Army Day, when events began peacefully with a wreath-laying at the Tomb of the Unknown Soldier. They ended with crowds shouting against everything to do with Yeltsin and his reforms, including a ban on the Communist Party itself. The protest leaders were hardliners who demanded the return of the USSR, waving pictures of Lenin and Stalin and chanting that Yeltsin was a fascist. They were joined by nationalists, capitalising on the pain of Russia's lurch towards a market economy. Many in the crowd were elderly, the pensions they had relied on suddenly worthless.

Yeltsin didn't shy away from the public anger. In mid-January 1992, Russia's first elected president had been on walkabout in various cities, addressing crowds through a loudhailer and seeking their support for his deep-cutting reforms. He blamed seven decades of communism for what he was having to do, asking for patience and understanding. In some places he found it, in others he was met with jeers.

But on 23 February, the communists had been denied permission to march through central Moscow. Their route to Manezhnaya Square was blocked by rows of OMON riot police, snow ploughs and rubbish trucks. When several thousand demonstrators tried to charge the lines, police beat them back with truncheons. The worst clashes were to the north, on Mayakovskaya Square, where several dozen people were injured, and a rumour spread that a senior military figure had died of a heart attack after being struck on the head. The day ended with a firework *salyut* to mark the military holiday as planned.

Roommate's diary, 25 February 1992

A lot of people were shocked by Yeltsin's readiness to bring OMON troops into the centre of Moscow and say it's a mark of his vulnerability that he quashed a peaceful demo with such force. There's talk of creeping censorship as TV programmes critical of the government suddenly have mysterious power failures.

Friend's letter home, 25 February 1992

Yeltsin and his government are not at all popular here … In a way it's inevitable, but I am now rather sceptical having been very pro when I came here. I don't know what to make of him. I don't know if anyone could do his job any better.

The next time there was a big rally in Moscow, three weeks later, I was in the thick of it. A photo from that day captures me standing on Manezhnaya Square beneath the Kremlin walls with red hammer-and-sickle flags all around. An American student with a fancy camera had managed to blag his way through to the press area by talking loudly at the police in English. I then slipped through the cordon behind him. The city authorities had decided to allow the gathering, anxious to avoid more clashes. The protestors were calling for Gorbachev and Yeltsin to be arrested for allowing the disintegration of the USSR and the speeches also raged against the West. One woman made a wild claim that the Yeltsin government was spiriting young Russians abroad as child labour. 'Her words hushed the crowd, moving many to tears,' my roommate Mishal recorded.

I wandered through the flags and people, taking pictures. On one of my shots from that day there's a home-drawn placard with Yeltsin tied to a railway line by a noose. The slogan also slams Yegor Gaidar, the author of Russia's shock economic therapy. The crowd's anger was clear, but the gathering was smaller than the organisers had planned and my pictures reveal a somewhat sorry-looking bunch. This time it all ended without violence.

Slava

Slava had a smile that showed off several gold teeth and hair that was constantly changing colour. Naturally dark-haired, one day he turned up at our hostel bleach-blonde. Another time he'd dyed his hair bright orange. He told us he was in trouble with the local mafia and the dye was so they didn't recognise him immediately as he drove around town, and didn't shoot. He couldn't afford to change his car, so he switched his hair colour instead.

Slava was the husband of a close friend who I suspect didn't know the half of what he was up to. He was my insight into the dark and wild side of 1990s Moscow, a land of immense opportunity that became a deadly scramble for wealth. As a journalist, it was the kind of story I would one day seek out, but at the time Slava was part of my Russian life. I've changed his name here, although he died years ago after a spell in prison.

As organised crime erupted, the English word 'killer' entered the Russian language. Businessmen who refused to pay protection money were shot. Others hired hitmen to kill their commercial rivals, just because they could. The first year I was in Moscow, the murder rate leapt almost 50 per cent.

Those were the years when the men who would become Russia's powerful oligarchs made their first fortunes, buying up state-run enterprises in the knock-down sale of the century. Future influential billionaires like Mikhail Khodorkovsky went from running a café to owning Russia's biggest oil producer, before falling foul of Putin. But for every emerging tycoon, there were many more men like Slava who occupied bit parts in a burgeoning criminal underworld and went nowhere.

I had no idea what Slava's business was, only that he would buy and sell anything. We called him *Nash Bank*, our bank, because when we arrived in Moscow he suggested we all gave him our dollars for safekeeping. At a time of empty shelves and long queues, Slava told us he could then find whatever we needed and deduct the cost from our 'account'. We declined the service, politely.

Diary entry, 1992

I always realised that Slava was involved in some kind of dodgy business – who isn't these days in Moscow? – and he was quite open about it, especially when he got drunk. He used to say that money is no problem, it lies on the street. All you need to do is pick it up.

Slava would often drop by our hostel with presents or to take us out for a trip, perhaps a dash up to the Lenin Hills to look down over the city as dawn broke. But one day he pushed open the door of Room 312, strode in and announced that he had a *zalozhnik* in the car outside. We all stared back at him blankly. Someone started thumbing through a dictionary, then read out the entry. *Zalozhnik*. Hostage. Pleased that we finally understood, ignoring our startled looks, Slava explained that someone had stolen a significant amount of money from his gang, so the two groups were now 'at war' until he got his cash back. To make sure of that, he was holding one of their group captive until the rival gang returned what they owed.

Diary entry, 1992

He had left this guy, who was only about twenty, outside in the car with the keys in the ignition, telling him that the hostel was surrounded and he was being watched and that some of his men were inside, armed and would shoot if he tried to get away.

It turned out that Slava's 'men' were us. A bunch of scruffy foreign students. He reassured us that he'd given his hostage a book to read in the car and a glass of Soviet *shampanskoye*, but he wanted three of our group to go down and pretend to be his back-up. 'You must not talk of friendship. Talk only of guns, war and business,' he instructed a skinny pacifist vegetarian and two Americans who could barely squeeze out a word in Russian. Out in the car, champagne-sipping captive in the back, Slava peppered the students with questions in broken English about 'business in Irkutsk', and the three did their best to look shady.

We would often exchange our dollars with *Nash Bank* as the actual banks never had any roubles and Slava was safer than finding a black-market 'speculator' on the street. I still have a note, written in green biro in English with random capitalisation. 'SARAH. I'll come two hours later! I Have a talk with you about dollars.' One time, counting out my cash in the gloom of their Lada, his partner opened the glove compartment and showed me a gun. The gang's life was precarious and dangerous, though to a young student a long way from home it was part of the adventure that was Russia.

When Slava's wife, my friend, was at her parents', he would call us over to the flat and cook the kind of food we saw nowhere else in those days: giant slabs of meat, or fried eggs for me, followed by big boxes of chocolate. He had a whole cupboard full of Magna cigarettes he claimed he'd been given for free, and he would drown us in vodka, praising me for drinking 'like three men'. I noted that compliment in my diary. 'Unfortunately it was an honour I was compelled to live up to at every meal.' We would then work our way through a VHS collection of pirated American films available in Russia for the first time and all dubbed by one monotonous, gravelly voiced man.

'Before driving me home to the hostel, [Slava] would slip a wad of roubles in his pocket, just in case ... or his Tic-Tacs, which he called anti-police pills,' I wrote. Everyone wanted to make money fast in those days, including the traffic police, and drivers could bribe their way out of pretty much anything.

Diary entry, 1992

Things have become a lot more serious. Slava declared at one point that three of the group of enemies had been shot dead and only when the rest were dead would he and his gang be safe again.

At some point, Slava and his friends became visibly stressed. They were desperately searching for dollars to buy guns. He began showing up less frequently at the hostel, his hair-dye ever more dramatic. When I asked Slava once if he'd ever shot anyone, he laughed and told me in English 'only in the butt'.

He sent his wife to live with her parents, telling his in-laws that her English friends had moved in, so there was no room. For a while, I heard nothing from either of them. When I eventually found Slava, he told me their home had been broken into and then 'bombed' through the window, so he and his wife had moved out for good. By then my friend was heavily pregnant and calling her marriage to the mini-mafia man the biggest mistake of her life.

A couple of days before I flew home from Moscow, Slava turned up in Room 312 carrying a gift. My suitcase was already stuffed full and I was planning to travel, in mid-June, wearing several jumpers and a duffel coat to save space. So my heart sank at the sight of the big box he was holding out. Inside was a full bathroom set in bright-pink plastic. Toilet seat, mirror and loo-paper holder. It was big and brash, like Slava.

The Moskva

One of my first flats in Russia as a reporter had a view of the ugliest church in Moscow, although I could see it only if I stood on tiptoe in the kitchen. In a country of delicately shaped and brightly coloured Orthodox churches, Christ the Saviour was plain and brutal in form, but its story mapped the drama of the nation. In 1992, I had been for a swim at the exact same spot.

The cathedral that stands on the Moscow embankment today is a replica. The original nineteenth-century church took forty-five years to build and lasted just forty-eight more before Stalin ordered it to be blown to pieces in 1931. Two demolition experts who refused to help destroy it were sent to the Gulag and several clerics who objected were reportedly shot. Stalin's plan was to replace the church with a towering monument to the superiority of communism, complete with a ninety-metre-tall Lenin on top. But construction was first delayed, then finally stopped by World War II, leaving Moscow with a giant crater. In 1958 that hole was converted into the biggest outdoor swimming pool in the USSR, known as the Moskva.

The heated pool was quite something in its heyday. Video footage from deepest winter shows smiling Soviet citizens bobbing up and down in their rubber hats, clouds billowing up from the warm water. From above it looks like a vast steaming pit melted into the freezing landscape of central Moscow. In the early days there were rumours that people would drown there, especially in winter, when everything was shrouded in steam. The story had it that they were being killed by a secret sect in revenge for the abuse of a sacred site.

By the time I swam in the Moskva myself, its heyday had long passed. The entrance from the changing rooms to the pool was underwater, so in winter you could swim straight through and avoid the icy poolside. The floor was slimy, as the management were running low on chlorine, and we tried not to put our feet down. In one spot, a couple were trying to have sex, barely submerged. 'As we swam to the far side of the pool the colour of the water changed dramatically from its normal green colour to an ominous shade of brown,' I wrote that day in my diary. 'We disappeared very quickly in the other direction, but when we came into very close contact with a floating human turd we decided to escape altogether.' Soon after that visit, the Moskva was shut down and drained for good, too expensive to maintain in a country struggling to meet far more basic needs.

A few years later, Yeltsin ordered the cathedral rebuilt on its original spot. Its vast size was a reassertion of Russian Orthodoxy after decades of official atheism, when churches all over the USSR had been turned into warehouses and museums or destroyed. After 2000, this concrete Moscow giant would be the church where Putin was filmed each Easter, head bowed in prayer and flickering yellow candle in hand. It was an annual image of piety that helped him project his story of Russian tradition and revival. In the mid-1990s, on a visit from St Petersburg, I had stood at the site of the old Moskva and taken photos as Christ the Saviour began to rise again.

Delayed Expulsion

SHEREMETYEVO AIRPORT, MOSCOW, 10 AUGUST 2021

09:41 I've just been told I'm not being allowed into the country … I've been designated a threat to national security … It's a permanent ban from entering Russia.

I spoke directly into the camera, holding my phone out in front of me on a rickety bench in the holding area of Sheremetyevo airport. Just a couple of hours earlier I'd been heading home to my husband in Moscow from a work trip. Now I was waiting to be put on my last ever flight out of Russia and my journalistic instinct had kicked in. The BBC didn't get thrown out of Russia every day: it hadn't happened since the Soviet authorities expelled Tim Sebastian in 1985, along with two dozen other journalists and diplomats. Like it or not, it would be a story.

I wiped my eyes, still puffy and red, and turned on my camera. As I described out loud what was happening I found myself fighting to blink back more tears.

It's a country where … I studied the language, I've been coming here for three decades and I have a lot of friends here, but apparently, for whatever reason, that's it. My whole story with Russia is over. My husband is still here, my dog is still here. My life is still in Russia. But I'm not allowed back.

Shortly after I finished speaking, two men approached. One was from the Russian airline, Aeroflot, and the other was a border guard who wanted to take my passport until I was put on a flight, effectively detaining me. When I reasoned that I needed my passport in order to book a ticket out of there, he decided that he would accompany me instead. As we walked towards the international terminal, I started to talk to my escorts. I told them I was no enemy of their country and no threat to its security. I told them what I thought of Russia's assault on the independent press and about the dire state of relations with Britain. It felt like my last chance to convince at least some Russians that their country was on a dangerous path.

The border guard urged me to stay positive, suggesting that being expelled was a chance to make a 'radical change' in my life. The Aeroflot man, on the other hand, was shocked that a journalist was being deported. He was in his mid-twenties, careful but sympathetic, telling me that he hoped 'the international situation' would get better. 'As you've had such a horrible arrival, the least we can do is give you a good send-off.' I joked that he could order a band to play me to the plane and he suggested whistling a tune instead, before deciding that would be 'a bit sad'.

As there were no more direct flights to London that day, a colleague booked me on a plane via Helsinki. The Aeroflot man said his goodbyes, telling me he hoped 'things will change'. That left the border guard sitting alone with my passport as I paced nervously. He refused a coffee, startled at my offer, saying it would be seen as a bribe.

At 11:41 my foreign editor called from London and told me under no circumstances to get on a plane. People were bashing the phones to try to prevent me being expelled. I bought another coffee and paced some more. The Helsinki flight took off without me.

Back home in our Moscow flat, my husband was a separate bag of nerves. His visa designated him as a 'travelling spouse' and as he was also in Russia on the say-so of the Foreign Ministry, he had to assume he would be told to leave. A friend suggested he pack a bag in case he had to go in a hurry, so he decided to get rid of some clothes. He ended up with a bag full of shirts which he took down to the security booth at the entrance of our apartment block. With minimal Russian, Kes mimed what he imagined said 'Sarah is being booted out of Russia', complete with a kick, and handed over the bag in case the guards could use the clothes. They thought I'd booted him out of the flat.

A notification on my phone announced that I had been booked automatically onto the next direct flight to London, in the morning. As an Aeroflot frequent flier after so many years in Russia, I wondered whether I could get an upgrade on my deportation. Mysteriously, a junior figure at the Foreign Ministry was suggesting to our office that things would be 'resolved' and we should just 'be patient', but no one quite believed him. *I can't help thinking they're messing with us again*, a colleague messaged.

A team from the British Consulate had arrived to demonstrate support. I'd been drinking gallons of tea, and they bought me more as we agreed that the chances of me entering Moscow that day ranged somewhere between minimal and non-existent. As time dragged, and we began to dare to hope, one of the team told me she would be happy to eat her hat. 'We'll have a hat-eating party.' When she went to find out about urgent Covid tests for travel, the Aeroflot staff told her they'd seen a video of my encounter with Alexander Lukashenko in Belarus and they wanted to know if that was why I was being expelled.

> 14:32 Am so tired. I would ideally like to be deported looking better than this.

Kes and I began messaging back and forth about practicalities, assuming that I would be in London within a matter of hours and that he and our puppy, Smudge, would be stranded. We had only three weeks left on our latest visas and had been living for some time with the nagging thought that they might not be renewed. But deportation was not a scenario we had planned for. The border guards had told me I would be sent home, but apart from a few months between two postings, I hadn't lived in the UK for over twenty years. My home at that point was in Moscow.

> 17:11 Kes to Sarah: Have you heard anything? This is killing me.

Some eleven hours after landing in Sheremetyevo, the consular staff persuaded me to check into one of the airport's capsule hotels. Just then, I got a call. Somehow, somewhere, something had shifted.

> 18:35 Sarah to Kes: I may be allowed in tonight, I don't know any more.
> 18:45 Sarah to colleague: It would be amazing if that's true, and even more amazing if not for a day.

I decided it was time for a drink. Sidestepping a restaurant called Magadan, with its worrying associations with the Gulag, I'd just ordered a beer from the sausage place next door when a group of border guards approached. Politely, they told me I could now make my way back to Terminal F and passport control. My head was spinning. For a while I stayed put, sensing the sudden need to reassert some control. My rebellion didn't last. Another group of men approached our table and the one with a bodycam pinned to his chest began barking commands. His machismo was presumably aimed at whoever would view the footage later, because when a woman started flirting with him on the train between terminals, his bad-guy routine disintegrated.

Nearing the line of kiosks at passport control, I froze. I had signed a piece of paper that declared me a national security threat and made it a criminal offence to enter Russia. I told my escorts I needed that paper to be ripped up before I crossed. They looked baffled, then irritated. Then they insisted it wasn't important. 'It doesn't mean anything.' But just that morning it had meant everything. They shrugged, led me back to the wobbly bench and told me to wait.

I was left to stew for almost an hour before I was summoned to the glass booth and my passport was stamped for what I supposed would be my last entry into Russia. The Foreign Ministry had already called me in the next day 'to talk'. But just after 20:00, more than twelve hours after landing in Moscow, I walked through the empty customs hall towards the sliding door of the exit. It opened. I was going home and I couldn't quite believe it.

> 20:26 Sarah to Kes: God knows what happens next, but at least I am in.

PART III

Diary entry, Dnipro, 26 February 2022

I can see tweets flashing up on my computer about Kyiv where my colleagues are hunkered in bunkers. *EXTREMELY HEAVY RUSSIAN AIR RAID EXPECTED IN KYIV WITHIN MINUTES.* There had been some pretence tonight that Putin was ready for talks. Moscow then claimed it had paused its 'operation' before declaring that the 'fascist government' in Kyiv wasn't interested in peace, and resuming its attacks. It seems Russia didn't manage the swift, victorious war it thought it would pull off and now plans to bombard Ukraine's capital into surrender. This is crazy. Even if Putin 'takes' Kyiv, what will he do with it? I think he has lost touch with reality and there is no one in his circle willing to stop him.

'V'

E40 HIGHWAY TO KYIV, MARCH–MAY 2022

When Leonid Pliats and his boss were shot in the back by Russian soldiers, the killing was captured on CCTV cameras in every terrible detail. It was the height of the fighting around Kyiv and the main roads into the city were a battlefield, including near the bicycle megastore where Leonid worked as a security guard. But what happened there was not an armed clash, it was an execution. I've watched all the camera angles available, and they show heavily armed Russian soldiers shooting the two unarmed Ukrainians and then looting the business as one man lies dead, and the other dying.

Our local producer, Mariana, managed to get hold of the footage from her contacts in the local territorial defence force and our cameraman spent hours matching up the various cameras and time codes. We then checked what we saw on film against the testimony of multiple witnesses. They included several of the people Leonid was able to call after being shot, as well as the men who tried to rescue him. We also visited the scene on the Zhytomyr highway running west from Kyiv and found bullet casings inside the showrooms and shattered glass from the soldiers' looting spree.

The attackers used a stolen van painted with the 'V' sign used by Russian troops and the words *Tank Spetsnaz*, or Special

Forces. Wearing Russian military uniform, they approached the territory of the bicycle shop with their guns up, fingers on the triggers. The CCTV footage shows Leonid walking towards them with his hands in the air, clearly indicating that he is unarmed and no threat. At first the soldiers talk to him and his boss through the tall green fence. The footage is mute, but from the images the men seem calm. They even smoke together. Leonid would later tell a friend he'd offered the soldiers cigarettes and that the Russians told him they didn't kill civilians. He and his boss then turn away and the soldiers do the same, as if to leave. But two of the Russians suddenly turn back, crouch down and shoot the Ukrainians multiple times in their backs.

The company director was killed instantly, his body dropping to the tarmac. But Leonid somehow survived to stagger to his feet. He removed his belt and managed to wrap it around his thigh, pulling it tight to slow the bleeding. Slowly, still holding one end of this tourniquet, he stumbled towards his cabin behind the showrooms and began phoning for help.

Vasyl Podlevskyi spoke to Leonid twice that day as his friend lay bleeding heavily and in terrible pain. 'I said can you at least bandage yourself up? But he told me, Vasyl, I barely crawled here. Everything hurts so much. I feel really bad.' Vasyl and I were talking in the grounds of a nearby village school, where even a marble plaque to the Second World War had a bullet through it. The recent fighting in the region had been ferocious, but Vasyl was still struggling to make sense of what had happened to his friend. 'This was the Russian military, not some gang. Soldiers are supposed to shoot each other. What have civilians got to do with it?'

Leonid had already retired, but he'd taken on the job in the bike shop to top up his pension and keep himself occupied. When the war started, his family were relieved he was so far out of the capital, where they assumed he'd be safer. But on his very first day at work, as Russian forces advanced along the E40 towards Kyiv, he got trapped. The local territorial defence asked the pensioner to act as lookout, so Leonid would sometimes climb onto the bike-store roof and report back what he saw. He assured his daughter he was fine, explaining that he'd moved into a Portakabin behind the shop and was making pancakes there to eat.

A few weeks later, when we went to investigate the shootings, I saw the cabin myself. By then, the stove and a rusty camp bed had been stacked up outside, along with some blood-stained sheets and Leonid's black woollen cap. Inside, I found a pile of detective novels.

When Leonid told his friend he'd been shot, Vasyl immediately called the territorial defence for help. These were volunteers who'd sent their families away to western Ukraine and stayed to defend the road to Kyiv and their villages. The two men tasked with reaching Leonid had run an air-conditioning business before the war. Now they had to figure out how to rescue a wounded man. But as the security guard was bleeding out in his hut, the Russians who'd shot him were still on site. The CCTV footage reveals the soldiers shooting their way into rooms around the complex and stealing bicycles and a scooter, which they shoved into the back of their van. They then made themselves at home in the office of the director they had killed, opening his whisky and rifling through his cupboards. It was some time before anyone spotted the security cameras in the room and realised that their every movement had been filmed. One man smashed the lens, but it was too late. Their faces had been captured, including that of a soldier in a 'Russian Army' T-shirt. After studying the footage in minute detail – the men's movements, their clothes and build – we believe that one of the men helping himself to a drink in that room was one of the two gunmen who had shot Leonid and his boss.

The territorial defence team had no choice but to pause their rescue effort until the Russians left. The Ukrainian volunteers were only lightly armed at that point, didn't even have proper body armour, and were easily outnumbered. The two men I met also admitted that they were terrified. 'We talked to Leonid on the phone, we tried to calm him. We told him, it's okay. Everything will be okay. You'll survive,' one of them, Sasha, recalled. But by then the CCTV camera in Leonid's hut shows him lying in a pool of his own blood. He'd been shot in the back, and the bullet had then ripped through his groin. Sasha realised that the best he could do was to comfort him. 'We said we were on our way. Maybe that helped him. Maybe. But unfortunately, by the time we got there, he was dead.' When the volunteer fighters finally reached Leonid, they counted ten bullet holes in his body. As they loaded him and his boss into a car, they had to take cover as another Russian tank rolled past.

The main road to Leonid's village was lined with charred trees, smashed buildings and the carcasses of burned-out Russian tanks. As we drove, we saw people pulling over to take photos beside the wreckage, celebrating how their troops had halted the terrifying advance. I watched a man using one of the cannons like a giant barbell, filming himself as he tested his strength. In that area, the Russian troops had daubed a white letter 'V' in Latin script on the front of their tanks. It was one of the symbols of their invasion, like the 'Z', and we found the two tags everywhere they'd been. The Defence Ministry in Moscow struggled to explain the letters' significance. At some point they decided 'Z' was from *Za Pobedu*, For Victory, and the 'V' came from *Sila V Pravde*. Strength in Truth. Knowing what happened under Russian occupation, the symbols were chilling. But like the war itself, they made no sense.

Leonid's ramshackle house was just as he'd left it in late February 2022, filled with scattered belongings and clothes. On one shelf was a chess clock 'made in the USSR' and an Orthodox icon propped against the wall. On another were dozens of books, tattered copies of Tolstoy and Taras Shevchenko, Russian novelist and Ukrainian poet side by side. Outside, we fed hot-dog sausages to a friendly Alsatian-style dog called Archie, tethered on a long chain in a yard that was dotted with bright-red wild tulips.

Leonid's daughter was in Poland when the war broke out. When we spoke in May, a couple of months after her father's death, Yulia still couldn't reach Ukraine because of the fighting. 'I beat myself up all the time. I didn't realise how dangerous that road was, or I'd have begged him to go to Kyiv.' But no one had known, and Yulia's father had reassured her that he was safe. 'My dad was not a military man. He was a pensioner! They killed a 68-year-old. What for?' She described Leonid as fit and healthy, 'with the blood pressure of an astronaut', and sent me a picture of him relaxing on his sofa with a big ginger cat lolling on one shoulder. She'd had to identify his corpse by photographs sent from the morgue.

Yulia was firm that she wanted those responsible for her father's killing to stand trial one day. 'But I'm not so much furious as full of grief and fear. These Russians are so out of control, I'm afraid of what they might do next.' Most of all, she wanted the brutality to stop.

Back in Kyiv, we showed the CCTV footage we'd obtained to the chief of police for the region, Andriy Nebytov. After the Russian troops were repelled, his forces had found the bodies of thirty-seven civilians along the road to Ukraine's capital, all of whom had been shot. Some had been killed in their cars, others as they tried to run for their lives. Later, I saw many of those car wrecks on a plot of wasteland where they'd been collected together temporarily. Some were clearly marked *deti*. Children. I approached one vehicle, but the sickly sweet smell of death was overpowering and I turned away quickly.

Even the police were struggling, their boss told me. 'The whole of Kyiv region is a crime scene. We have seen death before, of course, but not cold-blooded killings on this scale. People are in such pain, such grief, it's hard for our teams to take.' As we talked in his office in central Kyiv, an air-raid siren wailed to remind us that this particular crime scene was still a war zone. His team had recruited local journalists, experts in digital investigations, to help them trace suspects online, as the police collected physical clues on the ground. The prosecutor's office confirmed that it was investigating the killing of Leonid Pliats and his boss as a possible war crime. Just a few months into the war, it was one of more than 10,000 cases already registered.

Fallen Statues

There is a giant lump of granite outside the headquarters of Russia's FSB security service that was brought all the way from the Gulag. The Solovetsky stone was specially selected and transported to Moscow from a remote island in the far north, where thousands of political prisoners had once been held in a forced-labour camp. In the final year of Soviet Russia, the stone was placed on Lubyanka Square in remembrance of the victims of totalitarianism. On 30 October 1990, thousands gathered for an unveiling ceremony, lighting up the dusk with their candles as a funeral march played from a speaker mounted on a nearby bus.

The monument was the first of its kind in Russia, and although it was paid for by the Moscow city government, the idea and installation were all down to an organisation called Memorial. Formed in the last years of the USSR by a group that included Andrei Sakharov, the nuclear scientist who had become the Soviet Union's best-known dissident, Memorial was a driving force in Russia's early democratisation. The organisation's goal of recovering the names and stories of the victims of state terror came from a belief that modern Russia needed to confront and acknowledge its demons to ensure such crimes were never repeated. Memorial's focus later expanded from historic repression to monitoring modern-day human rights violations and political persecution. It saw the threat of authoritarianism as still present, a battle that still needed to be fought.

Memorial was bold from the very start. On a blustery night in October 1989 its members organised a candlelit march on the then-KGB headquarters, encircling a building that could strike fear in anyone. Some in the crowd were the relatives of people who had been imprisoned or executed; everyone was there to protest for more political freedom. They stood on Lubyanka Square for a full thirty minutes. Memorial soon had more than a hundred branches and thousands of members countrywide. People who had kept their stories of political repression secret even from relatives began to talk; in a whisper at first, then a crescendo.

When the Solovetsky stone was installed, a monument to lawlessness and repression was still standing nearby. Felix Dzerzhinsky, founder of the original Soviet secret police, towered over the same square, back straight and chin up, one hand tucked into his overcoat pocket. But in August 1991, with an attempted coup against Gorbachev collapsing, pro-democracy protesters converged on the giant Dzerzhinsky, determined to bring his statue down. City officials eventually intervened with a crane to lift 'Iron Felix' from his base before he could crash to the floor and injure anyone below. Rising on a rope, the secret policeman swung by the neck for a moment, to cheers and whistles from an ecstatic crowd.

A few months later I found Dzerzhinsky sprawling in the slush. By the time I arrived in Moscow as a student in 1992, the once-formidable statue had been dumped on its side in a park. His old pedestal was there too, still daubed with the word *palach*. Executioner. By then the muddy area behind the brutalist Central House of Artists, a short walk from our hostel, was littered with fragments of Soviet figures feared or revered only recently. The fallen heroes were unlabelled because at that point no Russian needed telling who they were. Just a few hundred metres away, a giant Lenin still loomed over the ring road from Oktyabrskaya Square, his coat flapping open behind him. Those in charge of the new Russia had decided that removing all the old statues, like renaming all the streets, would be too revolutionary.

I still have photographs of the toppled men, strewn in the mud. There's a chunk of one of Stalin's feet, the dictator's head with blue paint splashed in his face, and assorted bits of Lenin. A dappled-pink Stalin was eventually reunited with his foot and lifted upright. Over the years he's been joined by a big Brezhnev and a whole alley full of Lenins as the area around the gallery has been developed into a sculpture park. Known as Muzeon, it now mixes those icons of Soviet times with more modern statues and attracts crowds of tourists and school groups. The mud has been transformed into carefully tended flower beds and a lush green lawn. With ice-cream vans and cafés, falafel and French croissants, it's a popular spot on the riverbank, close to my old flat. In my last months in Moscow I'd walk our puppy there most days, playing chase beneath a vast Felix, now back up on his pedestal. The museum has added signs to introduce these historic figures to a new generation of Russians. One explains that a heap of stone heads behind barbed wire is a tribute to the victims of totalitarianism, but I'd often see young women draping themselves against the severed heads, pouting and posing for Instagram.

Every so often there would be an attempt to lobby for Dzerzhinsky's return to his original prime spot outside the FSB. His fans quoted opinion polls that showed how a significant number of Russians now saw him in a positive light, as the bearer of order. But even in Russia, such a blatant symbolic reversal was controversial, and the city government always resisted. In the end, on Dzerzhinsky's birthday in 2023, a slightly smaller replica of the famous statue was installed at the offices of Russia's foreign spy service in southern Moscow. But the Felix fans had scored a victory before that. For years, artists and curators at the Muzeon park had debated whether or not to remove the paint on Dzerzhinsky's pedestal that labelled him an executioner. One morning, staff unlocked the gates to discover that someone had broken in overnight and scrubbed the stone clean. The graffiti was gone.

It was after Putin's return to the presidency in May 2012 that Memorial began running into trouble. In July that year, he approved a law that meant any group receiving funds from abroad and engaging in political activity could be branded as a 'foreign agent'. Charities and non-governmental organisations of all kinds were included on a growing list, even a needle-exchange project set up to stop the spread of HIV/AIDs among injecting drug users. The slur was reminiscent of Stalinist times, when dissenters, real or imagined, were persecuted and purged.

Shortly before Putin signed the law, Memorial staff arrived for work one morning to find the words *FOREIGN AGENT* splashed in big letters on their office wall, next to a white love heart and the letters USA. In 2013 the organisation's human-rights wing was added to the official blacklist, and in 2016 Memorial's historical repression wing got the same 'agent' tag. Both were then obliged to mark all publications, including social media content, with their 'hostile' status. They began to be fined for every slip-up. In Putin's Russia, these once-potent symbols of the rejection of tyranny had been labelled the modern-day equivalent of enemies of the state.

Poisoned

MOSCOW, MAY 2015

Three months after Boris Nemtsov was assassinated on the bridge beside the Kremlin, his close friend and political protégé was fighting for his life in a Moscow hospital. By the time Vladimir Kara-Murza's wife made it to his bedside, his vital organs were shutting down. When Evgenia tried to find out what had caused such catastrophic problems, the chief doctor was blunt to the point of cruelty. 'Imagine a train. It crushes you. Does it matter what train it was?' She was told her husband's chances of survival were around 5 per cent.

As reports started coming in that the opposition activist was critically ill, I spoke to his father, a well-known journalist. Kara-Murza was in a coma, doctors were still doing tests and his father was cautious at first about suggesting any kind of foul play. An editor in London suggested the very fact an activist had fallen so ill might be a story, so soon after Nemtsov had been shot, but I hesitated. I didn't know Kara-Murza personally then, but I knew he'd been devastated by his friend's murder and a doctor had mentioned anti-depressants. I was wary of putting a BBC label on the suggestion of suspicious circumstances if there was even a possibility he might have overdosed.

A few days later, I spoke to Kara-Murza's father again. By then he was sure the 'nuclear reaction' taking place in his son's body was not down to any normal medication. After that interview, I filed my story. 'The father of a Russian opposition activist has told the BBC he believes the sudden, severe illness of his son is suspicious. "It's clear he's been poisoned," he said. "But by what or who, we don't know."'

At that point, the attempted assassination of the opposition politician Alexei Navalny with nerve agent was still five years in the future. But Kremlin opponents were already prone to sudden, mysterious ailments. In 2004 the campaigning journalist Anna Politkovskaya was taken violently ill as she flew to cover the siege of a school in Beslan by Chechen terrorists. She was sure she'd been poisoned. That same month in Ukraine, the pro-Western candidate for president, Viktor Yushchenko, was left in excruciating pain from a dioxin. His head swelled and lesions filled with pus appeared all over his body. The list goes on.

In 2015 Kara-Murza's medical team could not fathom the cause of his devastating symptoms. He was thirty-three and usually fit, but now he had doctors discussing heart failure, kidney problems and pneumonia. His family brought in an Israeli medic who confirmed the symptoms could have been caused by an unknown toxin but couldn't be more specific. The whole idea of poisoning is to make it hard to trace and treat, and Kara-Murza's medical team focused firmly on the second part. He was in a coma for a week with his wife at his bedside throughout 'guarding him like a dog'. The couple had met at school, become teenage sweethearts and married soon after they graduated from university. Evgenia describes her husband as her partner, lover and best friend. As he lay unconscious, she talked to him non-stop, sharing news from home about their three children in the hope he could hear. She remembers chiding him that he had to wake up because he still had a documentary to finish about Nemtsov, and she couldn't do it without him.

Finally, he defied the terrible odds and regained consciousness. It was several weeks before Kara-Murza was strong enough to leave hospital in Moscow. But in July 2015, Evgenia got him onto an air ambulance and out to the US. In hospital there she poured all her energy into getting him better, helping him to walk again and even teaching him to hold a spoon. Her husband was impatient. Back home and regaining strength, he would insist on staggering down from their bedroom to work from the sofa. 'He had all these lasting effects of the poison,' Evgenia told me, years later. 'So he would work and then throw up every half hour and then go back to work. And I would be there, feeding him spoonfuls of yoghurt.'

Kara-Murza was a child of *Perestroika*. The family were not well-off – his father was a journalist, his mother a translator – and he spent his early years in a communal flat where you had to queue for the shared toilet or to use the kitchen. Kara-Murza also remembers the long food queues and ration cards of the late 1980s. But some of his strongest memories are of the first stirrings of democracy.

He was ten years old in August 1991 when Soviet hardliners made their move against Gorbachev and his reforms. Across the USSR, *Swan Lake* played on television sets as crowds in Moscow surrounded the White House, preparing to defend the seat of parliament and their newly won freedoms. Kara-Murza's father and friends were among them, as was Boris Nemtsov. With tanks heading their way, they built barricades ready to resist any attempt to storm the building. Three protesters were killed on the first night, but the coup quickly imploded.

Those heady, dangerous days made a deep impression on the young Kara-Murza. His school was close to the KGB headquarters with the giant statue of Dzerzhinsky outside. After the failed coup, Kara-Murza clearly remembers walking to school past an enormous pedestal with nothing left on it but the anti-communist graffiti of protesters.

He was fifteen when he moved to the UK after his mother got remarried to a Yorkshireman translator of Russian. The headmaster at the teenager's public school in London remembered him as 'far and away' the most sophisticated, articulate and vociferous of his peers, although English was Kara-Murza's third language. At just sixteen he set himself up as UK correspondent for the *Novye Izvestia* newspaper by sending a fax and asking straight out for the job. Two years later, the cub reporter got to interview Nemtsov on a trip to London, and impressed the politician so much he took him on to help out. Eighteen years old and 'practically a nobody', Kara-Murza was struck by the respect Nemtsov had shown him. They became firm friends, despite the age gap.

That same year, Kara-Murza applied to Cambridge with earnest explanations about how the 'vividness' of his experience during the 1991 coup had sparked his interest in studying history. 'I have thus truly had the opportunity to witness history in the making,' he typed in his application, which I was able to see at Trinity Hall. At the top of the blue form is a photograph of his confident, smiling face. Under 'possible career' he printed 'POLITICS', describing that as his 'other great passion' after history.

Kara-Murza told me later that he'd set up his first political party in Moscow in 1994, calling it the Children's Democratic Party of Russia and trying to get it registered by the Justice Ministry. 'Even for those democratic days, this was too much. We were rejected.' He laughed at that memory. But applying to Cambridge, Kara-Murza was already sure where his future lay. 'I hope one day to achieve my greatest aspiration: that of leading the country in which I was born.' A reference from his school told the college his ambitions were 'not to be taken lightly'.

His tutors at Cambridge remember him as exceptional: precocious but popular, earnest but energetic. Two decades on, Kara-Murza's former director of studies, Clare Jackson, could also recall his 'exquisite' manners. He brought her premium vodka after his final exams, delivered, she remembers, in the finest manner of diplomatic gift-giving. A fellow student described him as a 'serious type' who stood out because he wasn't into 'sport and socialising'. One tutor thought it was at Cambridge that the young Russian first wore tweed, a quirky fashion choice that stuck for life. He graduated with a double first, which meant he'd achieved top marks throughout, including in a final-year paper on Margaret Thatcher. His supervisor recalls him as something of a fan, but then he was also a fan of *Fawlty Towers* and *Yes Minister*.

Neither Kara-Murza's college nor his contemporaries appear to have known that he was nipping back to Moscow mid-term, both to see Evgenia and to keep up his increasingly active role in Russian politics. His academic results were so good that no one was particularly worried about any extracurricular activity. As soon as he graduated, Kara-Murza returned to Moscow to run for a seat in parliament.

It was 2003 and Putin had been in power just three years, but there were already strong signals about the nature of his rule. That October the oil tycoon Mikhail Khodorkovsky was arrested and would later be sentenced to ten years. The way he was singled out was taken as a warning to other businessmen to stick to making fantastic amounts of cash and keep out of politics. The same year, Russia's last remaining independent national television station, TVS, was taken off air and in December, when Kara-Murza stood for election with Nemtsov's SPS party, the ballot was neither free nor fair. In those days, opposition candidates could still make it onto the ballot and Kara-Murza was even allowed on TV for a pre-election debate, but his microphone was cut. He was permitted some billboards around town, but the lights never came on and the short winter days ensured that they were invisible most of the time. The pro-Putin candidate for the seat duly won by a landslide. In the circumstances, Kara-Murza felt his second place was respectable.

With his political ambitions temporarily thwarted, he switched back to journalism as a day job and for a decade was based in Washington for a TV channel aimed at Russian speakers abroad. But Kara-Murza never abandoned his activism: these were the years when he and Nemtsov were lobbying US politicians for the Magnitsky Act, which was passed by Congress in 2012. The idea was to sanction those senior officials who violated human rights in Russia without a care, but who did care deeply about their property and bank accounts in the West. To hit the corrupt where it hurt, as Kara-Murza later explained it to me. 'There's few things they're so afraid of like losing their Western lifestyles. That's how they cope: steal here and spend there.' More lobbying brought similar, potentially powerful sanctions acts in the UK, EU and beyond.

Kara-Murza didn't return to Russia full time until 2014, when he was offered a role there by Khodorkovsky. Recently released from prison, the former oligarch was living in exile, now a sworn enemy of Putin. The job he had for Kara-Murza was in Moscow with his newly launched pro-democracy group, Open Russia, but Khodorkovsky warned his latest recruit to leave his wife and children abroad for safety. Kara-Murza thought him paranoid, 'afraid of his own shadow' after so long in prison. A year later, lying in hospital, he realised it was the best advice he'd ever had.

It took Kara-Murza six months to recover in the US from his poisoning, then he packed his bags and headed back to Moscow. His wife remembers it all as crazily fast. 'As soon as Vladimir could limp, he limped to the airport.' The activist was still using a walking stick and would never regain full feeling in his left foot and arm. He also suffered from dizziness and other symptoms. His determination to return to his work left Evgenia both scared and full of respect. 'I love and I hate him for his integrity,' she told me, later. 'His fight is bigger than his fears.'

By that point, there was plenty to fear. The climate for those in opposition to the Kremlin was becoming even more overtly hostile. In February 2016 Nemtsov's friend, and a former prime minister, Mikhail Kasyanov had a cake slammed in his face in a Moscow restaurant. A few days later he was pelted with eggs by a crowd calling him a traitor and yelling at him to leave the country. That April, the married politician and his lover would be publicly humiliated when a covertly filmed recording of them having sex was shown on national television.

In another disturbing episode, the Chechen leader Ramzan Kadyrov, whose allies were directly connected to Nemtsov's killing, lashed out against critics of the Kremlin as jackals and 'vile'. He published a video on Instagram of Kasyanov and another man in the sights of a gun, claiming they'd been filmed taking money from Western sponsors to fund subversive activity against Russia. The second man in the video was Kara-Murza.

Ever since her husband's sudden illness, Evgenia had been sleeping with her phone beside her pillow whenever he travelled. On 2 February 2017 she received another terrifying call. It was Vladimir, calling from Moscow, where it was 05:00. He was due to take a flight back to the US and his family that day, but had woken with the same symptoms as before. His heart was racing and he was struggling to breathe. Within hours he was back in intensive care and in a coma. This time the chief doctor's conclusion was clear and immediate. Kara-Murza had suffered 'poisoning by an unknown substance'. Whoever was responsible had probably banked on him being mid-flight when the toxin kicked in, which would likely have been fatal.

It was shortly after that diagnosis that I met Evgenia in person for the first time in Moscow, where she'd rushed again to be by her husband's side. His condition was still very unstable and she was scared, but she wanted the world to know what had happened in the hope that the spotlight might somehow help. She reminded me that Elena Bonner had done the same for her dissident husband, Andrei Sakharov, in Soviet times. We filmed a short and intense interview. Kara-Murza had known the risks in returning, I learned, but came to Moscow again anyway. Evgenia refused to hide behind double meanings or half-spoken words, and she was clear and sure that her husband had been poisoned deliberately. 'We know exactly what we're dealing with here, we know what kind of government we're talking about.' I questioned why anyone would want Vladimir dead when he was no household name, unlike Nemtsov or Kasyanov, and Evgenia pointed to his campaigning for the Magnitsky Act. 'I believe my husband's activity annoys many people. That's what I think could have provoked them to do it.' The sanctions targeted Russia's most rich and powerful. Putin's people.

As Kara-Murza lay on life support, the family took samples of his hair, nails and blood to send abroad for testing, though no one knew what toxin they were searching for or how long it might remain detectable. 'I knew we would probably never find that substance,' Evgenia told me. 'But at least we had this poisoning diagnosis. A true one.' From the US, the FBI confirmed it was investigating an intentional poisoning, but its full results on the toxin used have never been disclosed.

For several years, Kara-Murza's collapse remained a mystery: a sudden, near-fatal illness with no known cause. Probably a poisoning, probably for his political activity, but with no proof and no suspects. That changed after Alexei Navalny was poisoned in 2020. As the opposition politician recovered in Germany, the online sleuths at Bellingcat identified a group of FSB operatives who had been tailing him, part of an alleged hit squad. Navalny then personally placed a disguised call to one of the men, tricking him into revealing details of the poisoning. In early 2021, Bellingcat established that members of the same group had previously tailed Kara-Murza.

Soon after that report was released, I met Kara-Murza in a café in Moscow. At the time we both lived in one of the city's oldest neighbourhoods, not towering and intimidating like much of the Russian capital, but full of narrow streets and pretty churches painted in bright oranges and blues that stood out on even the greyest Moscow day. I was drinking coffee and Kara-Murza had soup, and the whole time he was eating I was remembering how he'd fallen sick the first time in a place just like the one where we were sitting.

The Bellingcat investigation was frightening reading. Tracing the FSB agents' travel records, the team had detected them following the activist before both of his sudden and devastating illnesses, as well as shortly before the assassination of Nemtsov. On 27 May 2015 Kara-Murza had been due to travel to Kaliningrad for a round table, but the men tailing him didn't buy tickets for that flight. It was the day after his first poisoning, the activist pointed out. 'They knew I wouldn't be going there. Realising that kind of gets to you.' Armed with the information Bellingcat had uncovered and more, Kara-Murza tried again to get the Russian authorities to investigate what had happened to him, but they refused to open a case. I asked him why he thought he was targeted, and by then he was certain. 'It wasn't because of some opposition lecture I gave in Kazan. This was about the Magnitsky Act.'

That day, as we chatted, I told Kara-Murza I wasn't sure I could have returned to the city where I was attacked. But he felt he had no 'moral right' to remain in Russian politics while 'sitting in safety abroad', tweeting from Washington. 'I have to be here and share the risks.' His refusal to leave Russia was also an act of defiance. 'Every time I enter the country, they check my passport for forty minutes. When I fly out, it takes three seconds. Stamp, go, get out. But you know what? We're not going.'

Enemy of the People

Georgy Yakovlevich Nesterenko
Arrested: 10 September 1937
Executed: 20 September 1938
Rehabilitated: 4 April 1956

Alexei Nesterenko had just been born when his father was arrested as an enemy of the people. It was September 1937, the height of what historians would label Stalin's Great Purge, but Alexei grew up thinking his dad was one of the millions who had died in the war. Many of his classmates had no fathers either. It was only when Alexei had to fill out a form for university that his mother revealed Georgy had been sent to the Gulag. For years after his arrest, she had written to Soviet officials pleading her husband's innocence and begging for his release.

It wasn't until Alexei was in his late seventies, twice the age his father ever reached, that he began to explore his family history. He was ashamed of how little he knew. The Memorial organisation helped him access his father's KGB file in the archives and Alexei sat leafing through its hundred or so pages in a cavernous reading room, confronted for the first time with the horror his parents had experienced. In the 1930s Georgy Nesterenko had been head of the planning department at a civil aviation institute outside Moscow and part of the new Soviet intelligentsia. The file Alexei was reading described his father's arrest and forced confession, under torture. The interrogators claimed to find 'counter-revolutionary' connections. 'They always had the same formula. It was all fake of course, but that fake was the basis for a death sentence.'

I first met Alexei outside the building where his father was subjected to a closed trial in August 1938. 23 Nikolskaya Street had housed a military court that mounted show trials for everyone from famous writers to students and bureaucrats. The hearings would last fifteen minutes at most, after which some people would be banished to the labour camps but the vast majority were sent for execution – more than 31,000 from this one city court alone. The rulings were based on pre-prepared death lists, many of which carried Stalin's own scrawled signature of approval. Alexei discovered that the sentence of 'ten years' imprisonment with no right of correspondence', the words on the official document his mother received, was code for immediate execution. 'It was a lie, thought up so that people wouldn't know their relative had been shot and wouldn't start sharing that information and making a fuss. Instead, they lived in horror, hoping just like my mother did that their relative would eventually come back.'

Georgy Nesterenko would never return. Imprisoned for a year after his arrest, he was executed straight after his 'trial'. After Stalin's death in 1953, Georgy's case was reinvestigated. According to the KGB file, the man who had claimed he recruited Georgy to work against the USSR withdrew his statement and the chief investigator then admitted to fabricating the charges against Alexei's father and many others. A prosecutor ordered the guilty verdict overturned and Georgy was officially rehabilitated. It was April 1956, eighteen years after he had been taken out and shot.

After uncovering his own family secret, Alexei became a fierce campaigner against plans to turn 23 Nikolskaya Street into an elite boutique selling perfume. The elderly man would take the metro once a week to stand outside the building on the cobblestones, whatever the weather. He held up a laminated photograph of his father and details of his false conviction. A slim man in a woolly hat, his nose red-tipped with cold, Alexei looked frail. But he was driven by a determination that the former courthouse where his father was handed a death sentence should be preserved as testament to Stalin's tyranny. 'You can't consider this site as anything other than a museum to those nightmare pages from our past.'

Alexei worried that too many Russians were still dangerously ignorant of their history, even wilfully so. The Soviet victory over Hitler in the Second World War has acquired near-sacred status under Putin, harnessed for his modern-day projection of Russian might. Stalin himself is increasingly talked of as a 'great war leader' or 'effective manager', rather than the author of state terror and repression. But Alexei believed selling perfume in the former military court that sent his father to the firing squad would be 'like dancing at Auschwitz'.

Memorial used to run occasional walking tours of Moscow that uncovered the history of political repression on the streets of Russia's capital. A topography of terror. I joined a couple of them in early 2020 and they made it impossible to look on Moscow with the same eyes, ever again. One route heads past the tall stone walls of Russia's modern-day FSB Security Service to a lettuce-green mansion. 'Thousands were shot by firing squad in the garages beneath that yard,' the guide told our small crowd, huddled around her in the icy cold. She explained that many of the dead had been sentenced at the court on Nikolskaya Street. I peered through a hole in the fence, but there is nothing at all to mark the spot.

Pulling a bunch of photocopies from her carrier bag, the guide then held up a photograph of Stalin's chief executioner with a chest full of medals. Some estimates suggest Vasily Blokhin personally shot up to 15,000 innocent people before he himself died of natural causes. A few days after the walking tour, I went searching for his grave and found it just inside the grounds of the Donskoy monastery. Blokhin's plot is decorated with lurid purple and orange plastic flowers and the dark marble headstone is etched with images of him and his wife. The executioner's face is locked in a half-smile. Just a few rows away in the cemetery are three mass graves containing the ashes of many of his victims.

When Alexei Nesterenko's mother died, he buried her at the same cemetery, imagining that his father's ashes would be there and hoping his parents could at last be close again. He learned later through Memorial that Georgy had been taken to a different mass burial site further out of town known as Kommunarka. There, nobody is quite sure where the bodies are buried, so relatives pin photographs of the dead to tree trunks in place of headstones.

Vera Golubeva

MOSCOW, AUGUST 2017

In Stalin's Russia, Vera Golubeva was sent to Siberia for telling a joke. Decades later, I sat with the 98-year-old in the yard of her Moscow apartment building as she described the six years she spent in the Gulag. The former school history teacher was warm and witty, but her youth had been stolen.

Vera's parents were arrested at the height of Stalin's Great Terror, taken away at night. When Vera was first detained herself in 1943, she was eight months pregnant. She gave birth prematurely in prison from the stress and three days later a guard brought her the dead body of her son. Vera told me her life was torture after that.

In 1948 she was arrested again and sent to the Ozerlag, a labour camp in the Irkutsk region, where she was forced to chop down trees and lay concrete railway sleepers in temperatures that could plunge to -56°C. The blocks were so heavy it took four women to lift each one. As Vera was physically unable to meet her quota of work she was fed starvation rations. Somehow she survived to tell her tale.

As we talked and filmed in Vera's yard, I noticed a neighbour shooting glances at us from a nearby bench and trying to listen in. When I stood to leave, the woman called out to me. Discovering that I was a foreigner, she instantly became suspicious. 'Was she criticising Russia? Was she saying bad things?' she demanded to know, jabbing a finger towards Vera. 'She'd better not have been. Or we'll give her what for.' As the neighbour shouted her threats, Vera was still struggling to get up from her bench. A frail and elderly woman whose life had been ruined by political hatred, in an era that was supposed to have passed.

We Can't Stop or They Win

KOSTROMA, SEPTEMBER 2015

On the day Boris Nemtsov was shot and killed, Ilya Yashin was forced to see his friend's body on the ground, eyes open but already lifeless. The young opposition activist was one of the first on the scene and announced the news to the world in a stark tweet. 'They shot Nemtsov. He's dead.'

Yashin had always looked to Nemtsov as a source of energy and inspiration. He might well have renounced politics that day out of fear or a sense of hopelessness. Instead, he told me, he felt a duty to go on. 'We have to keep on fighting. It's a question of the future of our country. If we stop, that means they win.'

As a teenage activist, Yashin had paint-bombed a memorial plaque to the former KGB boss Yury Andropov, a personal hero of Putin. Another time, he set himself alight opposite the Kremlin to send the message that 'all dictators burn in hell'. He'd been wearing a protective suit, but had to be taken away by ambulance after inhaling too much smoke. Now in his early thirties, Yashin had progressed to more traditional methods.

Two years earlier, with all other political platforms blocked to him, Nemtsov himself had downshifted to regional-level politics and won a seat in the parliament in Yaroslavl. Now Yashin decided to follow his friend's example and run for a seat in Kostroma. A few hours north-east of Moscow, it was the only region in all

Russia where the Parnas opposition party had been permitted to field candidates. Even then, they'd had to appeal to the courts. In those days, the authorities might allow a few genuine rivals onto the ballot to maintain a veneer of democracy, but they would then go to extraordinary lengths to stop such candidates from actually winning.

Unlike his officially approved rivals, Yashin had no access to state media and had to canvass for support in the old-fashioned way, on the doorstep. As most Russians live in giant apartment blocks, that meant calling people to meetings in their shared yard so that the candidate could hear their complaints and requests directly. But in Kostroma, Yashin's opponents got there before him. When he pulled up to the first location, he found his team rushing round gathering up copies of a pink and baby blue-coloured newspaper called *Kostroma Gay Pravda*. The main image on its front page was of a shiny golden 'strap-on' dildo, which the paper claimed had turned up in a search of Yashin's Moscow flat.

There were copies of the fake publication in every entranceway around the yard where Yashin was due to speak. It was so extraordinary I kept a copy: the pages are covered in phallic images next to headlines like *How to Spot a Gay in a Crowd*. It was the height of the *Gayropa* campaign, when Putin supporters would shout that Europe was trying to impose alien and perverse ways and values on Russia. Claiming that an opposition figure was gay was an easy smear. Even so, *Gay Pravda*, which proclaimed itself a 'periodic publication of the Kostroma region gay community', had taken some serious creative effort both to dream up and produce.

That level of commitment was even odder given the tiny challenge that Yashin or any of the opposition at that point actually presented to Putin. It was rare for more than a handful of *babushki* to turn up to meet prospective election candidates in their yards and those who did come were mainly gathering for a gossip. We once arrived to film with another opposition candidate in a suburb of St Petersburg and no one came to hear her at all. She was mortified. The impact of such electoral encounters on the actual vote had to be minimal, and yet Yashin's wreckers had apparently been instructed to take no chances.

That day in Kostroma the young politician didn't want to be seen in public speaking to the BBC, or even speaking English. The opposition were regularly denounced by officials and state media as a subversive 'Fifth Column' in the pay of the West, and Yashin didn't want to hand them any propaganda presents. Activists were also routinely threatened or attacked. A few months earlier, I'd met a man who'd filmed officials stuffing ballot boxes in a local election and who was then beaten so badly he needed emergency surgery to remove his spleen. So we decided to interview Yashin in his car between meetings, driving through Kostroma along roads lined with warnings of wild moose. As we went, he pointed to billboards plastered with his rivals' faces and their election promises. Everyone was on display up there apart from Yashin, who told me the only way of getting his message across was face to face, down on the ground. 'We have to shake thousands of hands.'

The 2015 campaign in Kostroma was part of an attempt to reinvigorate support for the opposition at the local level, ahead of national elections the following year. After the previous parliamentary vote in 2011, allegations of fraud sparked mass protests, which snowballed into the biggest challenge Putin had faced since taking power. The protests reached a peak during his inauguration in May 2012, when riot police clashed with protesters on Bolotnaya Square, just across the river from the Kremlin. The result was draconian punishment for a selected handful: long prison sentences to deter others from following their example. Three years later, as Yashin and his team prepared for the local vote, some of his fellow activists were still in prison or facing charges for the clashes on Bolotnaya. Others had fled the country and Nemtsov, who played a big part in the protests, was dead. 'Because of all these sad stories, people don't believe in politics anymore. They don't believe in change,' Yashin's campaign manager at the time, Leonid Volkov, told me. He said the Kostroma campaign was about generating optimism again.

In one city neighbourhood, Yashin's team had set up rows of folding IKEA chairs, red blankets draped over the back, in front of a Parnas party banner that pledged to make those in power work for the people. Russian national flags fluttered above it and a loudspeaker pumped music into the yard where six pensioners eventually took their seats. If Yashin was bothered by the tiny turnout when he strode out to speak, he didn't show it. He hoped they might spread the word. 'I've come to discuss the problems that bother us all, and most importantly, how to resolve them,' he addressed the elderly gathering through a microphone he could have done without. His speech, which he was making for the 130th time that month, focused on corruption and giant potholes. It also highlighted the gulf between state pensions and the salaries of senior officials close to Putin. 'We talk about social and economic problems. We don't talk about freedom of speech, for example. That's not what people are worried about. What worries them is how they'll get by the following day.'

It was a short drive to the next gathering of potential voters and once again the turnout was small. That didn't deter the saboteurs. Midway through Yashin's rally a young Black man appeared in a suit and hovered for a moment at the back of the crowd. I thought it unusual for very white, provincial Russia, but pushed the thought to the back of my mind. Then I saw a second man filming the event on his phone from a distance. Moments later one of Yashin's team spotted a car parked nearby with what appeared to be US diplomatic numberplates. When he checked, the licence plates were actually stickers, and he tore them off.

It was an extravagant piece of theatre supposed to suggest the whole Parnas party campaign was an American project and that Yashin's sponsors had come along to check up on him. Whoever had dreamed it up thought the only way to show a foreigner in the crowd was to find someone who was Black. It was crude, but the approach had roots in the 1990s, when someone would leak dirt on their political opponents to the press, damaging their reputation and slashing their ratings. Under Putin, such personal slurs became state practice as the authorities sought to discredit rivals of any kind. With full control over state television, the task was simple.

Yashin lost the Kostroma election. The official count gave Parnas just 2.6 per cent of the vote, below the 5 per cent threshold to enter the regional parliament. His team disputed the count and cited numerous blatant violations at the polls, claiming an electoral war had been waged against them. It was pointless and no one came out onto the streets in protest.

Diary entry, eastern Ukraine, 2 March 2022

Leaving a school that's now a hostel full of refugees, I see an email on my phone from another life. It's from a company I'd ordered cheese from before the war, for Dad's birthday. They want to inform me they sent an extra box by mistake. My head's still full of the stories of families fleeing the fighting but I carry on reading down the email about fancy cheese. 'We've had a think about what to do and in the context of all the horror and tragedy in the world at the moment … we won't be recalling the boxes. We hope they brighten your day.'

Diary entry, Kharkiv region, Ukraine, 3 March 2022

We've stopped for the night at the Forest Motel outside Kharkiv. There's displaced families in every corridor and every corner, even around the pool table. A receptionist who looks like Bet Lynch bustles about finding us tea and a few strands of tepid pasta. She instructs us to keep the curtains closed and lights off, so the Russian bombers won't spot us. People hover in the gloom, faces lit by the panels of their mobile phones. I stumble across some men in a back room and tell them I'm looking for the way to the bomb shelter. *Devushka*, they say. Girl. Don't worry. Nothing will happen here.

Fifteen-year-old Nika and her mum have just arrived after days under fire. Nika spent her time either hiding in the cellar or bashing out chords on the piano to drown out the sound of the explosions. She tells me she's scared now by every sound. Her first thought on waking each morning is to thank God she's still alive.

The Railway Station

DNIPRO, UKRAINE, MARCH 2022

The longest queue at the aid hub in Dnipro was of people signing up for guns to defend their neighbourhoods. The other was of locals bringing medical supplies and food, in case the city came under siege. But the strangest sight were the women shaving chunks of polystyrene with cheese graters and ripping rags into strips to stuff into glass bottles. They were making Molotov cocktails ready to throw at any Russian invaders. A young English teacher called Alina told me her original plans for that Saturday had involved a Pilates class and a party. Now she was making firebombs with her friends. 'This seems like the only important thing to do right now.' Life for all Ukrainians had been transformed with the first air-raid siren. Dnipro was some way from the eastern front lines, a strategic city with rocket factories and military hospitals, but its population mobilised in an instant.

Across Ukraine, city names were scrubbed off road signs to confuse enemy troops. In Dnipro shopkeepers piled sandbags at their windows and residents dragged tyres and boulders to block access to their yards. They were clearing out the basements of their tower blocks, installing mattresses, stoves and supplies so they could move underground during an air raid. In the meantime, they shoved their beds into the centre of their flats where they hoped they might be safer in a missile strike and prepared grab bags of essentials. Everyone seemed to act by instinct, although they'd never been invaded like this before.

One day the staff at our hotel reception called me over to ask my advice. Were they safe or was it time to leave? The women were anxious, close to tears, but they told me they'd been keeping an eye on our team. As long as we were in town, they judged it safe to stay. I warned them that we were not normal. They should find some other measuring stick.

The exodus from Dnipro had already begun. One day I stopped by the city railway station and found the platform heaving with people desperate for a place on the one evacuation train that had just pulled in. There was no timetable, no destination. All anyone knew was that the train was heading west, away from the front lines. A man lodged in the doorway of one carriage was attempting to marshal the crowds. 'Women and children only!' he yelled furiously, as the entire platform pushed forward. Most were carrying minimal belongings: a few bags stuffed with clothes and children's toys because they knew there would be limited room on board. But some had brought pets, including cats in bags. Somewhere in the middle of the crush I saw a glorious red setter dog. As women and children began squeezing on board, husbands and fathers passed pushchairs and blankets over the top of the crowd towards them. All the time there were the screams and tears of families being torn apart.

I remembered the novels I'd read as a child about evacuees in the Second World War and how romantic they'd made it seem as city children were sent to the countryside to escape the air raids. Now I was watching a real-life evacuation and it was heartbreaking. No men of fighting age were allowed to leave Ukraine, so couples had to say goodbye in that chaos with no idea when, or whether, they might meet again. Men pressed mobile phones to their ear with one hand, then pressed the other hand against the train window to connect with relatives inside. A father mouthed 'I love you' to his young sons through the dirty glass. Another told me he was sending his family 'to a better life', before turning away cursing those who had caused their suffering. I saw a husband try to laugh and joke with his wife so she would not see his tears. 'Everything will be okay, it will all be okay,' he kept repeating out loud, trying to convince himself.

Finally, the train was overfull. Doors shut and ready to leave. As the evacuees pulled out of the station, children waving, every single person left behind on the platform was in tears, my own team included.

PART IV

I'm Not the Enemy

MOSCOW, 11 AUGUST 2021

After I was released from the airport, my status in Russia was unclear and felt precarious. I had been allowed back to my flat, but there was no clear indication whether my near expulsion had been an unpleasant mistake or if I'd just been given a stay of execution. The next day I was called in to the Foreign Ministry to find out, and as I set off in the summer drizzle I wasn't brimming with good feeling or optimism.

The ministry is housed in one of Stalin's *vysotki*, the seven towers that were begun in the dictator's day to mark victory in the Great Fatherland War, as it was known in the USSR, and to project the might of the Soviet empire. Giant, stepped skyscrapers with spires that echo those of the Kremlin itself, the *vysotki* were intended to intimidate.

My meeting was in the building's more mundane and modern wing, where the ministry's spokeswoman, Maria Zakharova, held her marathon weekly briefings. They were rambling performances, their content toxic, and her audience soon shrank to reporters from countries closely allied with Russia who would bring gifts instead of probing questions. Zakharova had seemed extreme in her early days, posting endless tirades on social media when she wasn't posting pictures of herself working out in the gym, attracting hundreds of heart emojis from her fans. I used to think her prime role was to make her boss, Russia's long-time foreign minister, Sergei Lavrov, seem moderate by contrast. But by the time of the Ukraine war, Lavrov's statements were every bit as lurid and West-hating.

Zakharova didn't bother to expel me in person. The meeting was chaired by one of her deputies, Ivan Nechayev, who arrived with two colleagues, one in a Covid face mask decorated with a double-headed eagle. Both sat silent throughout but Nechayev didn't beat about the bush. 'We are obliged to inform you, Sarah, that you have been included on the stop list.' He spoke in Russian, apart from *stop list*, which apparently works better in English. 'These are mirror measures for the actions of the British government.' He produced a whole litany of complaints, including UK sanctions against Russian officials for corruption and human rights abuses. These were 'totally unfounded and fabricated' allegations, the functionary intoned, sticking to the script in front of him. He claimed that his ministry had sought a response that best 'mirrored' those sanctions and came up with me.

He also cited the case of a London correspondent for the Russian state news agency TASS who'd had to leave the UK two years earlier, when his visa wasn't extended. A candidate chosen by Moscow to replace him was then denied entry. 'We hoped the British authorities would think better of it and decide to let Russian journalists work normally in the UK … but the situation got worse,' Nechayev claimed. I let that pass a couple of times, then I had to speak up. 'He's not actually a journalist, though, is he?' I'd heard the complaint about this TASS man once before, when my editors protested to the Russian Embassy in London about me being moved to short-term visas. 'They didn't give him a visa because he's not really a journalist. But I am,' I repeated. Nechayev stalled. 'Sarah. Such conjecture … that's not a question to the Foreign Ministry press office, perhaps.'

After that meeting I looked into this man's case some more. It's true that in the summer of 2019 the UK paperwork of a Russian employee with TASS was not extended after some years working in London. But my own sources told me there was 'absolutely no equivalence' between us. This person had been deemed 'not conducive to the public good'. When I asked what exactly that meant, the reply was clear. 'We don't allow undeclared Russian agents to work in the UK.'

The man from TASS had been based in London for years but had no obvious social media accounts and just one byline on a photograph. It was an oddly low profile for a senior London correspondent at a major Russian news agency. Any internet search for my own name throws up articles from all over the world, with photos and videos as well as links to Facebook, Twitter and more. In a statement on my expulsion, the Foreign Office commented that Russian reporters who 'act within the law' continued to work freely in the UK.

Journalism could, of course, be ideal cover for intelligence gathering, allowing a person to move around easily and ask questions. TASS staff have a long record of that, stretching back to Soviet days. I have no way of independently confirming that it's what this particular individual was up to, but I do know that tolerance for Russian secret agents in the UK was at rock bottom. In March 2018 the former double agent Sergei Skripal had been attacked in Salisbury with the Soviet-era nerve agent Novichok, and there was clear evidence that men from Russia's GRU military intelligence agency had tried to kill him. A British woman, Dawn Sturgess, had died.

Nechayev claimed that the TASS man had been dismayed to leave London, deeply attached to his journalism and to his life there. But he never gave interviews, wrote articles or even posted on social media about what had happened. As it's a criminal offence in Russia to identify a spy, I didn't hunt for him too hard. I decided I was already in trouble enough.

On paper, though, Russia had produced a clear reason for expelling me. Many would take that at face value: a Russian journalist in Britain had his visa renewal refused, so Russia had done the same to a British correspondent in Moscow. The Foreign Ministry talked of Russophobia and a blow against free speech. If Britain relented and let the TASS man back, the story went, then I could also return to Moscow. They knew full well that was impossible. The other sanctions against me were apparently meant to mirror the TASS case, particularly the fact that I'd been declared a 'security threat'.

The implications of being directly linked to a suspected spy were intimidating, but at the meeting to expel me Nechayev feigned ignorance.

> NECHAYEV: No one is saying anything about you being a threat to national security.
> SARAH: I had to sign a statement saying so, that I am a threat to the national security of the Russian Federation. It's like you don't know what the FSB is doing.
> NECHAYEV: I didn't see what happened there.
> SARAH: You don't believe me? Your colleague has it right there …

I gestured towards the man in the eagle mask, who had a copy of the document on the phone lying in front of him. The BBC had sent it to him when it protested my treatment at the airport, but now this man stared straight ahead in silence. Nechayev was impatient. 'That was a technical moment. It was resolved positively. Yesterday has passed. I don't see what the problem is.'

The Kremlin later confirmed that I had been sanctioned, too, although my name has never appeared on any public lists. When we continued questioning the logic of that move at the Foreign Ministry, Nechayev became irritated. 'We are just trying to explain our position to you in the most pleasant way.' He said that he wasn't holding a press conference and didn't expect to be interrogated. My visa was due to end on 31 August and it would be my last. He offered to share the details of a 'wonderful company' which could help me pack.

> NECHAYEV: I am telling you, when you leave the Russian Federation, you won't be able to return. Ever.
> SARAH: As a journalist or as a citizen?
> NECHAYEV: As either.
> SARAH: Because I am a threat to national security?
> NECHAYEV: No. Why do you say that?

SARAH [angry]: Because I have a paper stating that from the FSB ... they gave it me in the airport.
NECHAYEV: [pauses] Things were not as tough there as they could have been. It all ended well. You entered Russia, as you wanted ... We helped you as much as possible, didn't we? Alexei and I had a tough day too.

The meeting at the ministry was part of my goodbye to Russia and I'd described my aim that morning in my diary. 'I want to make them think about where they are taking Russia.' It seems ridiculous, looking back, but I didn't want to go out meekly and make the task of those officials too easy. 'This is a war, a diplomatic war, and I'm sorry I won't be able to return. But I'm mainly sorry for Russia, that all these things are happening,' I told them. I said I believed they were making a mistake expelling someone who'd devoted years to trying to understand their country. *I'm not the enemy*. It was pointless. By then, Russia was seeing enemies all around and it had just added me to the list.

St Petersburg

1994–1995

Window on the West

When I applied to study Russian and French at university, I didn't mention either country in the 'achievements and interests' section on my form. Instead, I listed canoeing and abseiling, which I think I'd tried once. My work experience amounted to waitressing at the local pub and nearby motorway services. Under possible career, I wrote: 'UNKNOWN'.

Somehow, I got invited for an interview and was given a chance to prove myself. My main memories are of being interrogated in front of a blazing open fire in a small room. I stumbled through some live textual analysis and the French professor must have been happy enough. *Firm offer*. But a less flattering note on my file, which I dug out of the college archive, describes my schoolgirl Russian as 'very faltering'. Fortunately, the college acknowledged that I was off to Moscow for the next few months and should improve by the time I made it to Cambridge, so they let me in. The admissions tutor found me 'pleasant' but wondered whether I was 'up to it'.

It was a fair point. During the interview I was asked to explain why I'd chosen Fitzwilliam College in particular and replied with something honest about the high intake of state-school students like me. The men by the fireplace nodded. Anything else? As I continued to look blank, they had to inform me that Professor Anthony Cross, sitting in front of me, happened to be head of Slavonic Studies for the university. I had no clue.

A leading scholar of eighteenth-century Anglo-Russian relations, Professor Cross told me much later that he'd learned his own Russian at the JSSL during military service, like many men his age. The immersive Cold War course had changed the whole direction of his life. He remembered his own teachers as people with 'gruesome tales of life in the USSR' and a 'one-armed Pole'. In charge of them all was Elizabeth Hill, a British-Russian woman whose family had fled St Petersburg after the revolution and who would become Cambridge's first professor of Slavonic Studies. Her students knew her simply as Liza, a formidable figure with 'piercingly blue eyes' and a black Fiat that she nicknamed 'the Flea'.

My Russian did improve dramatically after my long stay in Moscow, as the interviewing panel had hoped. Once at university, I gradually pivoted away from any French papers, and when it came to my third year, to be spent abroad, opted to spend as much of it as possible back in Russia. Most students on my course were heading for provincial places like Voronezh, earnestly planning to immerse themselves in the 'real' Russia. But I was determined to steer clear of the backwaters and make for the classical faded beauty of St Petersburg. I'd been fascinated by the city's founder, Peter the Great, ever since I'd studied eighteenth-century Russia with Professor Cross. The despotic tsar would force guests to eat at his banquets until they were physically sick, then start eating all over again, but he was also the man of great vision who built an extraordinary European city on a giant Russian swamp to symbolise his opening up to the West. With its winding canals crossed by bridges made of winged dragons and pastel-coloured palaces designed by Italian architects, it became known as the Venice of the North.

I was enrolled at the St Petersburg Shipbuilders' Institute, an association that pleased me. Peter the Great had created Russia's first ever fleet and I'd read tales of his own trip to England three centuries earlier, to study shipbuilding in Deptford. The tsar and his retinue had trashed the manor house they'd been lent for the visit by an English writer, tearing up his lawns doing wheelbarrow races that ended with them pitching each other into the hedges.

I can't say my own language study at the institute made much impact. I never mentioned classes there in letters home, but I must have attended because I remember how we would take the metro a few stops down the line then drop in at a corner shop on the way. Every morning we bought a glass bottle of Pepsi from the same *babushka*. For months she would hand it over, stony-faced, as if she hadn't registered us, until one day for no apparent reason she cracked a giant smile and welcomed us into the shop as *moi devushki*. My girls. The sense of achievement was enormous. That hard-won Russian warmth used to feel a million times better than the *have a nice day*! that trips so breezily off American tongues.

By 1994 the shops were better stocked than I'd seen in Moscow two years earlier. We still ate lots of doughnuts and cabbage pies, though by then we'd get them from kiosks named after David 'Hot Wheels' Hasselhoff more often than *babushki* selling their homemade versions from carrier bags on the streets. I also have vivid memories of a visit to the Kunstkamera, which we headed for ahead of any more traditional sights. The museum must rank among the weirdest places in the world. My 1991 guidebook to Leningrad described it as a creation of Peter the Great, who decreed that its display cabinets should contain 'rarities, curiosities and monsters'. We knew it as the pickled-baby museum.

I hadn't been in town long when we met a group of Irishmen from County Cork who were converting a former Soviet butcher's shop into a bar, opposite the Mariinsky Theatre. As my classes were neither demanding nor very inspiring, a girl called Tess and I talked ourselves into a job. We began helping out as interpreters and general assistants, which was better for my Russian than any formal study. I've never forgotten the word for fire extinguisher, since I had to call round dozens of shops trying to find one for the pub kitchen. One day, when a builder slipped on the ice and cracked his head, the boss took Tess to translate at the clinic. As the Irishman sat bleeding and probably concussed, the doctor pulled out a new wristwatch from a drawer and insisted Tess explain the English language instructions before he bothered with the patient.

A few months later, the Shamrock was fully decked out in fixtures and fittings the owners had shipped over specially from Ireland and I was offered a job behind the bar.

The Shamrock

It's possible that I once pulled Vladimir Putin a pint of Guinness. Or maybe a half. When the man who would be president was working in the St Petersburg city government, I was working full-time at the Shamrock. Just three years after the collapse of the USSR, everything foreign was still new and alluring in Russia and the Irish bar was somewhere people went to be seen. The stars of the Mariinsky opera and ballet across the square were regulars, part of a crowd who would sip the Guinness and treat the watery Irish stew as if both were great delicacies. It's entirely possible that Putin came in one day when I was on shift.

It was 1994 and I was twenty years old with a rent-free flat in the heart of a beautiful city that came complete with a drawer full of someone's false teeth and their junk. My main task was to master the Russian language before I returned to college, which I did by spending as much time as possible with the local staff from the bar. Most evenings after work we would buy cheap alcohol and packets of crab sticks, quite a delicacy in those days. During the glorious, dusty St Petersburg summer, we might head for the embankment and watch the giant bridges on the River Neva arch open in succession to let the ships pass. Other days we'd go to some of the 'informal' bars that had sprung up in city squats around Nevsky Prospekt, and dance through nights that never grew dark.

On shift at the Shamrock, in breaks from pouring pints, I would plod my way diligently through a hefty green hardback copy of *Anna Karenina*, scribbling translations of new words in the margins. But I would also spend late mornings, after late nights, wrapped in blankets watching the latest Mexican telenovelas in my flat. In those disorientating days of high prices and high crime, I joined the many Russians gripped by trashy shows like *Simply Maria* and *The Rich Also Cry*. Ludicrously overacted and badly dubbed into Russian, the romantic dramas were pure escapism in a country that was falling apart at the seams.

On days off I discovered real-life Russians doing what I'd read about in my textbooks. I spent a week at Pioneer camp with friends in charge of a bunch of kids somewhere deep in the countryside, although it was just called 'summer camp' by then, as the Soviet youth organisation no longer existed. Another weekend I went mushroom-picking in the woods with the bar's security guards, who were also a rich source of new swear words. But I spent a good deal of my time at the Shamrock, a bar that imported 'the ale and the atmosphere direct from the Emerald Isle'. I found the newspaper cutting that made that claim in a shoe box of memories from Russia. The article was illustrated with a big photograph of the boss, Martin Healy, with a gleaming pint of Guinness and a quote: 'In future, when people ask where the Mariinsky is, they'll be told it's opposite the Shamrock bar!' He got a lot of flak for that comment from people who thought it disrespectful to Russian culture.

It wasn't Martin's first business venture in Russia. I tracked him down recently in Ireland, where he's now retired, and we talked by phone, his thick Cork accent still familiar after almost thirty years. He told me he'd arrived in Moscow initially to set up a betting kiosk at a football stadium when the Soviet Union was still just about intact. The Russians had known exactly what they were doing, even though gambling had been illegal for decades. That foray gave Martin a taste for the country as the communist stranglehold on the economy slipped. He explains his investment in the 'completely unknown world' of Russia as a 'mad' instinct. 'Something told me it was intriguing.'

In those early years there were around 400 Irish citizens registered in Moscow, mostly in construction. Russia's first Irish bar, also called the Shamrock, was there. It had opened in the dying months of the USSR, attached to a supermarket which, according to a newspaper report, was 'piled high with boxes of Rice Krispies ... imported milk and butter and fresh fruit'. Those were the days when other shop shelves in Russia's capital were mostly empty. In early 1992 I remember buying chocolate biscuits at the Irish supermarket as a treat, but it was too expensive for the everyday. Around that time, the *New York Times* declared that the 'first tendrils' of Western culture and materialism had 'woven their way' into the heart of Moscow, transforming the place with bright-coloured adverts for Baskin-Robbins and Coca-Cola in place of 'Milk' or 'Meat'. Clothes with the US flag were the height of fashion, as were carrier bags with English words or foreign brands not available in any shop.

By the time I started at the Petersburg Shamrock, the city was renowned as Russia's gangster capital. I guessed at the mafia's power, but at the time felt it wise to focus on serving drinks and not ask too many questions. I've since learned that to set up any kind of business then you needed a *krysha*, or roof, and you paid protection money to survive. The going rate was 10 per cent of turnover, but the *krysha* would decide exactly how much you were making, then calculate their cut. You couldn't argue because the criminals controlled not only the tax office but the hygiene and fire departments, too. Underpay and you'd find yourself with spot checks and massive fines at the very least. Martin had once objected to his *krysha* about a payment, pointing out that he'd bought and owned the bar space they were charging him for. The man replied, cool as anything, that he could sell him the city's Kazan Cathedral, too, but that wouldn't mean he owned it.

In order to trade, the Shamrock had to register a Russian operating company. The official fee was just $8, I was told, paid in roubles. But the actual amount to be handed over via an intermediary was a thousand times that, and in dollars. 'That was enough to buy a flat, or even two, in St Petersburg in those days,' an old contact reminded me, and the Shamrock was only a small enterprise. The registration fees would be paid to the department in charge of foreign investments at the mayor's office and although I have no way of checking, and the men of Cork do love a good story, I'm told a receipt for the Shamrock was signed by the head of that office at the time, Vladimir Putin.

The bar was popular in those early years, especially during high season at the Mariinsky. It was more restaurant than pub, adapted to the Russian taste, which meant waitress service at the tables rather than customers queuing at the bar then hovering in a corner. Russians like to eat when they drink, and they like to sit for that. The bar didn't make much profit, despite attracting a mixture of tourists, expats and curious locals. It wasn't only the protection racket that drained funds and gave the owners a headache: so much stock was disappearing out of the back door that Martin had to make staff do a detailed audit at the end of each shift. I would watch the chief barman measure and record how much alcohol was left in each bottle, even check the salt and pepper pots and the sugar, but it made little difference. I remember a whole side of salmon being 'disappeared' when someone took the rubbish out.

The year I spent in St Petersburg, the national murder rate reached a peak. By 1996, when Yeltsin was re-elected with a huge push from the West, it was almost three times the rate in the US. Alcohol abuse and social collapse were key factors in the surge, but so were contract killings. I asked my old boss if things ever got frightening for him and Martin admitted they did. He was often told to slide a wardrobe against his front door to prevent break-ins. He was also warned never to leave his luggage unattended if he was travelling, so that nothing could be planted, like drugs. One night the Shamrock was raided by armed FSB officers who put staff and customers up against the wall and searched them because they 'just wanted to show who was boss'. There were fights, too. When two rival gangs clashed in the bar, knives were drawn. One of the gangsters later told Martin he regretted not stabbing him that day. 'Talking about scary situations, there were loads of them.'

Martin had clung to the Shamrock for almost twenty years until, as he puts it, the bar was stolen from him. I don't know the details, only that he says he was tricked and stripped of everything. By then, Putin was running the country and the FSB had taken over running the protection business from ordinary gangsters. The spooks became the *krysha*. Putin's way was not to stamp out crime and corruption, but to control it. Other foreign businesses had folded far sooner, taken over by their Russian partners. 'They decided it was Russia for the Russians,' is how Martin describes the change. Given everything he'd told me, I was surprised he'd stayed in St Petersburg so long. 'It was a fantastic country as long as you weren't stepping on anyone's toes,' he explained, suddenly upbeat. He was haunted by no regret other than losing. 'I guess I was a stubborn Irishman. I thought I could hold my own.'

I kept in touch with some of the waitresses for several years, especially Nastya, who was beautiful and impetuous, verging on wild, and believed wholeheartedly in living for the day. Her wages never lasted the week, but that didn't stop her partying. Much later, when I began working for the BBC, she helped me with a story about Russia's demographic crisis. The report included visiting a police *vytrezvytel*, a sobering-up station, where we found ourselves surrounded by catcalling drunks, naked apart from their underpants.

The bar had also employed a couple of fierce-looking fixers who called themselves 'consultants' and used to drop in regularly. They didn't seem to like me being there, so I learned to keep out of their way. One, Misha, had a background in fine art and connections to the Hermitage museum, but as a fluent English speaker he'd discovered he could make better money in the world of business. He had a pronounced American accent, like all aspirational Russians at the time. When I caught up with Martin, I discovered that his old fixer was related to a furiously anti-Western MP who's a staunch supporter of the Ukraine invasion. Scrolling past Misha's pictures of his sausage dog on social media, I saw he'd added a Russian flag to his own profile two weeks after Putin ordered troops across the border. The caption was in English: 'I stand for peace, but I stand for Russia.' In the comments below, Misha declared that it was in fact the US who'd started the war, not Russia. He claimed he'd never been a supporter of

Putin until 'the hatred of the whole world' made 'patriots' of him and his friends. But he seemed just as upset that his account at Christie's auction house in London was no longer valid, since Russia had been placed under Western sanctions.

To Martin, Russia had been a mysterious land full of major opportunities as well as a source of endless stories back in Cork. My own Shamrock days taught me a street Russian that surprised and impressed my teachers in my final university oral exam. But 1990s St Petersburg was an education far deeper than any classroom. I saw the energy and enthusiasm as Russia embraced everything about the West. I also got parallel lessons in the harsh reality of Yeltsin's reforms, the crimewave and the social strains they spawned. It was the turbulence that would pave the way for Putin's claim to have saved Russians from Western 'humiliation' and given them the gift of stability.

I asked Martin if he'd ever seen Putin in the Shamrock in those early days. He didn't think he had, but then he met so many people he decided he wouldn't have remembered him. 'You might well have served him, though. Probably not a pint because he wasn't much of a drinker. But maybe you spilled a bowl of soup in his lap.'

Royal *Britannia*

When the Queen visited St Petersburg, I was employed as a volunteer telephonist on the royal yacht. The British Consulate had invited a few students to help out and my sole duty was to warn the crew if anyone contacted the ship to say there was a bomb on board. This didn't happen, and instead I watched through a porthole from the radio room as Queen Elizabeth, in a long fur coat and white gloves, walked up a Soviet-red carpet with Boris Yeltsin to climb on board *Britannia*.

It was October 1994, barely three years after the Soviet Union had collapsed, and this was the first visit to Russia by a British monarch. The event was heavy with talk of friendship and cooperation. At a gala dinner in Moscow, her first stop, the Queen had addressed Yeltsin in her glistening tiara and an aquamarine gown. 'You and I have spent most of our lives believing this evening could never happen. I hope you are as delighted as I am to be proved wrong,' she smiled down at Russia's first elected president, seated beside her. 'The message for our people is simple and important. In future we shall work together. Together we shall build a better future.'

On the bank of the River Moskva, the Queen laid the foundation stone for a new British Embassy. The building would be inaugurated in early 2000, after Putin had travelled to London and met the Queen himself on his first foreign trip. In Moscow, the all-glass embassy was designed to symbolise an open and friendly new era in relations, but it wasn't long before I would visit the British Ambassador and find the blinds in his transparent office pulled down low on all sides.

While the *Britannia* was moored on the English Embankment in St Petersburg, and the Queen was still touring Moscow, some of her sailors were busy leading the drinking games at our hostel. A girl in our group had found the crew looking lost on Nevsky Prospekt and brought them back. I've got a pile of photographs of the sailors in full uniform and the students taking it in turns to try on their white hats. In return for our crates of cheap Russian beer, the sailors invited us on board the *Britannia* the next day. There, as a friend told her mother in a letter home, we marched past hundreds of Russians taking photographs and headed up the gangplank for a private tour. We then settled in the sailors' mess for an afternoon of cider and cheese-and-onion crisps.

The Queen and Prince Philip eventually flew up to spend almost two days in the former imperial city, touring the Hermitage and visiting other tsarist palaces in their Rolls-Royce, greeted by crowds of locals waving little British flags. One news report recorded a well-wisher commenting that the visit 'doesn't just mean we have friendly relations, it shows we are actual relatives', a reminder that the near-identical-looking Russian Tsar Nicholas II and George V, the Queen's grandfather, were cousins. One of her stops was St Petersburg State University, where she met a group of students. Misha, the fixer for the Shamrock, was somehow there too. He snapped a photograph of the Queen, close enough to touch, in a bright-red woollen coat.

To mark her last night in Russia, she hosted a banquet on board *Britannia*. Hovering on bomb-scare duty by the phone somewhere in the bowels of the ship, I saw nothing of the dinner itself. But Douglas Hurd, then foreign secretary, had a seat at the table. In his memoirs, he remembers Boris Yeltsin turning up his nose at the white wine but gulping down the claret, which apparently lifted his mood. Waving away the gavel, Yeltsin had banged his giant fist on the table to propose the toasts.

The dinner conversation that night turned at one point to Ukraine and NATO. Three months later, Ukraine would sign the

Budapest Memorandum, agreeing to give up the nuclear arsenal it had inherited from the USSR in return for security assurances from Britain, the United States and Russia. In December 1994, all three countries duly pledged to respect Ukraine's independence, sovereignty and existing borders and to refrain from any use of military force. Two decades later, Vladimir Putin would annex Crimea and the world would do barely anything about it.

Almost seven decades have passed since thousands of national servicemen, my own university professor included, were drilled in Russian at the JSSL in order to protect Britain against enemy attack. By my own era, the opportunities linked to learning Russian were immense and the country warm and welcoming. Today we've come full circle, as language students at my old university are being sent to Kazakhstan or even Poland for their year abroad, not St Petersburg. We're back to fear and hostility.

Russia Obsessive, Unemployed

After university I struggled to find work using my language skills. When a friend spotted an advert for Russian speakers to appear as film extras in *The Jackal* with Sidney Poitier and Bruce Willis, we both signed up. I didn't get to utter a word. Instead I was handed fake leather trousers and a see-through shimmery shirt, and told I was meant to look like a hooker in a Moscow nightclub. My best efforts for the film's opening scene ended up on the cutting room floor.

I wanted to get into journalism but I was applying for even the most vaguely relevant job. When I eventually got an interview with Reuters, I blew it. The position was on the agency's international news team and when the panel asked me to list four world figures I would invite to dinner, living or dead, my mind would only flash up names related to Russia. Straight away I told them Gorbachev, Yeltsin and Stalin and I was floundering for a fourth. Realising I couldn't say Catherine the Great without looking like a Russia freak, I blurted out Maggie Thatcher instead.

Expelled

MOSCOW, AUGUST 2021

As a student I'd learned of the eighteenth-century Russian fascination with all things British, from rhubarb to landscape gardeners. But Putin's Russia reserved a special kind of anger for Britain, and the phrase *Anglichanka gadit*, England's doing the dirty, was a regular headline on state TV channels. I suspected some of the attacks were born of annoyance at Britain's relatively outsized influence in the world, when vast and once-powerful Russia now had to rattle its sabres hard to be heard. It also felt like we were a proxy punchbag for the US. But the TV presenters and politicians scoffing the loudest often had second homes in London and children in elite British public schools. One prominent anchorman even had a UK passport. Like a spurned lover, Russia was striking back.

By the time I was expelled, relations were awful. Even so, hitting the BBC was an unexpected blow, and for a long time I wondered why I'd been singled out. With a large pack of British journalists still in Moscow then, I couldn't help but feel it was personal.

The man at the Foreign Ministry had offered no clues. 'We decided that would be the most appropriate response.' Although he claimed it was retaliation for the TASS reporter who'd had to leave London, it was more than a year later that I got put on my first short-term visa. Colleagues had been renewed for a year in the meantime. Russian independent media assumed my lively clash with Alexander Lukashenko in Belarus had been a trigger, coming just before I'd been detained at Moscow airport. Their headlines all stressed my expulsion 'after questioning Lukashenko's legitimacy'. But the date of my ban on entering Russia, scrawled on the deportation notice, was two days earlier.

Could it be because I was one of very few British journalists, otherwise almost exclusively men, who was not married to a Russian? Perhaps, although it's difficult to believe the Kremlin cared too much about dividing families. Or was it my focus on political repression and spy stories? The authorities wouldn't like that, for sure, but it didn't hurt them. Later, I would try to make the FSB reveal its reasons in court, but the process became farcical. Any case would have to be held behind closed doors, as it supposedly concerned national security. I couldn't attend, as I'd been barred from the country, and even if a lawyer did manage to discover the reason for designating me a 'threat', he would be banned from sharing it, as it would be a state secret.

The meeting on the day I was officially told to leave lasted over an hour. I said what I could, but changed nothing, so when I stepped out into the yard I recorded myself speaking to the camera again. It was for the report I now knew I'd need to write on my own expulsion. The first few takes were angry, my face tense, and I struggled to express my thoughts. But the video I managed to record to the end has a different tone. It's regretful.

Video recording, 11 August 2021

I've just been told formally that my visa won't be extended. I was let back in, but only to pack. I have got three weeks to get out, and never return. [They say] they were forced to take this step, but they clearly weren't. This is an escalation. It just shows that it's becoming harder and harder to work as a journalist in Russia. But while I can leave, independent media are being shut down; journalists harassed and persecuted for what they report.

And whatever they say here in the Foreign Ministry about this not being personal, it doesn't feel that way at all. This feels like another step towards limiting freedoms in Russia and … increasing the tensions between Russia and the West. I find that extremely sad.

PART V

Diary Entry, Kharkiv, Ukraine, 4 March 2022

Drove into Kharkiv past a huge line of traffic heading out. Cars were three, sometimes four thick. Some were flying a Ukrainian flag. Lots had taped the word 'children' to their sides, hoping that will protect them. We met a young couple on the edge of town who said they'd spent days sleeping in the metro. They'd come up for a few minutes' air because the 'concentration of human misery' below ground became too much.

Bodies

KHARKIV REGION, UKRAINE, DECEMBER 2022

Oleh Podorozhny led the way through the dimly lit corridors of his morgue, past two men lying dead on metal trolleys and a dartboard pinned to the sandbags stacked at the windows. In the back yard, through the morning mist, the pathologist pointed us towards a white refrigerated container. Inside were the remains of civilians killed when Izyum was occupied by Russian troops. Weeks after the city was liberated, many of the dead still hadn't been identified.

Oleh warned our team to stand back as his colleague cracked open the heavy metal door of the container and the awful, cloying smell of death rushed out. The body bags were heaped on the floor, one on top of the other in a messy pile, because no one had time to build shelves. Some of the bags were muddy, as if they'd been dragged along the floor or even stepped on to reach other bodies towards the back. They had numbers and a few basic details scrawled in purple pen, but in some cases we were told the bodies inside the bags were in such a state it was impossible even to establish their gender.

With Ukrainian forces back in control in the north-east, the dead were being recovered from shallow graves all over the region. They were mostly civilians, killed in Russian missile strikes or shot. The main morgue was overwhelmed by the work of trying to identify them, so the dead of Izyum had been brought to this spill-over facility to wait to be claimed through DNA testing. Keeping the container cool, and the bodies from decomposing, was a major challenge, as Russia was constantly hitting Ukraine's power stations, disrupting the electricity supply. We couldn't stay there for long. It was unbearable.

Most of the unidentified dead of Izyum had been found on Shakespeare Street, buried in a pine forest on the edge of town. They'd been carried there by volunteer grave diggers, in haste and under fire, when the city was occupied. Some were placed in the ground without even a bag. Now the dead had been disinterred and sent for identification, leaving eerie rows of holes in the sand. A few had empty coffins poking out and there were wreaths of plastic flowers, scattered when the graves were reopened. The original diggers had marked each plot with a simple wooden cross, but often there was a description in place of a name, written in pen. *No. 284. Lenin Avenue, 35/5. Old man.* Was he killed by a missile, or did he die of old age, alone under occupation? I didn't know. Other crosses just had a number: *306, 352, 356*. I lost count. Now Ukraine was working to return the names to the dead.

Police teams were still locating an average of ten bodies a day. Serhiy Bolvinov, head of investigations for the Kharkiv region, told us that some of those buried on Shakespeare Street had died of natural causes during the occupation. But many had been killed in shelling or explosions. In seventeen cases he said there was clear evidence of torture, including fragments of rope around the neck or bound hands. By late 2022, 451 bodies had been unearthed in Izyum, including seven children. There were also a number of body parts.

We met in the lobby of an empty hotel, still wearing our coats and gloves but shivering inside the unheated building. Winter had been weaponised that year. Russia was conducting regular missile strikes on Ukraine's energy infrastructure that plunged whole regions into darkness and cold. After everything inflicted on his region, Bolvinov told me the level of anger towards Russia was very high among his officers. He only spoke Ukrainian now, on principle, even though he'd grown up speaking Russian like most people in Kharkiv, close to the border. I was meeting more and more people who'd made the switch. The police chief said he was directing his emotion into his work, determined that each crime committed during the occupation should be investigated and 'never erased' from memory. 'But it's very difficult and this work isn't over,' he admitted. Just that week, his officers had been called to exhume the body of a local man killed by a cluster bomb during the occupation. His wife had had to bury him in their garden.

The fighting in Izyum had been ferocious and the destruction was immense. A high-rise block of flats in the town centre had a giant hole blown through the middle. There was a children's playground on one side and the golden dome of a church now visible through the gap. Houses all around had been flattened and people had left candles and tributes in the rubble. A row of garages was daubed with big 'Z's, the tag sign of Russian soldiers. Ukraine's army had battled for seven months to force them out of town.

Living among the ruins were the families searching for those they knew had been killed, but whose bodies still hadn't been found. The police had set up an incident room inside a local art college after their own headquarters was destroyed. Inside, a silent cluster of people waited in a dark corridor to give their DNA samples and evidence. Officers called them in one by one and gently swabbed the inside of their cheeks. The test kits were then sent to a forensics laboratory to extract a DNA profile in the hope of finding a genetic match to a body at the morgue.

In the main room where all this work went on, there was a hush. The officers gathering data, many of them women, seemed to whisper their questions. Every conversation was intensely painful. I saw one woman stand and pause in the middle of the room, a hand over her mouth like she was holding back a sob. Tetyana's sister, Iryna, and nephew, Yevhen, had died in a Russian airstrike on their block of flats. They'd been sheltering in the basement, but that didn't save them. For weeks afterwards, the fighting was too intense to get close. When emergency workers finally reached the building to begin digging out dozens of bodies, Tetyana told me she spent days there hunting for her relatives. She managed to identify 22-year-old Yevhen by a tattoo on his arm, but it seemed her sister had been blown apart. 'I can't find even a piece of her,' Tetyana said softly. She wanted to bury the two together, whatever remained.

The war that had created Tetyana's nightmare was making the identification process painfully slow. At the Interior Ministry forensics laboratory in Kharkiv, we were ushered into the boss's office past a snow-dusted statue of Sherlock Holmes with his magnifying glass. Inside, I learned that many of the staff had fled when the region was invaded and their homes had suddenly felt too close to Russia for comfort. The laboratory was training replacements at high speed, but in the meantime those left were stretched to the limit. As well as trying to identify the dead, they were deployed to collect ballistics evidence at every explosion site. They also gathered clues when torture rooms were discovered in liberated areas. In the Kharkiv region, dozens of the fingerprints found at such scenes matched entries in Ukraine's criminal database. Some of the torturers were Ukrainian men from Luhansk and Donetsk, areas of the eastern Donbas that had been under Russian control since 2014.

The way people had died was complicating the scientists' work still further. Many had been badly burned in shelling and airstrikes, so the forensics teams were extracting genetic samples from bones, which was slow-going. They were also struggling to find close relatives of the missing and dead to provide DNA swabs, because so many people had left as refugees. On top of all that were the air raids and missile strikes. 'The high-precision equipment suddenly does this.' One of the scientists snapped her fingers to show what happened in a power cut. 'Then we have to start all over again.'

For the families, the wait was agonising. At the DNA swab site, Tetyana told me a neighbour had recently buried seven family members, killed in the same strike as her own relatives. He'd told her that holding their funerals had lifted a great weight from his shoulders; he was finally able to sleep again. Searching for her sister, Tetyana was longing for the same relief. 'If I can just get through this moment, then maybe it will be easier.'

* * *

The body in grave 319 in the forest was eventually identified as Volodymyr Vakulenko, a children's writer and poet. He had been detained in late March 2022, beaten and interrogated by Russian forces and then released. The next day, witnesses saw two soldiers leading him away again. They said he shouted, 'Glory to Ukraine!' and was bundled into a car with a 'Z' on it. When Izyum was liberated in September and the graves exhumed, two bullets were found in the poet's remains.

Nine months after Vakulenko was shot, his family were finally able to give him a funeral. Bending over a closed wooden coffin covered in a Ukrainian flag, the poet's mother damned those who had killed her only son as 'jackals'. 'God teaches us to forgive, but I will never forgive the murderers.' Olena Ihnatenko hugged a photograph of her son close to her chest. In the image he was wearing a traditional embroidered shirt, a *vyshyvanka*. 'I will live in the hope and belief that the investigation finds who's responsible and that the killers will be punished. I will live for that dream.'

After Vakulenko's death, Victoria Amelina, a fellow writer, went searching for the diary he had kept during the occupation. She recovered the notebook from where he'd buried it beneath a cherry tree in his garden, and delivered it to the local literary museum. There, a woman in white gloves placed the chequered pages carefully on a velvet cloth for me to read. They were tatty and covered with crossings-out, but the words spoke of the poet's fears as a prominent Ukrainian patriot in a small village under Russian occupation. 'It is extremely dangerous for me to be encircled by the enemy,' Volodymyr worried in one scribbled entry. His final lines describe seeing a flock of cranes overhead, shortly before his arrest. 'Through their chirps I seemed to hear, "Everything will be Ukraine! I believe in victory!"'

In June 2023 the woman who had recovered the notebook was killed by a Russian strike on a busy restaurant in Kramatorsk, eastern Ukraine. Victoria Amelina was in the region documenting war crimes, which had become her focus since the start of the full-scale invasion. She believed that those crimes included an attempt by Russia to eradicate Ukrainian culture.

Russia

2000–2005

The *Kursk*

BARENTS SEA, AUGUST 2000

The day Russia admitted that the *Kursk* nuclear submarine had sunk was the day I arrived in Moscow as a journalist. I'd spent the past couple of years at the BBC's Russian Service, tucked away in a corner of Bush House, editing radio interviews by cutting and splicing reels of quarter-inch tape with a razor blade. There was a back room full of chain-smoking Russian intellectuals and some former Soviet dissidents who might have told me fascinating stories had I not been so intimidated. Instead, I became adept at removing the 'ums' from other people's interviews and rescuing stray breaths I'd accidentally cut out of the tape and let drop to the floor.

In 2000 I'd been plucked from that role and propelled to Moscow as a news producer. It was the year that Vladimir Putin was sworn in as president, and I arrived with little idea of what was expected of me beyond speaking Russian. It was the job I'd long coveted, combining journalism and the biggest country in the world: a place of extremes, so often so important but still so poorly understood. But that first day I dithered nervously on the seventeenth floor of a giant block of flats in an anonymous city suburb until a colleague called from the office to wonder whether I was ever planning on showing up. Before long I was up in the Arctic covering the first big story of my career.

The *Kursk* disaster contained all the traits of Putin's rule in an early, still-evolving form: an instinctive dishonesty, wariness of the West and a chilling disregard for human life. The crew who survived the blast would slowly suffocate as Putin and his navy first covered up the disaster for two days, then bungled the rescue effort. Just three months into Putin's presidency the loss of an atomic submarine, the pride of the Russian fleet, was a stinging humiliation. But as I headed for Murmansk, it was also to report on a personal tragedy for the families of the 118 crew. The story of the men trapped beneath the waves would captivate Russia and the world for eight grim days.

On 12 August the *Kursk* was taking part in an exercise in the Barents Sea, off the north coast of Russia, which involved 'attacking' a ship on the surface with a torpedo. At 11:28 the instruments on that ship, the *Peter the Great*, recorded a strong underwater explosion that the captain later described as like being tossed on the waves. The commander of the Northern Fleet, Admiral Vyacheslav Popov, felt his legs buckle, but a crew member convinced him there was nothing to worry about. Two minutes later there was a second, even more powerful blast that was detected as far away as Norway.

An official inquiry would eventually conclude that a torpedo on board the *Kursk* had disastrously malfunctioned after a hydrogen peroxide leak. More missiles detonated as the submarine sank. Ninety-five men died instantly but further down the vessel there were survivors. They began moving towards the tail end of the submarine, where there was a rescue hatch.

At 13:15 Captain Dmitry Kolesnikov scribbled a note on paper ripped from a collection of detective stories. *Our condition is poor. We are weakened by carbon monoxide ... our reserve oxygen is running out ... we won't last more than a day.* He placed the note in his pocket, listing the twenty-three crewmen now squeezed into an area meant for just three. With no specialist kit, swimming to the surface was impossible. They had to stay put and hope someone was coming for them. But it was almost freezing, the poor air would have been making them sick, and the ships above had not even realised their plight.

At 14:00 Admiral Popov took a helicopter to the shore and updated a huddle of TV cameras on the naval exercise. 'We are working according to plan. I am fully satisfied with the first stage.' At 15:15, four hours after the disaster, Captain Kolesnikov wrote another note, this time to his wife. *Olechka, I love you. Don't be too upset.* Twenty-five minutes after that, Admiral Popov was informed that the *Kursk* had failed to surface.

The Northern Fleet then dithered all afternoon and all evening until declaring an accident at 00:30 the next day and calling a rescue ship. It was nine hours' sail from the scene, but there was still reason for hope. The *Peter the Great* had registered a series of bangs from inside the *Kursk*. Someone was calling for help.

Almost a full day after the explosion, the defence minister interrupted Putin's holiday in the southern resort of Sochi to inform him of an 'abnormal situation' in the Arctic. Putin later claimed he was told the rescue was going fine, the navy had all it needed. In fact it would be another two hours before the rescue ship reached the scene, its outdated equipment was next to useless for the task, and the Northern Fleet had no deep-sea divers. Had Russia admitted the accident immediately and asked for foreign help, it might have saved lives. But secrecy and pride were the priority, as one military analyst told us at the time. 'No one got killed for losing sailors' lives, but for giving secrets to NATO you get sent to Siberia.'

By this point, rumours of the disaster had reached the families of the crew, but they had no official information. Someone inside the *Kursk* was still banging for help, still conscious. A rescue capsule was lowered to the submarine but failed to latch onto its hatch. Putin stayed on holiday in Sochi.

The navy press service issued its first public statement two days after the disaster. It revealed little. 'A problem has occurred with the *Kursk* atomic submarine in the Barents Sea. It is lying on the seabed. There are no nuclear weapons on board. The radioactive situation is normal.' The wives and mothers of the crew began to gather in Vidyaevo Officers' Club and were assured that the men were alive, but by 09:00 the knocking from inside the *Kursk* had stopped. When countries including Norway and the UK offered to assist with the rescue effort, Putin insisted that Russia could cope. He stayed in Sochi.

On the fourth day, Russians were getting conflicting reports about signs of life on board and the men's chances. The sinking had sparked discussion about the state of a military built up in the Cold War but maintained on a budget a fraction of its former size. Public criticism grew as further attempts to latch a Russian rescue vehicle onto the *Kursk* failed, and on day five, following a phone call with US President Clinton, Putin agreed to accept outside aid. The UK and Norway immediately sent ships with kit, specialists and deep-sea divers, but the chances of finding anyone to rescue by then were very low.

The next day, Russian officials reported that the entire front section of the *Kursk* had been ripped open, dashing the desperate hopes of many relatives. Newspaper coverage had become scathing about Putin's absence and his delay in accepting help, portraying the president as indifferent. One paper jibed that he had spent the week on pressing matters, such as appointing an ambassador to Jamaica. Only then did Putin break off his summer holiday and return to Moscow.

On 20 August the Norwegian divers reached the *Kursk*. They managed to open the hatch in a matter of hours, but the space below was full of water. There were no survivors.

The families of the 118 crew were based in Vidyaevo, a military town closed to foreigners, so we had to report on the disaster from some distance. Our teams ended up in a basic Soviet-era hotel in Murmansk, where the receptionists offered the men a choice at check-in: 'coffee or a prostitute?' They got insistent women hammering on their doors late at night in any case.

Among the rare bits of footage to emerge from Vidyaevo was a video clip of a distraught woman named Nadezhda Tylik yelling at a government minister. 'They are dying in that tin can for fifty dollars a month!' The woman's son, Sergei, was on board the *Kursk* and her anger supplanted any fear about speaking out. 'We have nothing here. Nothing.' As a nurse with a syringe tried to lead her away, she turned back towards the stage, shaking with fury, to address the naval officers. 'Tear off your epaulettes right now! You don't deserve them, you swine!' The nurse then injected her from behind and three men stepped in as Tylik's legs gave way. They almost carried her out, and as she sobbed quietly, someone ordered the camera to stop filming.

Our news teams debated at length how to interpret what we were looking at. Those who'd spent less time in Russia saw the injection as a uniquely sinister move. An angry woman, sedated to silence her. Most British newspapers agreed, running front-page images the next day of the nurse, needle poised like a still from *One Flew Over the Cuckoo's Nest*. Others saw crude Russian medicine in practice, where consent was always an alien concept. Tylik herself would later tell conflicting stories. But watching the video still gives me goose bumps. The mothers' grief in that room was raw, and the official charged with giving the families answers and explanations had nothing.

The next recording to leak out came when Putin finally made it to Vidyaevo, ten days after the disaster. There were just a few shaky snippets on camera from inside the Officers' House, but a print journalist managed to hide in the crowd and record audio of the whole encounter. Putin was several hours late to meet the bereaved families, as he would be studiously late for world leaders his entire career. He strode into the auditorium, his face lean, not puffy as it is now, in dark shirt and jacket. All the crew had been declared dead, but some women were clinging to hope that there were survivors. Squeezed into that room, after waiting far too long, they now stood and shouted directly at Putin. Burly men, strategically placed in the crowd, tried to pull them down but Putin realised that they needed to be heard. 'Let her speak!' He promised the families compensation and shared their shock at discovering the lamentable state of the military. 'I had no idea things were so bad.' The heated exchange is extraordinary to watch two decades later, when only carefully vetted people are allowed anywhere near Russia's president.

Journalists, as well as the families of the crew, were demanding to know why Putin had refused international help for so long and why he'd stayed on holiday as the crew of the *Kursk* was drowning. For days, TV channels and newspapers had been exposing the holes in the official account of the disaster. Then the 'Telekiller', TV presenter Sergei Dorenko, went to work. He spent two days in Vidyaevo, where he discovered that the men who ventured out beneath the ice for weeks on end to serve their country were returning to homes with leaking roofs and no radiators. His fifty-one-minute report cut together images of peeling paint and shabby blocks of flats with the giant atomic submarines sitting in the dock. 'When Putin came to visit, there was running water,' Dorenko intoned. 'When he left, they turned it off.'

Then he played Putin's statements on the disaster. Between each one the camera cut back to the studio where Dorenko looked straight down the lens and accused the president of lying. In one clip, Putin announced that contact with the *Kursk* was lost at 23:30 on 12 August and 'a search was initiated'. Dorenko informed his viewers that the two explosions had been twelve hours earlier, and so huge they were impossible to miss. 'The president's explanation does not account for the facts, and yet facts would be very useful in such a delicate matter.' His conclusion was withering. 'The authorities don't respect any of us. That's why they lie. And they only do that because we let them get away with it.' He was sacked after the programme went out.

Dorenko's 'killer' reputation came from targeting other prominent figures. In the late 1990s, he had set about blackening the name of Boris Nemtsov, who was then a deputy prime minister. For weeks, Dorenko 'poured dirt' on the politician from his TV news bulletins, interviewing women who would claim Nemtsov had hired them to sleep with him. The prostitutes' lies were so convincing that Nemtsov's own mother believed them. But Nemtsov said the presenter later admitted to paying the women $200 each for their appearance. The attacks were part of a power battle between the oligarchs who owned the TV channels and a government of young reformers. To Nemtsov, Dorenko justified his actions easily. 'I'm the contract killer. And you were my hit.'

In 2000 the TV presenter had a real scandal to uncover, and his report on the *Kursk* disaster was a shocking tale of chaos and cover-up, secrets and lies. But two years later, military prosecutors closed the criminal case into the death of the crew. Some senior officials had lost their jobs over the faulty torpedo, though other positions were found for them. Twenty years on, I caught a TV interview with Admiral Popov in which the former commander of the Northern Fleet talked of the *Kursk* tragedy 'lying heavy' on his heart. But he'd gone on to become a senator and continued peddling his conspiracy theory that the *Kursk* had been hit by a foreign submarine. He never produced a scrap of evidence.

As for Putin, he had seen very clearly that journalists could be dangerous.

Diary entry, 16 May 2001

Today I met Putin. In the flesh, for the first time. Or rather, I saw Putin. It was a press conference on the results of an EU-Russia summit. The questions were predictable (freedom of speech, Chechnya). Putin's answers were well-rehearsed and we'd heard them many times before. As for the man himself, he was far slighter and much fairer-haired than I'd imagined. His feet didn't touch the ground from his chair and he fidgeted almost constantly.

A Reporter

MOSCOW, 2000–2004

In 2022 many people were shocked that Russian troops could bring such blanket destruction to their Ukrainian 'brothers'. But they had done the same before to their own citizens in Chechnya. From 1994 under Boris Yeltsin and then again from 1999 with Putin, Russian troops bombed and ravaged part of their own country to stop it breaking away. Even the mass looting by soldiers in Ukraine was not new. Two decades earlier in Chechnya, Russian forces had made off with people's washing machines, fridges and cars.

Putin's military campaign was already underway when I arrived back in Russia in 2000. But the Kremlin had learned a vital lesson from the first Chechen war, which had ended with Yeltsin forced to sign a humiliating ceasefire. Powerful journalism from on the ground had undermined support both for the fighting and for the president himself. The second time round, the whole area was declared a 'counter-terrorism operation' zone, off-limits to all reporters without extra accreditation and on an authorised tour.

One woman ignored all the rules. Anna Politkovskaya went to great personal risk to report what was happening in Chechnya for *Novaya Gazeta*, describing the terrorisation of the local population through enforced disappearance, torture and rape. She would express profound anger at the brutalisation of a people and the deadly cycle of violence and revenge, as well as at her own powerlessness to stop it. With barely anyone else left reporting from inside the republic, Politkovskaya felt she had no choice but to continue.

Diary entry, 27 March 2002

Interviewed Anna Politkovskaya from *Novaya Gazeta* this evening. She's been to Chechnya forty times to report on the war, although it is incredibly dangerous and no one else is doing it. The Kremlin has taken control of all information from Chechnya, but she refuses to play their game. She has been threatened, intimidated. But she keeps going back. Amazing.

The first time I met Politkovskaya, she was at a desk covered in messy heaps of papers and files. Slim with greying hair and glasses, she had just returned from another solo trip to Grozny and I'd come to ask her about what she'd seen. She described Russia's 'mop-up' operations, the *zachistki*. These were the security sweeps in which Chechen men were rounded up as suspected militants, then disappeared. Secret burial places were regularly unearthed, often near former Russian bases. 'I witness very grave events and no one else is reporting on them. I can't not write about it,' Politkovskaya told me when I began to record. 'Everything in Chechnya is exactly as ever. It's just that the world has forgotten about it. People die every day. I see no sign the war is over. It's being reignited with new force.' She then informed me curtly that I shouldn't be interviewing another journalist on what they'd seen in Chechnya. I should be going there for myself.

The BBC had a big Moscow bureau in those days: four correspondents, four producers, a bureau chief and two camera crews, as well as support staff. There was also a separate Russian-language service, all based in the business centre of a slightly sleazy hotel then favoured by gangsters. Down in the lobby, long-legged women in red shorts and boots would strut back and forth, handing out Marlboro cigarettes.

Upstairs in the office I had started off as a news producer, which involved everything from suggesting stories to correspondents to making them happen: finding interviewees and arranging logistics. If the reporter didn't speak Russian, I would translate or conduct the interviews. 'All the hard work and none of the glory,' as I described it in a letter home. But I also called it the 'best job' I'd ever had, taking me all over the former USSR. I'd left the UK with an earnest promise to my partner Kes that I'd be back in a year, or two at the most. I would end up being abroad for the next two decades.

Moscow was no longer a city of empty shops and empty wallets. As of March 2000 it had its first IKEA, and tens of thousands of people queued outside in the snow for opening day. The store was on a main road out of town previously notorious as a pick-up spot for prostitutes. When cars pulled into the lay-bys, women would emerge to pose for the drivers in a shivering row in the headlights. By 2000, those sex workers were disappearing, perhaps moving into the city's many clubs and strip bars. One place I knew had women swinging on trapezes above the dance floor and that November I wrote to Kes, describing a perfectly run-of-the-mill nightclub with pool tables, which also featured 'two semi-naked girls on a platform' and a man in white tights with pink fluffy wings.

For many Russians the struggle wasn't over. It was less than a decade since the USSR had collapsed and the oil price so critical to the economy was only just beginning to rise. In the depths of that first winter we reported from towns suddenly plunged into the dark and desperate cold as Soviet-era infrastructure crumbled. In Karelia, in the north, families were living indoors in their hats and overcoats. In one woman's house I bashed together frozen beetroots in an attempt to capture the sound of the cold for a radio report. Even the toilet water had turned to ice. Across Russia, the social problems were just as serious, including drug use, HIV and alcoholism. Even in the capital, when spring came, the corpses of homeless men would be discovered in back yards where they had fallen down drunk months earlier, then lain, covered in snow, until the thaw. Wage delays were another hangover from the transition years. In one region, companies that ran out of cash were paying their workers in whatever they produced. For staff at a fertiliser company, that meant heaps of manure.

Russia provided an endless flow of stories. For one report we followed travelling hair collectors who were buying up ponytails to sell on to Western markets, where they were used to make expensive extensions. It was often *babushki* who turned up with their first plait, cut off in one piece then kept carefully in a drawer for decades. By then the pensioners needed the cash more than the tissue-wrapped reminder of youth. Long blonde tresses were the most valuable, but the collectors had once been offered a horse mane by a man insisting it came from his wife. I met Gulag survivors in Arctic Vorkuta, a town like a deep-frozen Lowry painting, and there was the 2001 summer summit in Slovenia when George Bush said he'd looked Putin in the eye and got 'a sense of his soul'. He thought he could trust him.

A month earlier and less world-defining had been a mad dash to Archangelsk on the trail of a couple of hundred thousand stranded seals. A news agency had published pictures of the fluffy white pups with a warning that they faced imminent death by mass starvation and the BBC switchboard was then jammed with calls from viewers wanting to save them. As a producer I was supposed to make that happen, but it turned out that the Russians who'd raised the alarm had no plans to intervene. 'In this area, the seals are hunted and clubbed to death at two days old anyway, so they're hardly sentimental about them,' I wrote home. But our audiences were. With ITN hard on my heels, I ended up racing north and chartering a helicopter so a team could fly out over the White Sea to search for the poor creatures. They landed back a few hours later with the news that the seals had saved themselves: the weather had changed and they were floating off towards their feeding ground, probably slightly terrified by the British TV crews on helicopters trying to get close enough to film. When they did, they discovered that the pups were no longer fluffy white and impossibly cute, but 'fairly unattractive slugs with fins', as I put it. 'I'm not sure the great British public would have been quite so keen to rescue them.'

I was learning my job fast from some of the best. Caroline Wyatt, then Moscow correspondent, could flip masterfully from covering geopolitics to writing about a man taking a drunken wee at -40°C and freezing himself stuck to a metal bus stop. I once took her to a run-down morgue before breakfast for a story on the demographic crisis and there was also a memorable exhibition of Soviet underpants. But in late 2000, as we were covering the shutdown of the last reactor at the Chernobyl power plant, I realised I'd left all our nuclear safety kit locked in a car round the corner. As the countdown from ten began, I decided that being a producer was probably not my calling.

It wasn't long before I was spending my weekends and spare time out and about hunting for stories that I could report for myself. I would then hide away in a radio studio, overwriting my scripts and endlessly practising what I thought was a good 'reporter voice' until I was ready to go on air.

In early 2002 I told the story of Moscow's street children, who were an unmissable and pitiful sight then, especially around the train stations. I wrote about 'tiny figures ... [who] wander among the crowds begging money, or loiter near cafés angling for leftovers'. Most were high on glue, some just five or six years old. A thirteen-year-old called Dima spent most nights underground, close to the central heating pipes. Shortly after that report went out, a correspondent colleague left for a stint in Washington and my boss asked me to step into her place. 'Six months to try and prove myself as a reporter, then who knows what will happen? I'm overjoyed.'

Diary entry, 25 March 2002

Nightmare day spent trying to make my recordings on wine and Moldova into some kind of story. I'm wondering whether or not I'm really cut out for this reporting lark. It's almost beyond me. Used the phrase 'daily struggle' in two pieces. Argh.

Diary entry, 26 March 2002

Played wine story to Chris and he liked it. Hurrah.

My first solo TV report was about internet brides. We filmed in Crimea, meeting intelligent, beautiful Ukrainian women looking for a route to a better life abroad. That came in the form of two dozen unreconstructed Americans hunting for the 'traditional' wife they couldn't get back home. I'd got the story idea from a friend in St Petersburg who was searching for a husband the same way but kept finding men who were already married. She wound up with a devout Christian almost twice her age who arrived in Russia with Bibles for all her friends. Olga was a university graduate but she saw no future in her country, fretting that all the decent men had been snapped up, leaving only paupers and bandits. As she'd grown up in a poverty that she longed to escape, she plumped for the evangelical older American with two washing machines.

By that point I had moved out of my high-rise in the suburbs, swapping a view of more tower blocks and busy roads for one of Christ the Saviour Cathedral, recently reopened and just visible from my 1920s Constructivist block. 'I noticed today that I adopt a completely different disposition in Russia,' I wrote in a diary, noting that Moscow was still a place where you had to brace for battle to achieve even the smallest things. 'I start scowling, too, and assume that everything will be a struggle. It must be the same for everyone, even the shopkeepers. It's a vicious circle.' When I left Russia in 2005 for other foreign postings, I realised I'd stopped frowning.

Anna Politkovskaya's comment about reporting from Chechnya for myself had stung because it was true. Our teams deployed from Moscow to other wars, working in both Afghanistan and Iraq in those years, but access to Chechnya was heavily restricted. I would squelch through the mud of giant refugee camps in the neighbouring republic of Ingushetia, talking to Chechen women about the horrors they'd fled and the men who'd disappeared or been killed. On one escorted trip to Grozny, when our convoy stopped at a roundabout to let people film, my producer Dasha and I darted off into a nearby housing block and ran up the stairs. We knocked on doors until we found someone to interview, minus the minders. It took a while for them to realise we'd disappeared. Politkovskaya would not have been impressed, but it was something.

In 2003 we were invited back to Grozny to witness the 'election' of Ahmad Kadyrov, father of Ramzan. He'd been a separatist leader in the first war, before switching to back Moscow in the second. The vote was supposed to be proof of 'normalisation' in Chechnya, although that claim was immediately undermined when we saw Russian soldiers sweeping the road outside their base each morning for freshly laid landmines. The elections were a farce: Kadyrov's face was plastered on posters everywhere and any rival who'd been polling higher than him had either been disqualified or withdrawn quietly. The Kremlin's candidate duly secured more than 80 per cent support, which Putin hailed as proof of the desire for peace. The following year, the new Chechen leader was killed by a bomb set to explode beneath his seat at a stadium.

Many Russians lapped up Putin's gangster-like vow to 'wipe out' Chechen insurgents wherever they were found, 'even on the shitter'. People were scared as attacks on Moscow and other cities intensified. Some were carried out by female suicide bombers, who became known as the 'black widows' – women who committed acts of terror after their husbands or brothers were tortured or killed. As Putin went about restoring order in Chechnya in his own style, most Russians would not be confronted with the human suffering that caused, because state TV no longer reported it. Many people would hear nothing of Russian military casualties either. In the first Chechen war, the Soldiers' Mothers Committee helped women rescue their conscript sons directly from the front line, becoming a focal point for protest against the war. The second time, the soldiers' families were much more reluctant to speak out. 'We have adapted to this war, this cruelty,' a committee member called Elena told me. 'These days, families suffer in isolation and they receive their bodies alone.'

I remember one of my own encounters with a soldier's mother very starkly. It was the first time I'd interviewed anyone in such pain. Anna's son Sergei had been in a military hospital for Russian troops injured fighting in nearby Chechnya. In August 2003 someone drove a truck full of explosives into the compound and blew up the hospital, killing dozens of soldier-patients and staff. When we met, Anna had just been told that all she would get to bury of her son were the soles of his feet. There was nothing else left of him. We sat talking for a long time and Anna didn't know who to blame. 'Maybe all of us,' she concluded. 'For shrugging and saying, "well it wasn't me today", then staying silent.'

Anna Politkovskaya would report the stories of mothers like Anna, as well as the suffering of Chechen families. She was compelled to speak out about all she saw, despite the very real risk that brought. 'In Chechnya, I've had officers tell me they want to shoot me,' the journalist revealed that day in 2002 when we met. 'I get intimidating calls, people hovering in my hallway. There've been so many threats, there was a time when my editors decided my life was really in danger. But I'm used to it. If the FSB is so opposed to me, it only proves that what I'm doing is effective.' She was no hero, Politkovskaya told me, just a reporter doing her job. But from the wreckage of another Russian war, the words she wrote then from Chechnya read like a warning forgotten, or ignored.

School No. 1

BESLAN, NORTH OSSETIA, SEPTEMBER 2004

As Rima talked, she pulled her eight-year-old grandson Alain closer to her side, stroking his hair and calling him her little hero. He stood gazing back at her through huge dark eyes. For three days the pair had been trapped with Alain's sister Jaqueline and more than 1,200 others inside the sports hall of Beslan School No. 1, held hostage by heavily armed men beneath bombs strung between the basketball hoops. Another device was attached to a detonator, which one of the terrorists kept a foot on at all times. The hostages were predominantly women and children. Most of the men had been killed by female suicide bombers at the very start of the siege, their bodies then dumped out of a window.

The heat in the packed gym was stifling. The gunmen had denied their hostages food or drink and threatened to shoot anyone who they caught with water. But the one time that Rima made it to the bathroom, she soaked her shirt under the tap and then returned to squeeze drops into the children's mouths. It wasn't enough. Through sobs, she told me she'd had to get Alain to urinate in a shoe then make him drink it. Each night, she stayed awake clearing space for the children to sleep in the crush.

Rima was in floods of tears as she spoke and I was crying silently as I recorded her, because in Beslan it was impossible not to. In that community that was barely more than a village, there was tragedy all around. Rima's next-door neighbour had lost his entire family in the siege. They had been sitting beside her in the gym and Rima told me she was ashamed to have survived. 'There was a little boy near the door covered in blood and, let God forgive us, we had to climb over his body to get out.'

Our small BBC team reached Beslan on the first day of the siege, on a plane full of emergency workers. It was my first major deployment as a reporter and the most intense experience of my life. It was September 2004 and Vladimir Putin's vicious war on Chechnya had recently burst beyond its borders in a string of terror attacks that culminated in the siege of Beslan School No. 1 in the North Caucasus. The way he handled the crisis would offer more crucial early lessons in Putinism, including that he would spare nothing or no one to crush those who challenged him.

The challenge was serious. The day before the school siege, ten people had been killed and dozens injured in Moscow when a Chechen woman blew herself up outside a metro station. A week before that, the woman's sister was one of two suicide bombers to detonate explosives mid-air and blow two passenger planes out of the sky. In August there had been a double suicide bombing at a music festival in Moscow and, just a few months earlier, another woman blew herself up, killing more than forty people on the metro. But the news that children had become the target was especially shocking.

On the flight from Moscow we met Kazbek. He introduced himself when he realised we were journalists, and showed us photographs of his young children, Jacqueline and Alain, who were among the hostages with their grandmother. It was the first day of the school year, when little girls wear huge white ribbons, the boys' hair is carefully parted and there are celebratory speeches, songs and balloons. In Beslan that morning the yard had been filled with parents and grandparents as well as the children when the masked gunmen rushed in, shooting into the air. They then herded everyone into the building.

By the time we pulled into town it was 3 a.m., but the Dom Kultury, a kind of community centre, was full of relatives. Some bunched together talking in whispers, others slumped in seats, staring silently ahead. The men were chain-drinking plastic cups of instant coffee. A doctor told me there'd been no panic so far, but he had stocks of sedatives just in case. Almost twenty-four hours into the siege, the gunmen were refusing to allow even water to be delivered to the school. There were at least three babies among the hostages, the doctor knew, maybe more.

When we discovered that our hotel rooms had been given over to emergency workers, Kazbek invited us to move in with his relatives. No one was sleeping in any case, and he thought they'd welcome the distraction as well as any information we might find. As a journalist, you often arrive on a scene after a major incident has taken place and report the aftermath, but Beslan was like nothing else I've ever covered. We lived through the siege with Kazbek's family, starting from when we pitched up on their doorstep just before dawn and they insisted on feeding us soup and buttery Ossetian pies. I will forever associate that taste with the warmth and kindness of Beslan, even in the midst of its anguish. Our hosts kept apologising that they hadn't had chance to buy fresh bread.

By the time I went on air at daybreak, there were at least a thousand people milling around helplessly at the Dom Kultury. It was clear that the authorities were grossly under-reporting the number of hostages. That day they gave an official count of 354, which never changed, but locals told us the true figure was at least three or possibly four times higher. As well as the children and their teachers, there were parents, grandparents and siblings inside. The fact the authorities were lying, and state TV channels repeating that, was making people angry and scared. They feared it meant that troops were preparing to storm the school, so playing down the scale of potential casualties in advance. It also infuriated the terrorists, which was dangerous.

The families had good reason to worry: in 2002, a group of gunmen had rushed on stage in a Moscow theatre in the middle of a musical called *Nord-Ost*. Firing into the air, they took around 800 people hostage. The group were demanding the withdrawal of Russian troops from Chechnya and they threatened to execute the theatre audience. Images from inside the auditorium showed women suicide bombers dotted among the theatre-goers, jet-black chadors against the bright red seats, and heavily armed men pacing the aisles. A survivor we met later called Ksenia said the women had told them their husbands and brothers were being killed in Chechnya, so Muscovites would now suffer too.

Outside the *Nord-Ost* theatre, with tanks on the streets and snipers hunched on surrounding rooftops, crowds of frightened relatives began a protest, calling through a loudhailer for the authorities to comply with the gunmen's demands. *Down with the war in Chechnya!* Instead, the siege was ended after two days when special forces pumped a mystery gas into the auditorium to knock everyone out. They then stormed the building to shoot the hostage takers, many of whom were already slumped in their seats.

But those who focused on defeating the terrorists failed to prepare enough ambulances or medics for their hostages. One hundred and thirty people died in the rescue attempt. Some suffocated as they were carried out unconscious, floppy bodies flung over shoulders, then loaded onto buses or slung on their backs in the street. Most died because the authorities refused to tell doctors what gas they had used, or to reveal the antidote. Putin regretted that they 'could not save everyone', but in his terms the operation had been a success. 'We proved that it's impossible to bring Russia to its knees,' he declared, in what would become a motif of his rule and the justification for much that was yet to come.

Two years later in Beslan, there was a lot of nervous talk about *Nord-Ost* among relatives of the school hostages. No one wanted another deadly demonstration of Russian strength, especially one involving so many children.

The militants who stormed the Moscow theatre had called for Anna Politkovskaya to act as a mediator and help shape and convey their demands. 'They knew I would not lie,' is how the *Novaya Gazeta* journalist explained that request to a BBC radio programme a few months later. The men also expected to die, and they wanted her to hear their stories. They thought she could portray them as heroes. She told them they would be universally damned.

In 2004, as the school siege began in Beslan, Politkovskaya took a flight south. She wasn't only going as a reporter; she thought she might use her extensive contacts from years of working in Chechnya to help negotiate an end to the stand-off. She'd already been in touch with a representative of the Chechen separatist leader, Aslan Maskhadov, as someone who might influence the hostage takers. But on board the flight, Politkovskaya was suddenly taken ill. As the school crisis played out, the journalist was in hospital dipping in and out of consciousness. When she recovered, she and her doctors were sure she'd been poisoned. At the time, I remember being too focused on the siege itself to raise more than an eyebrow at the news, and even now there is no firm evidence that it was poison. But it is entirely plausible that someone was ordered to stop Politkovskaya reaching Beslan. The Kremlin didn't want to negotiate and they certainly didn't want a Russian journalist there who did not lie.

As time passed, the mood darkened in Beslan. Our reporting team had grown and we had moved into the house of another of Kazbek's relatives, opposite the Dom Kultury. Tamara had orange-dyed hair and a single cow that she rushed to bring inside when she heard explosions. On the square, the crowd of relatives were becoming desperate. They wanted the authorities to comply with any demand from the terrorists, but those demands were never fully articulated in public. Every couple of hours, an official would emerge and people would surge towards him with their questions, but he would mumble something barely audible then disappear. The families grew increasingly convinced that no one was working hard enough to protect their children, a fear that surged with every burst of gunfire from the direction of the school.

The release of a small group of hostages gave some hope, but it was no act of mercy. The crying of tiny babies had pushed the gunmen to breaking point, so they let their mothers take them out but forced the women to leave any older children behind. One mother who was freed described the terrorists as like animals, with mad eyes, and confirmed that the school gym was stacked with explosives. By this point, parents were trying to get sent into the school in place of their children, but the gunmen refused any exchange. They still wouldn't allow in any food or drink, or even let anyone collect the dead bodies from the school grounds. Still the official count from the crisis headquarters was stuck at 354 hostages.

It was late Friday morning and I was live on air for an extended radio programme when we heard the first big blast, followed by screams from Beslan's mothers. With my producer, Dasha, I did my best to describe what was unfolding: women and small children running for their lives through hails of gunfire; locals piling the injured into cars to rush them to hospital; soldiers bringing in heaps of body bags. And all the time, more explosions, gunfire and wailing.

Live radio report, Beslan, 4 September 2004

> People are trying to get closer to the school. There is absolute panic. The children are inside and they want to go and get them out, despite the explosions. They are trying to storm the military cordon and being pushed back all the time.
> Locals here blame the hostage takers themselves, of course, but they're also blaming the security forces. They are angry that a school full of children is at the centre of a very fierce battle and mortar attacks.

At one point, when we'd taken shelter in the yard of Tamara's house, an armed man burst through the gate. There had been reports all day that some of the hostage takers had escaped, so, live on air, I stumbled as I described the scene. 'There's a man with a gun. A big gun.' He soon vanished back into the chaos. By midnight we already knew of 200 dead. That number would rise above 330 and 186 of them were children.

The day the siege collapsed, Vladimir Putin flew in late at night and visited a hospital under cover of darkness. He told Beslan that all Russia was mourning with their town, but he avoided all crowds, any questions and any blame. 'He came far too late,' I heard. 'He should have stayed with us.' But by the time the sun came up in Beslan, Putin was gone.

That day, I found parents hunting for their children among the corpses at local morgues. There were no official lists, only chaos. 'Making us open all the bags to check inside is killing people,' a woman told me. She described a mother she'd seen stroking the heads of her two dead children, drained of the strength even to cry. There was real anger by then at the authorities for failing to prevent the attack, for failing to negotiate, and for failing to get more children released from the school.

More than 700 former hostages were in hospital, including children with terrible burns and shrapnel wounds. But the walls of the Dom Kultury were still covered with pictures of the missing, their young smiling faces beside a contact number in case anyone had news. Then the funerals began. I remember little Alina laid out in an open, white coffin in her yard. The eleven-year-old was being buried with her dolls. There were so many cars with coffins that there was gridlock on the road to the cemetery.

One evening, very early on, police removed the barricades from around the school to let people up to what remained of the sports hall. The entire roof had collapsed in flames and the shattered gym walls were sprayed with shrapnel and bullet holes. I saw children's belongings in the ruins, a hairbrush and a girl's bow. As people sobbed, they placed candles, icons and flowers on the fire-blackened floor where so many had been killed. Beside blown-out windows they left piles of food and drink for the dead, who had been denied both for three days. Among it all were notes asking the children for forgiveness.

Some years later, a gold-tinted shroud was placed over the school ruins, left as a shrine to the immense suffering of Beslan, a small town still haunted by big questions. During the siege the families had been assured that troops would not storm the building and the official version contends that the security forces only moved in after the terrorists detonated their explosives. But many people still dispute that. Just as unfathomable for parents is why the troops used such deadly force, firing on the school from tanks and using flamethrowers when there were still hundreds of hostages inside. It also emerged that there had been advance warning of a terror attack that day, and yet the gunmen were able to drive up to School No. 1 unchallenged. Only one of the attackers was caught alive and brought to trial. No official was ever held responsible for the huge loss of life.

In 2017 the European Court of Human Rights ruled that Russia had failed seriously in its duty to protect the hostages. The case had been brought by bereaved mothers, brave enough to challenge the authorities because they felt they had nothing left to lose. I sat with some of them in Beslan as they celebrated the damning verdict from Strasbourg with piles of hot Ossetian pies. The shelves all around us were stuffed full of files, all the documents the mothers had gathered in their hunt for justice. But the ECHR ruling brought no new investigation in Russia itself. No soul-searching. Nothing changed.

I've often wondered what would happen to a government in a Western democracy after an attack like Beslan that ended with far more hostages dead than terrorists. I don't believe it would survive an inquiry or the next election. But Vladimir Putin didn't have to worry about any of that. He was the strongman Russians had returned to the presidency just six months earlier with 72 per cent of the vote, when Beslan School No. 1 had been used as a polling station. Many Russians had elected a man then who 'refused to let Russia be brought to its knees' and would 'wipe out' terrorists, and their views didn't change after the disastrous handling of the siege.

What did change was a decision by Putin to cancel direct elections for governors in Russia's regions. He claimed that having them appointed by the Kremlin would bring more security, although the governors had no link whatsoever to the school siege. As MPs gathered in parliament to vote on the move, opposition politicians picketed the building, warning that Russians were trading their freedom for security. They talked of a creeping dictatorship. Vladimir Putin talked of unity, order and control.

Kazbek's family survived the siege with no physical injuries, but for a long time he struggled to cope with what had happened to his children. One day he called me to say he'd brought them to Moscow, to demand more help from the authorities, and that they'd all been sleeping in the street in his Lada. I would return to Beslan many times over the years, a journey that never got easier. But Kazbek's beautiful children got to grow up. Alain went on to study theatre in Moscow and Jaqueline became a mother herself, sending me smiling photographs with her newborn.

Please Don't Judge

UKRAINE, 2022–2023

In the early weeks of war, we came to know one Ukrainian family quite well: a couple, their two teenage daughters and the girls' grandmother, as well as their dog, cat and budgerigar. They came from the mainly Russian-speaking east, where Sonya handled the wages at the coal mine and Oleg, a gentle giant of a man, drove a truck. When the war started he was in Dnipro in the south-east and we talked a lot about his worries for the family, closer to the front line. When Dnipro itself was struck by a missile, he decided to dash home to get them.

As he did, we headed for the shoe factory that had been hit and I was confronted by my first bomb site of this war. There were just a couple of factory walls still standing; the rest was smashed and blackened bricks, with acrid smoke still rising. The night guard and his dog had been killed. There were still traces of them on the floor and no traces of any military target.

That night, Oleg's family moved into a room in our hotel and I'd sometimes crouch in the corridor with them during air raids, stroking their spaniel for comfort and missing my own. Sonya told me how a couple of days earlier she'd been at work at the mine, counting out the cash, and couldn't understand why no one was coming to collect their wages. Suddenly there was a giant thud as a missile landed nearby, and she realised that everyone else was in the bomb shelter.

The couple's eldest daughter was usually glued to her phone, messaging her boyfriend who'd stayed behind and was now telling her about Ukrainian tanks in their town. On my own phone I saw that in Moscow the Sakharov Centre had declared Russia's invasion shameful and a sign of a 'morally bankrupt' society. Established in the 1990s, it would soon be forced to close.

Oleg's family couldn't afford to flee to safer, wealthier western Ukraine, where rental prices had shot up as huge numbers were displaced there by the fighting. As Russian speakers, with car licence plates from the eastern Donbas, they were also worried they wouldn't be welcome, seen as pro-Moscow and disloyal, even though their own town had never been occupied. Their comments were a hint that the old east-west tensions still lingered in some places, even with the entire country under attack.

In late March 2022 the family left Ukraine as refugees. Oleg had to stay behind, like all men of fighting age, and there were clinging goodbyes at the border. I kept in touch after they arrived in Germany, worried how they'd cope when they had never been abroad before, spoke only Russian and Ukrainian, and were suddenly dependent on complete strangers. Sonya tried to sound cheerful, writing that their host was nice and had dogs too and that there was even a beach and woods nearby. But it was hard being a long-term houseguest and she worried constantly about Oleg, fearing he would end up being drafted and sent to the front.

The girls began going to school, but by June Sonya was admitting there were moments when she just wanted to go home. Some women were returning to their husbands in Ukraine, but Sonya had nowhere to go. Their town was still holding out against the Russian advance, but the fighting was close and the danger immense. I heard about an extreme removals service there, people who would dash into a town under fire to collect furniture or find important documents abandoned in the rush to leave. The price depended on the degree of risk.

A few months later I discovered that Oleg had left Ukraine and joined his family. I didn't ask how he got out, but he wasn't the only one. The tales of Ukrainian men's and women's bravery on the front lines are many and they are real, but so are the long rows of fresh graves in city cemeteries. Soon I was getting photos of Oleg studying German in their new hometown, standing at a whiteboard with a big marker pen and the words *Preis* and *Kleid* carefully spelled out behind him. Sonya had begun sketching again and sent pictures of a cartoon dog in the colours of Ukraine's flag. The family moved into a separate flat and in December they sent photos of everyone gathered around a fir tree in their Christmas best with a few presents and a bottle of Martini Rosso arranged at their feet. I messaged that I was happy they were together again and safe.

Their reply came just before the one-year anniversary of the invasion.

Message from Sonya, 18 February 2023

Dear Sarah! Please forgive me that I haven't written for so long ... Germany is a wonderful country but unfortunately, due to many circumstances, we have decided to move to Russia. Please don't judge us too harshly. We are moving because of the health of our loved ones. On top of that, Oleg's mother is now in Crimea and also needs him ...

We found out that our flat is gone. Not just the flat, half the building. Mum's place was destroyed too. Burned down. But we are not getting upset. We are together, we are alive and we have many friends. That's the main thing. Life goes on. We really hope to see you again. Look after yourself and your loved ones. Huge 'Hi!' and may God protect us all.

I was too shocked to reply straightaway. A few weeks later, Sonya wrote again. She was already in Russia and sent photos of the spaniel playing in the snow. 'She is very happy with the changes!' It wasn't only the dog. Sonya said she felt 'at home' in Russia, unlike in Germany. Things in the shops were familiar, people spoke her language. 'We are from Donetsk region, they treat us as their own here.' Across the border right then, Russian and Ukrainian tank crews were blowing each other up. Oleg had once described Russia's attack on his country as 'worse than Chechnya', pummelled by Moscow in two ruthless wars. Now he'd moved to the country doing the pummelling – of his own hometown.

Several months into the war, I'd found Ukrainians in the eastern Donbas camping in their cars, waiting for permission to cross back into Russian-occupied areas. Many had fled the fighting at the start, but adapting to life as a refugee was extremely tough. They had run out of funds, or energy, or both, and wanted to go home even though an invading army was in control. Two pensioners sucking little fish from a can told me their grown-up children were living abroad as refugees. The couple had left them in Europe to head for the ruins of Mariupol, the port city besieged by Russian forces for months. Home, they assured me, was the most important thing, wherever it stands. Only they weren't sure theirs was still standing.

But Sonya and Oleg weren't even going home. They were taking their children to Russia, a country at war with their own, under international sanctions and increasingly isolated. That point was underlined when they had to walk across the border from the EU because there were no longer any flights. 'We are taking only the positives from this situation and trying to move forward,' Sonya wrote. She said that her youngest girl had been ill, blaming the damp German climate, and that the weather in Russia would be more suitable. She hadn't wanted to go to Poland because she'd heard the government there might send men like Oleg back across the border, and that scared her. Russia wasn't mobilising Ukrainian refugees to fight, even from the Donbas. They weren't to be trusted in the ranks.

I tried to understand, not to judge, as Sonya had asked. But mixed in with chat about the family and photos of the dog, her messages began to read like Russian TV talking points. 'All this didn't start in 2022 ... We saw how the Donbas region was oppressed,' Sonya wrote. 'We even paid more for our communal services in the Donbas than they paid in Kyiv and Dnipro.' Maybe she would pay less one day, under Russian rule, but for that Sonya's house and much of her town had already been wiped out.

A few hours after that exchange, my phone started vibrating with alerts from across Ukraine as the air-raid app went off. It was a cue for people there to head for their basements and bunkers. Russia was launching its biggest barrage of missiles on its neighbour in weeks and this time it included the hypersonic *kinzhal*, the dagger, I'd seen Putin unveil in a big speech a few years earlier. He'd boasted then that the missiles were undetectable, hailing Russia's supremacy over the United States in designing and deploying them. Now Putin's pride and joy were evading Ukraine's air defences to smash into its power plants and its homes.

Diary entry, London, 23 March 2022

One month on from the war I'm home in the UK and extremely tired. In bed, scrolling through the news incessantly, I see that an independent Russian journalist has just been killed in Ukraine. The same photograph is on all the reports. Oksana Baulina is young and striking, with a big mane of dyed-red hair. She was in Kyiv filming at the site of a Russian missile strike when they fired again. Oksana was the seventh journalist to die in Ukraine in just four weeks of war. She was the first who was killed by her own country.

Journalists Should Die Old

Before 24 February 2022, I'd never called Vladimir Putin a liar on air. But when he launched an invasion of Ukraine claiming he had to 'save' Russian speakers from 'genocide', it felt important to be clear. There was no genocide and this was no 'Special Military Operation'. That was a false justification. This was all-out, unprovoked war.

Putin's war on truth had begun more than two decades earlier. Just a few days after he was sworn into office in May 2000, armed and masked security officers raided the headquarters of NTV, then owned by an oligarch. The channel's reporting from Chechnya had infuriated Yeltsin, and it had bothered Putin since he launched his own war there. NTV was home to Russia's very own *Spitting Image*, known as *Kukly*, which had a particularly unflattering puppet of Putin. It was also where Sergei Dorenko would expose the official lies fed to Russians about the sinking of the *Kursk* submarine.

The takeover battle for NTV took many months. Departing journalists would cling to free speech for a little longer by moving to other independent channels. But those soon closed down too, ostensibly because of financial problems, and by mid-2003 the taming of Russian television was complete.

By the time of the pro-European protests in Kyiv in late 2013, known as the Maidan, state-controlled channels in Russia had developed into fully fledged Kremlin propaganda. Putin needed

Ukraine's revolution to fail: he couldn't bear to 'lose' Kyiv or for opposition groups in Russia to be inspired by the crowds there. So Russian state media, which were widely followed across the border, were deployed to exacerbate difference and whip up hatred inside Ukraine. Television helped turn a dispute over the country's political direction into burning anger and deadly violence, which Moscow then called a 'civil war'.

On one notorious occasion, a Russian channel invented a claim that a child had been crucified by Ukrainian nationalists. State-run news agencies were at it too. Reporting from Donetsk, I saw a pro-Moscow crowd set upon pro-Kyiv protesters as they tried to walk down a central street holding Ukrainian flags. Later that day I read that Ukrainian nationalists had attacked a crowd of innocent Russian speakers. It was a lie, but it was effective.

For audiences back in Russia there were chat shows with guests shouting about Ukraine as a Western puppet state, governed by 'Nazis'. News programmes drummed home the message that revolution led only to chaos, conflict and disaster. After the full-scale invasion in 2022, Russian TV went into overdrive again. For months, schedules were taken over almost entirely by news programmes and talk shows devoted to Ukraine. Instead of cutting away to escapist soap operas and classic films during the day, viewers got back-to-back shriek shows about the war. Putin had justified his invasion as 'de-Nazifying' Ukraine and his media machine needed to keep reminding people of the 'fascists' they were up against.

The channels would often broadcast hate speech. At one point, Anton Krasovsky of RT's Russian-language service called for Ukrainian children to be drowned or shoved into huts and burned alive. Even his hawk of an editor-in-chief had to accept that he'd gone too far and suspend him, but only after the show had been recorded, edited and broadcast. RT had considered Krasovsky's murderous calls perfectly acceptable until they were translated into English, clipped and went viral, causing outrage.

Over the years, I have often wondered what drives those who work in state media and how deeply they believe in the message they convey. I wonder whether they would switch in an instant, fed a different script and new instructions. Anna Politkovskaya was scathing on that topic. 'Their only commitment is to their financial wellbeing,' the *Novaya Gazeta* correspondent believed. A choice between Gucci and Versace, or 'old shabby clothes'. Back in 2004, she perceived no ideological commitment at all. Today, the most prominent names from Russian state media are under economic and travel sanctions. Many have lost access to lives and homes in Europe. But there's been no wave of resignations, no public change of heart. Just one TV producer broke onto set with an anti-war poster during a live news broadcast and later fled the country to avoid prison. Perhaps the rest believe in what they preach. Perhaps they have to tell themselves they do, to make the sacrifice worth it. Speaking out is certainly dangerous, but silence is not. Those who still take the Kremlin's cash did have a choice, and they made it.

Social media now spread the vitriol even further. Clips of hate-spitting TV performances have become anti-hits on Twitter as users outside Russia have struggled to believe their eyes and ears. One of my colleagues has the painful job of translating such shows for a branch of the BBC known as Monitoring: 'Watching Russian state TV so that you don't have to,' as Francis puts it. Every extract he publishes on social media rapidly racks up large numbers of views.

Opposition activists will often argue that Russians don't support or trust their politicians, pointing out that opinion polls are deeply flawed in an authoritarian state. They believe most people are just keeping their heads down because they know they are powerless to bring change and because open dissent is dangerous. I agree, to a point. But I've also seen the immense power of propaganda. It hangs in the air all around and it takes immense self-control not to breathe in even a little of it.

Even before the invasion in February, whenever Russians thought of Ukraine, many would automatically associate the country with fascists. Somewhere in the minds of many would be the false notion that Russian speakers were in danger, even in Kyiv, and that Russian culture was being cancelled by Ukrainian nationalists. They were sure the government was only in power because the West had staged a coup to install its puppets and that it was now trying to weaken Russia by 'stealing' Ukraine from under its wing. Those had been the TV talking points and the social media message for years, and people quoted them back at me endlessly.

On the rare occasions that a chat show invited a guest who was not pro-Kremlin to the core, it was purely as a whipping boy or girl to be shouted down and mocked. I remember one liberal commentator, years ago, telling me he agreed to go when they called because 'if even one person hears what I say and is persuaded, it will have been worth it'. Even then, I remember thinking he was a masochist.

Proof of the success of this war on truth came with the 2022 invasion, when I discovered that Russians who had family members across the border could be convinced that Ukraine was in the grip of 'Nazis'. I regularly met people in bomb shelters and among the ruins of Ukrainian towns and villages whose own relatives in Russia were demanding to know why they were still protecting a 'fascist' government. Often earnestly, but sometimes in anger, these people would urge the Ukrainians to surrender as quickly as possible to Russian troops so that they could finally be 'liberated'.

In parallel with its propaganda war, the Kremlin has waged an assault on the remnants of the free press in Russia. Journalists have been labelled foreign agents, modern-day enemies of the state and even traitors, and independent media have been banned. After the invasion of Ukraine, the 'fake news' laws criminalised the truth and it became illegal even to call the war a war. Major news sites including the BBC and social media platforms were blocked, and independent Russian journalists began leaving their country for safety.

All of this is why, reporting from eastern Ukraine, I called Putin a liar. I argued against even mentioning Russia's denials and distortions from places like Bucha, where we had seen the evidence of atrocities with our own eyes. Because I fear that every time you repeat a lie, even to expose it, someone somewhere will believe it. Putin has made lies a potent weapon in a war with real victims; now the only defence against the denials, fake news and falsehood has to be solid journalism, hard facts and the truth.

On 7 October 2006, Anna Politkovskaya was shot dead as she entered her Moscow block of flats. The gunman fired four times, hitting her in the chest and head. He dropped his pistol and fled the scene. Eventually, five men, including three Chechen brothers, were found guilty of organising and carrying out the killing. But the person who hired the hit squad has never been found, just as in the murder of Boris Nemtsov a decade later.

Like Nemtsov's killing, many would suspect the involvement of Ramzan Kadyrov, the boxer and thug who took over running Chechnya after his father's assassination in 2004. He arrived to meet Putin in the Kremlin then wearing a sky-blue tracksuit. To Politkovskaya, Ramzan was a 'complete idiot, bereft of education [and] brains', but he was also extremely dangerous.

In 2018, I would confront Kadyrov myself. I'd heard he was opening a ski resort in the Chechen mountainside once controlled by separatist fighters, so I signed up for a press tour. At the time, I was reporting on allegations that gay men were being detained, tortured and even killed by Kadyrov's security forces. I'd interviewed some of the victims in a Moscow safe house, and their accounts of abuse were chilling. A leading human-rights activist had also been detained, the case against him clearly fabricated. So when Kadyrov hopped off his shiny new chairlift in a gaudy ski suit, I was standing in his path in the snow. His grin faded. To my questions, Kadyrov snapped that human rights activists were all stooges of the West who had 'sold out' their country. 'You know who defends human rights here,' he threw his head back to cackle with his sinister, adult-kid laugh, mimicked by all the men huddled round him. I persisted for a while, unaware that his heavies had already dragged away my cameraman, Matt, by the scruff of his neck. Our team was then stuck in the mountains for several hours, worrying about how badly we had angered him, as Kadyrov and his guests ate hunks of barbecued meat and cooed over a display of motorcycle stunt riders flying through the sky over bursts of bright orange fire.

Much of Politkovskaya's later reporting had focused in depth on the abuses committed by the Chechen leader and his men. Kadyrov declared himself 'saddened and shaken' by her death and warned against unfounded accusations. Vladimir Putin claimed she had minimal influence on life in Russia and implied that the journalist wasn't worth killing. The day Politkovskaya was shot was Putin's fifty-fourth birthday and some thought her silencing was meant as a gift.

Politkovskaya's journalism was highly engaged, often polemical. Critics, usually men, would call her too emotional. But she was not operating in a world of objective, impartial journalism. Politkovskaya was raging against a system she believed was rotten and dangerous. For every article she wrote, she would make a calculation: if it might change something for the better, that justified the risk she would take to get the story. So as state TV channels broadcast a soap-opera version of life in Chechnya, Politkovskaya pursued the truth and then thrust it at her readers, in all its often graphic, gory detail.

Rereading her writing now, I'm sure she changed the lives of the people she listened to so intently and whose stories she told, especially in Chechnya. It's why they sought her out. Her readers will surely have been changed too, by what they learned. But Politkovskaya could not change Russia itself. After Chechnya, Ukraine 2014 and Syria, her country has gone to war again. Civilians are being shelled and shot and tens of thousands of soldiers on both sides maimed and killed. Again, millions of Russians are hoping it won't affect them directly, and staying silent.

Against the odds, though, a new generation of independent Russian journalists has emerged with the same drive and passion as Politkovskaya. Many now work as best they can from abroad, for safety. A few have remained, like Elena Milashina at *Novaya Gazeta*, who continues writing about abuses in Chechnya, despite being assaulted and subjected to a mock execution. Two months before Russia invaded Ukraine, the newspaper's editor, Dmitry

Muratov, was awarded the Nobel Peace Prize. Six staff at *Novaya Gazeta* have been killed since its founding, and Muratov named them all in his acceptance speech. He described a free press as the antidote to tyranny and ended with one wish: that journalists should die old.

PART VI

Tarusa

13 AUGUST 2021

For days after the border guards let me go from the airport I was dazed. I kept replaying in my head the meeting at the Foreign Ministry confirming my expulsion, sliding between upset and anger. That evening, over commiseration drinks with colleagues, there had been speculation over whether Russia would let anyone in to replace me, and I'd protested at what felt like indecent haste. But mostly I raged at Russia, angry to be torn from a country I was attached to and the story I'd always wanted to report.

On Friday the thirteenth an activist from the punk protest group Pussy Riot was detained, Russia and China held joint military drills and talked about expanding ties, and Bloomberg reported the news of my expulsion. They'd picked up on a story the previous night on state TV. 'Sarah Rainsford is going home,' the Russia 24 presenter had announced, somewhat gleefully I thought, in front of a clip of me from a very old TV report. He'd called it a 'landmark deportation' ordered 'amid simmering tensions', because Britain had 'crossed all our red lines'. Journalist friends in Moscow began sending sympathy and seeking details. As they wrote up their stories, they also fretted a little about what it all meant for them.

At that time, expelling a foreign correspondent was still a significant move. It had been a decade since Luke Harding of the *Guardian* was forced to leave, the first Western reporter to be kicked out since the Cold War. He was refused entry at Moscow airport, then deported, before the Kremlin called that an 'administrative error' and allowed him back. He eventually left Russia before his visa expired, denying anyone the pleasure of expelling him twice. Harding is sure his treatment was in response to his journalism, particularly his in-depth coverage of the Wikileaks revelations of high-level Russian corruption. Three years later, a correspondent for Poland's *Gazeta Wyborcza* was ordered to leave Moscow after eighteen years because Warsaw had expelled a Russian correspondent on suspicion of spying.

The climate for local Russian reporters had been worsening for some time, but I think we foreigners were still slumbering, kidding ourselves that we were somehow untouchable. We imagined that Russia needed the foreign press as part of its facade of normality. But no one cared about appearances anymore.

Long before I was detained, we'd booked a holiday at a woodland retreat a couple of hours' drive from Moscow. It had become a favourite spot to go with the dog, on the site of an old Soviet children's camp on the River Oka, with huts and cottages dotted in the trees. The small town of Tarusa nearby had been a regular haunt of the poet Marina Tsvetaeva in the early twentieth century. Later it was a sanctuary for all sorts of literary dissidents and anti-Soviet types, located beyond the 101st kilometre from the capital that was the safe distance to which Russia banished its least wanted. As the news of my expulsion spread, we decided to head to Tarusa as planned, to try to get away from it all.

Behind the scenes, the BBC had been protesting and pressing for my ban to be overturned, holding off on a public comment until all chances of reversing the ruling were exhausted. It felt like a hopeless cause, but then I'd never thought I'd be allowed back into Russia at all. Our levers in Moscow were minimal, though, and August is a bad time for diplomacy. Foreign Secretary Dominic Raab was on holiday in Crete and his staff were nervous about disturbing him. Later it was reported that the minister was delegating calls on even the imminent Taliban takeover of

Afghanistan to an aide. When he resurfaced, Raab was asked on the *Today* programme about Russia's action and pressed to explain what he was doing. He called my expulsion 'a response to us holding them to account for the various malign things they do'. He would eventually write to his counterpart, Sergei Lavrov, to express his concern about press freedom, but by then our tickets were bought and our life in Russia packed away in boxes.

A senior diplomat I talked to agreed that expelling me was meant to scare the rest, extending the attack on the press in Moscow from local to foreign reporters. She also saw it as part of a depressing downward spiral. 'It's about the future of Russia. It's awful for the Russian people most of all, but also for everyone who sees a different Russia and wants it to succeed.' She called it the 'Closing Down Russia' project and I thought that was pretty accurate.

The official BBC statement went out late that evening, when it was clear that Russia's decision would not change. It condemned the move as a 'direct assault on media freedom'. As I briefly became the news, I read articles online containing mistakes and half-truths. But I was nervous of sharing details, especially about being called a security threat. I'd asked for the BBC's own coverage to be low-key while I was still in the country, so that evening there was a short news despatch on a Radio 4 bulletin, just before the sport.

I hadn't planned to comment on my situation at all until I left, apart from a tweet thanking people for their messages of support. *Being expelled from Russia, a country I've lived in for almost $1/3$ of my life – and reported for years – is devastating.* But as our car crawled towards Tarusa through the weekend dacha traffic, a message popped up on my phone. Mishal Husain wanted to know whether I'd speak to her for the *Today* programme the next morning. I decided that it was time to correct the record, as far as I could.

Interview on BBC Radio 4 *Today*, 14 August 2021

SARAH: This is not a failure to renew my visa, although technically that's what it is. I'm being expelled, and I've been told I can't come back. Ever.

MISHAL: That's quite something ... I first met you in Moscow when we were living there when we were eighteen, but it's been a big part of your life ever since. So to be told now you can never come back, what effect does that have?

SARAH: It's devastating personally. But it's also shocking. Russia has never been only a posting for me. It's a country that I've devoted a huge amount of my life to trying to understand ... I calculated just now, it's almost a third of my life that I've lived in Russia ... I've loved trying to tell the story of Russia to the world. But it's an increasingly difficult story to tell.

Mishal and I first met in Moscow in 1992. She knows what Russia has meant to me like few others and she teased that out as I sat beneath the trees of the old pioneer camp. It was a relief to say some of it out loud. At the end, Mishal asked me to reflect on the changes I'd seen since the two of us had arrived in Russia all those years before. It felt like delivering an obituary for a country lost.

You'll remember how in the early 1990s people were queuing to sell their belongings to have enough money to buy food ... They were terrible, turbulent times ... But it was also a time of new and exciting freedoms for Russia, and my career as a journalist has charted the path through which those freedoms have been reduced and reduced and reduced ...

We wake up every day and hear news of someone else who's had a police search of their flat; someone else who's in court; someone else who's left the country. The number of people leaving is extraordinary. I've never seen anything like it. So yes, I'll be leaving, and I'm extremely sad I won't be able to come back. But it makes me sadder that Russians feel they don't have a future here. That's not the country I came to thirty years ago, and it's certainly not the one I started reporting on twenty years ago.

Under Surveillance

NIZHNY NOVGOROD, SUMMER 2018

When Russia hosted the World Cup it was briefly transformed into what it might have been. In the summer of 2018, police officers in Moscow gave patient directions to fans from Colombia and Peru. In Saransk, a host city way off the tourist track, a young woman ran up and kissed me just for being there. Cuban friends, visiting from Havana, danced salsa in a metro carriage and no one batted an eyelid. There were even safe spaces for LGBT fans. For one month, life in Russia was excellent.

When Qatar came under scrutiny for its human-rights record at the next World Cup, Gary Lineker suggested that the BBC, himself included, had pulled its punches in Russia. But we'd reported in great detail on the human-rights abuses and repression for many years. Our bureau had been covering Russia's brutal defence of Bashar al-Assad in Syria since 2015 and just months before the 2018 World Cup we were hunting down every possible lead on the Salisbury poisoning, the nerve-agent attack on a former double agent. After the British government identified Moscow as 'highly likely' to be responsible for the assassination attempt, no minister or member of the royal family would travel to Russia for the football.

In the run-up to the tournament there was an intense focus on the darker side of Russian life. Everything from racism and

LGBT rights to political repression hit global headlines. Football hooliganism came under an especially bright spotlight after the violence at Euro 2016, when MMA-trained Russian thugs had clashed with mainly boozy, out-of-shape England fans in Marseille. For officials in Moscow, bending over backwards to show the best of Russia to the world, the negative coverage was infuriating.

Some England fans were unhappy with the press, too. As the tournament started and I was reporting from the streets, I got heckled for supposedly blackening Russia's image unfairly. 'You lied to us. You told us not to come. Fucking BBC!' After one comment, I remember shouting at the group to come back after the World Cup and see the other Russia for themselves. They were annoyed at the small England following, outnumbered by fans from places like Panama and Tunisia. But I suspected that was as much down to bruising memories of Marseille as any of our Russian news coverage. I was always convinced that Russia's ultras would be on their best behaviour when the international party hit town. No one would be allowed to spoil Putin's World Cup.

As the country geared up for the competition, we began visiting the host cities in a kind of warm-up tour of our own. Saransk didn't have much to speak of, but it did have a fantastic bus shelter from Soviet times shaped like a giant lightbulb, in honour of a local factory that produced a third of all the bulbs in the USSR. Nizhny Novgorod was more mundane in bus-stop terms, but we planned to film the brand-new riverside stadium and a big spruce-up in the city. In cobbled streets full of 'Welcome to Nizhny' signs, we chatted to locals taking pictures with World Cup mascots and dropped in to the local kremlin to hear what the deputy governor hoped to gain from the tournament.

It was shortly after we left that interview that we realised we were being followed. Our cameraman, Matt, saw the cars first. After several years working in China he'd become adept at spotting surveillance, and we soon had a list of all the car numberplates that reappeared on our tail wherever we turned. Sometimes there were three teams following at once. When we climbed out of our van at a vantage point over the city, next to a giant sign spelling out #Nizhny2018, two men emerged from their own vehicle and hovered at a distance. They mostly stood with their backs to us, phones pressed to one ear in the modern-day equivalent of reading a newspaper, but they weren't even trying to be discreet.

As they persisted in harassing us, our attention inevitably shifted from how Nizhny was preparing to greet the world's football fans to the extraordinary surveillance operation that had greeted our own team. At one point, as we filmed on a hill far from any crowds, a TV crew rushed towards us, though we hadn't told anyone where we'd be. In times gone by, local journalists were curious, sometimes even excited, to see the BBC in their town. So were local people. The older generation would reminisce about learning English with the BBC or listening to banned Western rock music. Seva Novgorodtsev, a BBC Russian Service DJ, was a legend in even the farthest corners of the ex-USSR. But by 2018, people were so used to state media portraying the BBC as part of some anti-Russian plot, many had grown wary or even hostile.

This wasn't my first unpleasant encounter in Nizhny. Two years earlier, we'd travelled there close to the first anniversary of Boris Nemtsov's murder. The attractive city on the broad river Volga had been the opposition politician's home, and one of his allies, former prime minister Mikhail Kasyanov, was due to hold an event we wanted to film.

As we waited for him, we were interviewing a local opposition figure when a group of nationalist activists burst in. Encircling us, they began jabbing their fingers at our faces. 'What are you filming, BBC? How bad life is in Russia?' They then chanted four numbers repeatedly. *1-9-3-7*. I couldn't understand what on earth they meant until I made out another word. *Chistki*. Purges. The nationalists, their faces creased into snarls, were chanting '1937'. It was the year when Stalin's Great Terror began, the round-up and execution of imaginary enemies of the people.

After threatening to 'purge' us, the group then wanted to send us to the Gulag. 'If you prepare a revolution, you go to Magadan!' They managed one last patriotic burst before they grew tired. 'Our country, our rules! Fatherland! Freedom! Putin!' After that they filed outside to gather in an oddball picket beneath the giant feet of a Lenin statue in the square.

The prime target of their hostility that day, Kasyanov, never showed up. When I called to find out why, he admitted he'd already left town. 'It's dangerous. They're following me everywhere, trying to kick me.' The previous day he'd tried to hold a press conference, only to end up shut in little more than a cupboard with his bodyguards for several hours, scared to emerge.

In 2018 we decided not to change our reporting plans, despite attracting uncomfortable attention once again. We'd arranged to visit the local branch of Alexei Navalny's team because I wanted to know what opposition activists made of Russia hosting the World Cup. I wondered whether they saw the prestigious event as 'sportswashing', as some Western commentators were suggesting; whether it was positive PR that Russia did not deserve. As we were setting up to film, the doorbell rang and a woman announced through the intercom that she was from Russian state TV 'here to see our colleagues from the BBC'. Again, we hadn't informed anyone of our filming plans.

We carried on with our interviews and some of the Navalny supporters did tell me they'd prefer fans to stay away during the World Cup. They wanted to punish and isolate Putin at a time when activists like them were under intense pressure. But most were in favour of hosting the tournament. They didn't want the Russian people to be ostracised and suffer because of the actions of a government they never chose. Perhaps just as much, they wanted something to enjoy and be cheerful about. With the whole world focused on Russia for four weeks, at least they might not get arrested.

It was already dusk by the time we wrapped up, but as we headed for our van, a woman appeared suddenly from nowhere, calling out to us all by name. She was filming on her mobile phone, so I guessed her cameraman's shift had ended and he'd left her to lurk in the bushes alone. She was remarkably persistent, posing questions that sounded strangely sinister through her rictus smile. 'How do you like Nizhny Novgorod? How do you like our stadium?' We slid the van door firmly shut, without comment, as she filmed.

The overt surveillance continued the following day as we went to interview players from the local football club and then drove to the former flat of Andrei Sakharov. In 1980 the Soviet authorities had sent the nuclear scientist-turned-dissident into internal exile in Nizhny, which was then known as Gorky. The aim was partly to keep him away from the foreign press who were descending on Moscow ahead of the Olympic games: the Kremlin didn't want awkward headlines and talk of human rights to spoil the party.

'Sakharov was kept under visual surveillance through the window and the KGB listened in to all his conversations,' the museum's curator Lyubov Potapova explained as she showed me round the ground-floor flat on Gagarin Street. My idea was to film the museum as somewhere curious that World Cup fans might visit, but I'd also wanted to see it for myself. The dissident's bedroom looked straight onto another apartment block across the path and KGB agents had been stationed there round the clock to keep an eye on him. There was also a trailer full of agents further along for extra surveillance and police stationed outside his front door to stop and check all visitors.

When I tweeted about our museum visit, someone chirped back that Sakharov's flat had been spacious by the standards of the time. That old Soviet propaganda line ignored the more pertinent fact that however many square metres Sakharov occupied, he was forced to live miles from home, against his will, with no link to the outside world. His radio and TV reception were jammed and the KGB were listening in even when he went to the toilet. In 1985 Sakharov began a long hunger strike to demand medical care for his wife, Elena Bonner, which ended with him being pinned down by several doctors and force-fed.

In December 1986 a telephone was installed at the flat so that Mikhail Gorbachev could call Sakharov to inform him that he was being released and could return to Moscow. Four decades on, the white dial-phone was still there beside the tatty brown leather armchair where the dissident received the news of his freedom. There was also a state surveillance team back in place outside Sakharov's flat, an operative on every corner. Only now they were watching us.

A Spy Story

MOSCOW, DECEMBER 2018

Paul Whelan was in Room 3324 of Moscow's Metropol Hotel when the Russian friend who would betray him turned up unannounced. The American was on holiday, and that day he was due at the wedding of a fellow former US Marine and his Russian girlfriend. He'd been to Moscow before, spoke a few words of Russian and liked to think he knew his way around. So that morning he'd offered to lead a group of wedding guests on a tour of the Kremlin, including some of the Russians. They took in the cathedrals and the museum, then crossed Red Square to wander through the glamorous GUM shopping arcade and nearby streets. The pretty yellow lights hung for Russia's World Cup party just six months earlier were still dangling.

It was around 16:00 and Whelan was back in his room when Ilya Yatsenko knocked at the door. The American had already seen his friend that week and wasn't expecting him. He thought it odd, but invited him in. Minutes later, FSB agents in balaclavas burst into the room and pinned the American to the floor. In English, one of them announced he was under arrest for espionage. For a split second Whelan thought it was some kind of joke. Then he counted eight, maybe ten, men in his room and even more in the corridor. Bundled out of the hotel in handcuffs, through the rear door, Whelan disappeared without trace for three days.

On New Year's Eve the FSB announced that an American had been arrested for 'espionage activity'. I was on call that day, and this was big news that grew even bigger when it emerged that Whelan held four passports, from the US, UK, Canada and Ireland. His FSB interrogators would claim they were fake, produced by US intelligence for undercover espionage missions. But Whelan had been born in Canada to British parents with Irish roots and they'd all moved to the US when he was small. He once told me he had a bit of each of his four countries in him. He grew up watching the Trooping the Colour on TV each year for the Queen's official birthday, with tea and biscuits.

Whelan would be locked up at the FSB's Lefortovo Prison for the next twenty months. For twenty-three hours a day he was kept in a cell measuring 9.5m² with one other prisoner, the lights never turned off. Exercise was one hour on the roof. Under interrogation for weeks, Whelan was pressured to confess that he'd been trying to obtain Russian state secrets. The FSB were also fishing for information on the US military. He wasn't allowed to call home that entire time, deepening the isolation. Even his lawyer was appointed by the Russian state, a man who had a small golden bust of Putin on his office shelf when I paid him a visit there. Whelan's family didn't see the point in sapping all their resources on a private defence lawyer when the trial outcome seemed predetermined. Whelan agreed, but it left him with no one in his corner he could really trust.

The first time I set eyes on Whelan, he was being led into a Moscow courtroom by officers dressed in black from head to toe and in balaclavas. It was early 2019 and Russia's foreign minister had already declared that the American had been caught 'red-handed', not waiting for even the pretence of a trial. But as the 48-year-old approached us that day in handcuffs, side-parting and blue anorak, cradling a carboard box with his prison lunch, he looked like a confused librarian.

By this time, Whelan had been in custody for almost two months. I called out in English to ask how he was coping and he managed a weak smile. His guards then locked him into a metal cage in court. Just before the judge arrived to rule on his custody arrangements, the press were allowed into the room to film. It's a very uncomfortable feeling, pointing your camera at someone who has nowhere to hide. But those few moments are usually a prisoner's only sight of anyone but lawyers and interrogators. It can be their one chance to speak out. The press were forbidden from addressing the accused, but I always tried my luck.

That day, when I started talking to Whelan through the bars, his eyes flicked towards the guards. 'I don't think the FSB will let me speak.' But I had to ask how he responded to the espionage charge. 'Communication is forbidden,' a bailiff barked in my direction and the American shifted uneasily in his cage. 'They don't want us to say anything. You get the picture.' The judge then entered the tiny courtroom and began reading the ruling and no one bothered to translate. I let Whelan know he was remaining in custody. 'It's not going to get any worse if you speak!' I tried, and he laughed at my persistence. 'I think it could. If I talk, I'll be in a bad way.'

The spy story was unfolding against a hostile political backdrop. By 2018 tensions between Russia and the West ran higher than ever since Soviet times. Washington was accusing Russia of meddling in its 2016 presidential elections, while the Salisbury poisoning in the UK in March 2018 had prompted a mass flushing out of Russian intelligence officers from all over Europe. When Whelan was arrested, he called himself a political hostage. There was immediately speculation that he was some kind of pawn.

In Russian spy cases even the defence lawyers are banned from revealing details, on pain of prosecution. To find out any more, I needed to make a connection with Whelan himself. That meant each time the FSB brought him before a judge to extend his detention, I would squeeze into court for the few moments of the hearing that were open. As Whelan's hopes of release evaporated, he grew bolder. He began to bring handwritten signs condemning his arrest, holding them through the bars of his cage for us to film. He denounced the espionage charge as absurd, declaring that he was in a 'kangaroo court'. Russia thought it had captured James Bond on a spy mission, Whelan declared. 'In fact they abducted Mr Bean on holiday.'

He would sometimes call out for me or my cameraman by name and I sensed the FSB officers in court eyeballing me through the slits in their balaclavas. Once, as Whelan was being led back out to the prison van, he threw a document for me to catch right in front of his handlers. It was nothing secret, but the guards didn't know that.

The FSB would eventually leak details of its case, including a claim that Whelan was working for US military intelligence. They said he'd been seeking a list of students at the border-guard institute, which I knew his friend, Yatsenko, had attended. At the next custody hearing, I shouted over a thick wall of bailiffs to ask Whelan for his response.

Moscow City Court, 17 September 2019

WHELAN: A person turned up at my room. He put something in my pocket, then I was arrested. That person was an FSB officer. Someone I had known for ten years.
SARAH: Were there state secrets on the drive?
WHELAN: I have no idea. I never looked at it. I didn't know I had it until I was arrested. This is 100 per cent a provocation. A really bad one.

When the judge returned and began mumble-reading his decision to keep Whelan behind bars, the American erupted. 'This is garbage. There is no evidence at all. It's ridiculous.' The judge raised his voice, so Whelan did too, drowning him out. 'As my cousins in England would say, *this is total bollocks*!' At that, the TV cameras were removed from court.

By the time Whelan went on trial in Moscow in 2020, behind closed doors, a Covid lockdown had added an even thicker layer of secrecy. Press and public were barred from the building until the verdict. The judge had refused all forty witnesses requested by the defence and no one beyond that courtroom had seen any of the evidence presented. Whelan says that's because there is none. But on 15 June 2020 he was pronounced guilty of espionage and sentenced to sixteen years. It was to be served in a high-security facility for the most dangerous offenders.

* * *

Five months after his conviction, Whelan called me from his prison camp.

Phone interview from IK-17 prison, 24 November 2020

I can tell you I am innocent. No crime was committed. There was no evidence. No witnesses were allowed. But all they had to do was pass this whole matter through a show trial and they came up with a conviction …

[I'm in] an old Gulag camp. Things are very old. It's overcrowded. We don't have enough facilities. We only have cold water, not enough toilets or sinks for all the people. It's a very, very grim existence.

The American was being held at prison colony IK-17, 300 miles south-east of Moscow. For the first time I was able to ask him questions without shouting across a courtroom. We spoke by phone several times, often at length. Sometimes he clearly wanted to get a message out, but occasionally it felt like he was ringing to let off steam or hear an English voice. He didn't answer everything I asked. He would claim that was for safety reasons while he was in Russian custody, which could feel like a ruse to dodge difficult issues. But that first time we spoke, Whelan was anxious for me to take down one thing in particular. 'The prisoners here call this place "Colony Pizdets". If you can work that in, it would make them smile.' The equivalent would be something like 'Fucking Shit-Pit Prison'. Whelan reminded me, more than once, to mention that.

When Whelan first visited Russia in 2006, he was a serving US Marine on a tour of duty in western Iraq. His family saw nothing odd in his holiday choice, telling me that wanderlust is in their blood as British-Canadian-Irish-Americans. Besides, an old Marine friend of Whelan was in the team protecting the US Embassy in Moscow, giving him somewhere to stay. He told a Marines' magazine that, as a single man, the break was a chance to 'experience the diversity of culture'.

For two weeks he toured art galleries and military museums and made his first Russian friends. After he left, he went on to expand that network via social media. He chatted to people using an online translator. 'It mostly started as language exchange. Football teams in England, music, movies, things like that.' The next time he travelled to Russia, two years later, he had many more people to see.

Phone interview from IK-17 prison, 6 December 2020

Being able to visit Lenin's tomb, the Kremlin, the Tretyakov, all those things ... were interesting to me. Russia was where I had friends ... I collect old Soviet-era *podstakanniki* [cup holders], but I don't collect secret information. I have all sorts of souvenirs, but I have never asked anyone for secret information or expected anyone to give it to me.

Whelan created a webpage describing his early trips, and his enthusiasm is almost childlike. The page is covered in exclamation marks. 'Having grown up during the Cold War, it was a dream of mine to visit Russia and meet some of the sneaky Russians who had kept the world at bay for so long!!' one entry reads. He posted his own guide to the Cyrillic alphabet and some basic Russian words, and there's a whole section dedicated to the big-eared Soviet cartoon character Cheburashka. There's also a photo of the FSB headquarters. 'This is Lubyanka, where the KGB has our spies locked in the basement!' A decade later it's where Whelan would be interrogated.

The content matches how the American's contacts, friends and family would describe him to me later: a curious globetrotter who made friends pretty much everywhere, including among men with a shared interest in the military. 'He said it's beautiful and he liked the cold and he had quite a few friends there,' an ex-colleague remembers asking about his trips to Russia. There's a photo of one of those friends on Whelan's webpage, a young soldier called Maxim. Visitors are invited to click and learn more about the Russian's 'hobbies and military service'. Maxim then explains how his 'new friend Paul' is helping him with his English and describes touring Moscow together, eating sushi and pancakes filled with caviar.

In the days after Whelan's arrest, I scrolled through his account on VK, the Russian equivalent of Facebook, trying to learn more about him. His friends there were almost all male, significantly younger than him, and some openly displayed their military connections. I messaged a selection of them, asking about Whelan, and one sent a paragraph of expletives in return. Most ignored or blocked me, but six replied. They were nervous about saying much because of the espionage charge and no one was prepared to meet in person. But all were shocked by the arrest.

Vadim said he was studying at a military academy when Whelan first got in touch, 'because he was ex-military too'. They'd only ever chatted online about 'ordinary, everyday things'.

Yury was a supermarket night-guard with no military connections. He met Whelan once for a few hours in 2008 when the American was touring various cities. 'I don't believe that Paul is a spy,' Yury messaged, in broken English. 'I don't know anything what might be interesting to a foreign spy.'

A Moscow hairdresser who tagged his Instagram posts #browneyes also had no obvious military links. He'd chatted to Whelan a couple of times about travel. They never met.

A second Yury was more forthcoming. In 2018 he was still in the navy and his VK profile was full of photos in uniform. He told me Whelan had first messaged a decade earlier when Yury was at cadet school. 'He was friendly and really liked our country, its history and our traditions and people!' this man wrote, explaining that they mostly spoke about 'military things and politics'. They messaged regularly, Whelan even sent New Year's cards, but they never met. Yury was stunned to hear of the American's arrest. 'No way! He's the kindest soul. If he's a spy, then I'm Michael Jackson!!!!' A couple of days later, he deleted his profile and disappeared.

When the FSB began dripping details of its case to state news agencies, the anonymous source made a big deal of Whelan's ties to Russia and the fact that his social media friends were not 'pretty

Russian girls'. The leaks claimed these were targets to cultivate, identified for him by US intelligence. 'They had evidence I knew Russian people? So what? None of that is illegal,' Whelan retorts. He had even introduced some of these military friends to his parents when they visited Russia together in 2009. If he was actually attempting to 'turn' enemy agents, he was oddly public about his interests and encounters.

His parents also met Ilya Yatsenko. He and Whelan had been chatting online, but when Whelan took his parents to visit Sergiev Posad, outside Moscow, it was a chance for the virtual friends to meet. A short train ride north from Moscow, the town of beautiful Orthodox monasteries is a tourist draw. It was also Yatsenko's hometown. The Russian turned up that day with a friend, both keen to know 'real people' from the West. They'd requested gifts: a bottle of Jack Daniels for Yatsenko and a Beatles album on vinyl for his friend, which Whelan had to carry carefully all the way from America.

He says they all stayed in touch online. 'It was all very casual. A lot of the chat was focused on football, or general culture and the news.' He even helped Yatsenko's brother with his English. It would be almost a decade before he met his friend again in person.

Whelan told me he visited Russia twice in 2015, but Yatsenko was away in Crimea. By then the American was working in global security for a US firm. He travelled extensively for work but says his Russia trips were just for fun, sometimes using up his air miles. In January 2018 he was back, posting Instagram pictures of the Kremlin cathedrals and the Bolshoi Theatre. The American got a kick out of playing the tour guide to Yatsenko and other Russians from out of town, taking them ice skating and to the John Bull pub. 'It was just normal touristy stuff. Running around with a foreigner was funny for them too.' He also returned to Sergiev Posad for a couple of nights at Yatsenko's parents' home. I've seen the enthusiastic emails he sent back home then, attaching photos of the fireplace and Sultan, the family's giant dog. He particularly enjoyed the *banya*, or sauna, he wrote, and 'running in and out of the snow!'

All this time, Whelan was aware that his young friend worked for the FSB. Yatsenko was a border guard, more passport-stamping than front-line intelligence, but it was part of the security service nonetheless. The American wrote breezy messages home, joking about that. 'I will be with guys from the FSB, so should be okay!' he said in one exchange I've seen. In another, he mentioned that Yatsenko had studied at the 'FSB school'.

In one of our phone calls, I challenged Whelan on that. I wanted to know why a former US Marine, or any American, would knowingly hang around with an FSB officer. At first, he professed ignorance. 'I knew this person worked for the border guard … but no one ever presented themselves as an FSB officer.' When I told him I'd seen messages from him that showed otherwise, he didn't want to comment without the context. 'If I'd known someone was involved with that organisation, I wouldn't have dealt with them,' he insisted. At that point, Whelan had high hopes he'd be swapped for a Russian prisoner abroad, and it's possible he didn't want to jeopardise his chance of getting out. Maybe he just didn't want to look daft for being too trusting. But whatever he knew about Yatsenko's exact job, he never tried to conceal their relationship.

I did attempt to track Yatsenko down. It's illegal to reveal the identity of a serving Russian intelligence officer, so I was nervous about actually finding him. I got hold of several phone numbers, but he never answered. Then, with my team, we took a train to Sergiev Posad, retracing Whelan's route and hunting for the FSB man's house as he had described it. We failed, which was deeply frustrating, but also a kind of relief. I'd been worrying what kind of trap we might be walking into.

Whelan's defence is just that: that he was trapped by Ilya Yatsenko. In December 2018, when he landed into a freezing Moscow for his American friend's wedding, Whelan says Yatsenko met him at the airport, which he hadn't expected. The two ate sandwiches in the Metropol lobby and the next day 'ran around a bit' at a city shopping mall. On 25 December the Russian wanted to join Whelan and other friends for Christmas dinner, so they went to the Goodman's steakhouse opposite the hotel. That day, Whelan snapped a photo of a geeky young man in polo neck and sports jacket with a side parting and cleft chin. He's smiling straight into the camera, fork raised over a juicy chunk of beef, half-glass of red wine to one side. Whelan forwarded the picture of Yatsenko to a mutual friend with the caption 'Dinner with Tovarishi'. It seems a strange move if he was midway through a mission to acquire classified material.

It's possible the young Russian was primed to set Whelan up from the moment they met, and that his FSB bosses were just biding their time. It's also possible that Yatsenko himself disclosed the friendship to the FSB at some point, in return for some reward. Whelan himself thinks he was pressured. When Yatsenko appeared as the key trial witness, Whelan says he stood with his back to the cage and delivered a speech he had memorised. It was the FSB story: that the American was a military intelligence agent who had asked him to supply state secrets. There were no recordings, no written notes. It was one man's word and he refused to look Whelan in the eye. 'It was a put-up job. He was going through the motions.'

Phone interview from IK-17 prison, 6 December 2020

SARAH: What do you think of him now, this friend?
WHELAN: He is definitely not a friend. I don't know how he was dragged into this, and I don't care. But I know in court, he lied and signed his name to statements that were not true.

A few days after his arrest, the US Marines revealed a secret that Whelan had concealed even from his twin brother: the man who still flew the Marines' flag at the gate of his parents' house had been given a dishonourable discharge back in 2008. I've read the transcript of the court-martial hearing and it shows that Whelan pleaded guilty to charges which included attempting to obtain $5,000 cash in lieu of leave days he hadn't used. It was money he wasn't owed. In his closing speech, the prosecution counsel declared Whelan 'a thief, a liar and a cheater'. His defence lawyer countered that his client had 'served valiantly and honourably' for over a decade, including two tours of duty in Iraq. He had cashflow problems and the court papers mentioned depression. But when the judge asked Whelan whether he had any excuse, he replied, 'Not at all, sir,' and agreed that his actions were unlawful. He was found guilty. Whelan's brother, David, was 'stunned' at the revelation, describing his twin's behaviour as utterly out of character.

When I asked Whelan himself about his dishonourable discharge, he was evasive. 'I can't confirm or deny anything while I'm in Russia.' He hinted at some kind of conspiracy. 'There is a story there and when I get home I'm more than happy to share it with you.' But he wouldn't be drawn. 'Yeah, unfortunately I can't discuss that when I am standing in a Russian prison. We can discuss all of that when I get home.' Back in 2020 he was hopeful that day would come soon. Five years after his arrest, we still haven't had that conversation.

Whelan now spends his days sewing fake-fur hats and making industrial uniforms in his Russian labour camp, singing Eminem tracks as he works. IK-17 is a cluster of low-rise barracks and a church surrounded by forest, in a region dotted with prisons. The inmates are up at 06:00, six days a week. There's fifteen minutes of light exercise, then breakfast, work, lunch, work, roll call, dinner and bed. 'It's Groundhog Day, day after day.' At night, he gets woken every two hours by guards shining a light in his face and taking his photograph, because he's been singled out as an escape risk.

Despite everything, Whelan was often upbeat in our phone calls, making quips which he'd end with a *ba-boom!* in case I missed the joke. It amused him to recommend good spy novels from the pile he was reading in prison. He also told me that he was keeping his spirits up, and showing his defiance, by singing all four of his national anthems each morning at full volume, until the guards yelled at him to stop. A 'bit rusty' on the Irish anthem, he usually sang something by the Pogues. It turned out he'd done the same in Lefortovo, when the FSB kept him in solitary confinement. 'I try to be as positive as I can,' he told me, though that doesn't always work.

I once asked about his fellow prisoners and he told me they were 'murderers, rapists, robbers. People who've killed multiple times. And lots of people in their twenties in for drugs.' He believes he is safe for as long as the Russian government wants to extract a price for him. 'If something happens, it would be bad for everyone.' Whelan has always been sure that Russia wants to trade him for one of its own, in the US. He says that the FSB told him so and the trial judge repeated that after delivering his verdict. Whelan's state-assigned lawyer talked openly about prisoner swaps to us journalists throughout. They all assured Whelan it would happen soon.

It has worked before. In 2017 a retired Norwegian border guard named Frode Berg was convicted of espionage and exchanged two years later following a presidential pardon. I went to meet Berg in Oslo right after his release and he told me how Norwegian military intelligence used him to deliver cash and instructions for an agent codenamed Natalia. In return, Norway got data on Russian submarines. The case exposed how at least one country was using civilians for high-risk espionage in Russia, but the FSB had been on to Berg from the very start.

Whelan's interrogators were pressuring him to confess like Berg had done, and be swapped. But the American resisted. 'I told them, no way. This case is totally made up.' He told me later that there were serious negotiations for an exchange in any case, after his conviction in 2020. But Donald Trump rejected the terms and Whelan was dispatched to his labour camp to start his sentence.

Phone interview from IK-17 prison, 13 April 2021

> I remain innocent of the charge, so it's getting a little tiresome being here. I'm not happy that I've lost twenty-seven months of my life to this. I know it will be resolved sooner or later, but … the fabricated case against me is just blatantly wrong.

In April 2021 Whelan told me Joe Biden's administration was 'quite positive' they could bring him home. I had to break it to him that there had been another round of diplomatic expulsions, tit-for-tat. He brushed that off. 'It's basically the lowest point of the Cold War; it can only get better!' Isolated in his prison camp,

I think he struggled to grasp the downward rush in relations. By then, Biden had agreed with a TV interviewer that Putin was 'a killer'.

My last call with Whelan in Russia was on 10 May 2021 and on that occasion we didn't even mention the possibility of a prisoner exchange. The following month, Biden and Putin would meet in Geneva and discuss 'stabilising' relations. By the end of the year, Russia was amassing troops on the border with Ukraine, poised to launch its invasion. I had been expelled and Whelan remained behind bars.

So was Paul Whelan more Mr Bean, or James Bond? In espionage cases, it's hard ever to be sure. But this one seems to rest solely on the testimony of an FSB officer in a closed court. Whelan's discharge from the Marines shows a record of dishonesty that seems incompatible with high-risk espionage. His military background means he'd have struggled to work under the radar, and Whelan never even tried. He posted pictures online, wrote home about his trips, even introduced a member of the FSB to his parents. He did seek out military men, but he contacted other Russians, too, with no links.

Perhaps Whelan got a buzz from hanging out with the FSB. He loves a Cold War thriller and there is a little of the Walter Mitty about him. A former colleague, who describes Whelan as kind and patient, also remembers him turning up to support her at her factory in Mexico with armed guards, posting them outside restaurants when they ate. She felt that Whelan's macho approach was over the top, and that he enjoyed that. Another friend told me Whelan was 'a little quirky' and liked to 'push the line a little bit', and wondered whether some comment or quip might have been dangerously misconstrued.

Whelan's twin, David, is adamant his brother is no thrill-seeker and believes he was ensnared by Yatsenko deliberately. 'It sounds incredibly naive to someone who lives in Moscow … but my sense is that Paul really thought they could be friends,' he told me in one interview from Canada. 'The FSB thing wasn't a big deal until he was entrapped.'

Ivan Pavlov, a lawyer who specialises in espionage cases, suggests Yatsenko would have been looking for his opportunity with the American from the start. 'The temptation is high: promotion, more stars on the shoulder. This is how FSB careers are made. We call it "rearing a calf". He reared him, cultivated him. But then you need to cull him.'

The US government has formally declared Whelan 'wrongfully detained'. John Sullivan, US Ambassador to Moscow from 2019 to 2022, was always clear with me that the case was a 'gross injustice'. But Ambassador Sullivan also argued that Whelan's arrest and imprisonment do more than mirror the deep crisis in relations between Russia and the West. They were a reminder of the utterly arbitrary nature of rule in Russia today. 'This is happening to an innocent man. If they can do it to him, they can do it you. To anyone.'

Journalism is Not a Crime

MOSCOW, JULY 2020

When Ivan Safronov was accused of treason, it came as a deep shock to other independent Russian reporters. They were sure the case was a fabrication, intended to intimidate every one of them. Safronov's former newspaper, *Kommersant*, condemned the charges immediately. When journalists protested outside the FSB headquarters, denouncing a 'cannibalistic state', more than two dozen were detained.

The investigative outlet *Proekt* got hold of some of the files from Safronov's case. The FSB was claiming that he had shared details of overseas deliveries of Russian military equipment, and of Russian activities in Syria, with two foreign contacts. This data supposedly included state secrets, which these contacts then sent to foreign intelligence services. But when *Proekt* compared the information Safronov had allegedly shared with data freely available online, it found that everything had been reported previously, including by the Defence Ministry.

At the time, talk of enemy agents and spies was peaking and so was the number of arrests. But Safronov's lawyer, Ivan Pavlov, told me he was sure he hadn't encountered a single 'real' spy in all his years defending people accused of espionage. 'It's a war, do you understand? And when there's a war, everyone is seen as the enemy.' Pavlov described the FSB as 'the mightiest' intelligence service with 'secrecy, provocation and falsification' in its arsenal. If you got caught up in a case of treason or espionage, the lawyer warned me, then you were in 'the most complicated story of your life'.

As I was reporting on Safronov's arrest, I tracked down the last Russian journalist who had been tried for treason, two decades earlier. Grigory Pasko had also been a military correspondent and was eventually released from prison after an international outcry. But he saw no such chance for Safronov. 'Now Vladimir Putin doesn't care what anyone thinks,' Pasko said. 'There are no brakes, no restraints now.'

Pasko was right. Despite the protests and pressure, and the publicity, there was no leniency for Safronov. Instead, Russian justice set a grim new record. In early September 2022 a court in Moscow sentenced the journalist to twenty-two years for treason. His own lawyer had fled the country a year earlier, as a criminal investigation was also launched against him.

Safronov had been offered a deal by his interrogators: confess and cut your potential sentence in half. He refused. He used his closing statement in the trial to say that he would serve his time with dignity if he was jailed. But speaking from his glass cage in court, he stressed that his only crime was journalism. 'To find me guilty means an end to freedom of speech for a long time.'

Tarusa

14 AUGUST 2021

After my interview went out on the *Today* programme, Russia's Foreign Ministry spokeswoman publicly accused me of 'manipulating information'. Maria Zakharova claimed that I'd not been expelled forever; my accreditation had simply not been renewed. Indefinitely. 'A journalist, even a British one, who has lived a third of her life in a Russian-speaking environment, should understand the difference.' She spelled it out: I could return to Russia just as soon as the TASS man who'd been forced to leave London was reinstated.

What Zakharova didn't explain was why that would never happen. She didn't mention that the Russian reporter had been identified as a possible spy. She skipped over the FSB document that labelled me a security threat and made no mention of either my detention at the airport and near deportation, or the additional sanctions for 'anti-Russian activities'. A friend called from Moscow to tell me I was being discussed on the news. I suggested he switch off. But in the independent press, speculation about the unnamed Russian reporter grew.

Tweet by Ekho Moskvy radio journalist, 14 August 2021

The entire Foreign Ministry and Maria Zakharova are beating their chests in defence of a secret Russian journalist who has not been given a visa to England. Who is it? Why is he so valuable to the motherland? Why is Zakharova squealing about it? Why is his name unknown, and his feats so significant?

A response to that tweet revealed what many Russians must have assumed. 'This secret Russian journalist is called Stierlitz,' the user joked, referring to the fictional undercover Soviet agent often cited as Putin's inspiration for joining the KGB. All the spy talk was making me jumpy. I told myself that it was just words, that *security threat* was the only box the border guards could tick to bar me from Russia. A high-placed Russian contact assured us I'd be fine, 'unless she does something extraordinary'. After years reporting on arbitrary arrests and prosecutions, including a surge in spy trials, I was now waking in the night imagining all sorts of crazy scenarios. 'Another day feeling sick to the guts,' I wrote in my diary on 15 August. 'Happy Sunday.'

Some time before, when I was reporting in depth on Paul Whelan's arrest, I'd thought someone had broken into our Moscow flat. Whoever came in left a large unflushed deposit in each toilet, which was a well-known calling card of the FSB. Other people I knew, diplomats and those close to them, had experienced multiple forms of intimidation over the years, from pictures turned upside down on their walls to an FSB lapel badge left by the bed. In one case, a man's photo, taken on the metro without his knowledge, was posted on a gay pick-up site describing sexual acts he would supposedly like performed. The same person recounts coming home one evening to find the landing outside his door 'awash with blood, gallons of it'. Assuming it was from an animal, not a murder scene, he stepped over it to get into his flat and didn't bother calling the police. Another tactic was to approach foreigners' cleaners, beauticians or even doctors seeking highly personal and potentially compromising material. The only reassuring thing in any of this is that when agents made such an approach, not every Russian agreed to comply.

I had avoided worrying too much about our own apparent intruders by wondering instead whether those responsible came prepared for such missions with pre-filled bags. Perhaps they had to rely on good timing. I remembered how, at the 2014 Sochi Olympics, it was FSB agents who had to handle the frozen urine samples from Russian athletes. They'd pass them through a hole in a laboratory wall in the middle of the night to cover up a massive doping scheme. I assumed there must be a special 'dirty' unit in Russia's intelligence service, probably not a place any spook with aspirations would want to end up.

When I reported what had happened at our flat to my boss, the BBC security team gave me a mini speaker with a motion sensor that was supposed to trigger a camera if anyone came close. I could never make it work and by the time I was expelled my husband was using it to play his Cuban salsa.

Diary entry, 16 August 2021

Head into Tarusa. Chat to two girls in the coffee shop who fuss over Smudge. One learned English for ten years but is too shy to try it. They tell us there's a culture house in town where they do great poetry readings. Down the road there's a cat with a small fish in its mouth and another one sunbathing on the balcony of a pretty wooden house. Some old ladies are gossiping on a bench in flowery housecoats. A man passes and shouts, 'Hello girls!' and they all giggle.

Diary entry, 17 August 2021

Russian Imperial Ballet summer-school girls pass by in matching yellow T-shirts and blonde plaits. They get down to deep stretching as Smudge watches, chewing grass. I love Russia in summer. Deserted cities and hot dusty streets. They could have kicked me out in winter. It would have been much easier to be expelled at minus 20 on a dark, short and depressing day.

We took Smudge for long walks in the woods and the dog's playfulness was a distraction and comfort. But it was proving impossible to relax. I'd begun contacting removals companies and researching how to get a puppy and two adults out of Russia at short notice with Covid flight restrictions still in place. Now, on top of everything, a lawyer had advised that my 'national security' designation could be a problem. Formally speaking, he told me that by entering Russia after being informed that I'd been banned, I had committed a crime. 'This is of concern.' The punishment was a fine or up to four years in prison. 'For Sarah to be in the Russian Federation during this period of uncertainty is not advisable,' he wrote.

I hadn't slipped through any border fence or dodged any guards. I had a stamp in my passport. But it was impossible to banish the lawyer's words from my mind completely. 'Perhaps I am overstating the risk, but in my opinion, a negative development in this situation is highly likely,' he wrote. 'All the conditions are there for it.'

It was clear that pretending we were on holiday wasn't working. On day four we gave up and set off from Tarusa to begin wrapping up our Moscow lives.

PART VII

Diary entry, Kyiv, 1 May 2022

Someone is having loud sex in the hotel room above me. It must be journalists, there's no one else here these days. But she's so loud, maybe she's a prostitute. Either way, noisy sex should be banned in a war zone. When their bed bangs against the wall it's like a distant explosion. And she keeps screaming.

Diary entry, London, June 2022

100 days after the war began there's still an impressive number of Ukrainian flags on display in London. Some people even stitched them into their bunting for the Jubilee celebrations. But stories from Ukraine are beginning to slip down the news bulletins, pushed by domestic politics. At a party this weekend no one asked me a thing about the war: what it's like? What do people say? What might happen? All the talk over drinks was the usual middle-class British stuff: houses, food, prices. It felt like people didn't care as much as their blue-and-yellow flags and bunting suggest. I know not everyone wants to hear horror stories all the time. But it can be hard to accept that when you come home.

Ukraine's Missing Children

DINKLAGE, GERMANY, MAY 2023

Sasha Kraynyuk spoke quietly as he described the day when Russian soldiers took him from his school. For six weeks, his mother Tetyana had no word of him, no idea where he'd gone. Forced separation would be upsetting for any child, but for those like Sasha with special educational needs, it was particularly tough. The fifteen-year-old remembers the moment the soldiers came very clearly. 'They were in military uniform, with masks and guns. They put us on buses,' Sasha told me hesitantly, rubbing his hands back and forth on his thighs as he talked. We'd travelled to meet him in the small German town of Dinklage, where his family were now living as refugees. 'If I'm honest, it was scary. I didn't know where they would take us.' When I wondered about missing his mum, Sasha paused for a long time, then asked to change the topic. 'It's pretty difficult to think about that.'

The story of Kupyansk Special School is part of a growing body of evidence in the case against Vladimir Putin as a suspected war criminal. Just over a year after he ordered troops into Ukraine, the Russian president was indicted by the International Criminal Court (ICC). It did not base its case on allegations of torture by Russian soldiers or their targeting of civilians. Nor did it indict Russia's president for bombing vital infrastructure and plunging cities into freezing darkness mid-winter. Instead, Putin was accused of the unlawful deportation of children to the Russian Federation from occupied areas of Ukraine. 'There are reasonable grounds to believe that Mr Putin bears individual criminal responsibility,' read an ICC statement that announced the warrant for his arrest.

Moscow's reaction ran the usual gamut of scorn, denial and defiance, with senior officials threatening retaliatory arrests against ICC representatives. Russia insisted that its motives were purely humanitarian, that it was removing children from front-line areas for safety. But the criminal charge added to Putin's isolation, preventing him from travelling even to allied countries that are parties to the court. They would be obliged to turn him in.

Neither the details of the case nor the number of children involved are publicly known. But many of the stories our own team investigated in Ukraine involved vulnerable young people like Sasha, taken from schools for those with special educational needs or from care homes, and forcibly removed to Russian territory. In multiple cases we examined, there was minimal or no effort to locate relatives. Ukrainian children would be told there was nothing at home to return to. Many were subjected to a 'patriotic' Russian education. The pattern was clear: whenever Russia occupied an area of Ukraine, it immediately claimed everything there as its own, including the children.

When the Russians invaded their region of north-eastern Ukraine, Tetyana kept her son home at first for safety. As September approached, the occupying administration began insisting that all children should return to school for the new academic year, when they would begin to study using the Russian curriculum. The same was happening across all occupied areas. When Ukrainian teachers refused to collaborate, staff would be brought in from Russia to replace them.

Tetyana was reluctant to send Sasha back to school, but the teenager was bored stiff after months at home in their village with no internet and only Russian state channels on television. Tetyana had even begun to think the takeover might become permanent, that the Russians might stay. So in early September she took her son to Kupyansk and dropped him off at school. Days later, Ukrainian forces launched a surprise operation to retake the region. 'We heard the noise from miles away. The booms. Then the helicopters and the firing. It was a terrible din. Then I saw the tanks and the Ukrainian flag.' Unable to contact her son, Tetyana was frantic.

The fighting was so intense she couldn't reach the school for several days. By the time she made it, Sasha had gone. 'I cried every day, called the hotline and told them I'd lost my son and wrote to the police. We tried to find him through volunteers.' For a whole month, there was nothing, until a friend spotted a local TV report online, filmed soon after the children had disappeared. It announced that thirteen students from Kupyansk Special School 'who'd been left truly alone' had been moved further east for safety. They were now at a similar facility in Luhansk, an area under Russian control. The children's faces are blurred on the report, which shows a presenter asking about the fighting. When a girl starts to cry, the presenter thinks she's remembering the shelling. Then, one by one, the other children pipe up and say they just want to go home.

It would be another fortnight before Tetyana's phone beeped with news. Sasha had been moved again, to a school in Perevalsk, she read, and his mother could call the director's phone to talk to him. She rang the number immediately. 'Sasha was happy to hear me, of course. But he really cried. They had told him his home was destroyed and he'd been afraid we were gone too.' Communication with areas of heavy fighting is not easy, but the Kupyansk children had passed through three institutions in Russian-controlled territory before anyone had even tried to reach their relatives.

Investigating the cases of missing children, we did find some instances where Ukrainian parents chose to let them stay in Russian-held areas, at least for a while. They were usually families who lived close to the front line and were scared to bring the children back into danger. Occasionally the children themselves didn't want to return. Some were from troubled homes and preferred to stay with foster families and away from the air-raid sirens, even if that was in Russia. I met one teenage girl who'd travelled across half of Europe to collect her younger brother, only for it to take several days of persuasion to get him to go back to Ukraine with her.

There was never any question Tetyana would bring Sasha home. But the school director in Perevalsk informed her she'd have to travel there, into Russian-controlled territory, to get him. All the children had been taken without permission, but this director was demanding a whole pile of documents in order to send them home. Many families didn't have those papers to hand, let alone a passport to travel, and sorting anything out was extra-complicated in a war zone. They'd need around €1,000 to fund the long trip, and most of those caught up in all this were not well-off. One grandmother we spoke to had sold a cow to help pay for her journey. Later a Ukrainian charity would get involved and arrange transport and funding. But Tetyana couldn't wait. She had never even left her region before, but she now set off alone into enemy territory to rescue her son.

The direct route to Perevalsk was impossible because it would have crossed a front line. She was forced to loop the long way round, travelling west through Poland and the Baltics before crossing into Russia on foot. At the border there, the FSB Security Service went through Tetyana's phone and questioned her about Ukrainian troop movements, though she could tell them nothing. They then quizzed her on life under Russian control, asking which side had given the best aid parcels. Tetyana chose her words carefully. 'What could I say? I needed to get through.' Finally released, she travelled on by car, heading south through the country that had declared war on her own, until she crossed into the occupied eastern territories of Ukraine. 'It was pitch dark, there were checkpoints, men in balaclavas with guns. I was so scared I took pills to calm me. I was like a zombie.'

Tetyana had an extra reason to be frightened as she raced towards her son. 'I was afraid that if they moved Sasha into Russia, I'd never find him. I was afraid he'd be put in a foster family, just like that.' In late September 2022 Putin had announced the illegal annexation of four Ukrainian regions, including Luhansk, where Sasha had been taken. Before that, he'd also amended the law to make it easier for Ukrainian children to get Russian citizenship and be adopted. Now Russia was removing children from care homes in the annexed areas and placing them in new families.

The transfer was carried out in plain sight. Russia's children's ombudswoman, Maria Lvova-Belova, filled her Telegram channel with images of her escorting Ukrainian children across the border. There were multiple videos set to rousing tunes. Each new group was greeted by foster families with gifts and hugs. The message was clear: Russia was saving the children. But a scroll through Lvova-Belova's channel quickly revealed that this was no mercy mission. Both online and in public comments, the ombudswoman referred repeatedly to children in occupied regions of Ukraine as 'ours', meaning Russian. She even adopted a teenager from Mariupol herself, posting pictures of the boy with a new Russian passport. In March 2023 Lvova-Belova was indicted by the ICC as a war criminal, alongside Putin.

After five exhausting days on the road, and many stressful weeks apart, Tetyana was finally drawing close to her son in Perevalsk. She'd been delayed many hours by the Russian border guards, and the road through Luhansk was terrible, with no lights and lots of potholes. The school director was getting impatient. At one point she snapped that she was leaving for the weekend and Tetyana would have to wait until Monday to get her son back. Struggling on through the snow, she had to beg the director to stay. When Tetyana hugged her son to her tightly at last, Sasha didn't say a word. He was crying from happiness.

The family had been back together for several months by the time I went to see them in Germany in early May 2023. A tall, shy boy, Sasha smoothed his long fringe into place every few minutes like any self-conscious teenager. Tetyana fretted that he was still withdrawn and had developed grey hairs from the stress. Sasha told me he'd found rural Germany too quiet after Ukraine at first, unable to get used to life without bombing and shelling. But he was starting to settle.

Tetyana was still struggling. In their flat, over a pile of sprat sandwiches, she talked of her fears for her eldest son, who was still in Ukraine and could be called up to fight at any moment. She wanted nothing more than to go home to him and her husband, but Kupyansk was under heavy fire again. In late April 2023 Russian missiles had destroyed the local history museum there, killing two women. Before that, Sasha's old school was badly damaged when shells landed nearby. Since then the fighting had intensified.

The Ukrainian authorities were now investigating Sasha's abduction as a suspected war crime. Tetyana showed me photos they'd sent her from the school where Sasha ended up in the occupied east. In several of the pictures, the children were wearing Russian military uniforms. One image stood out in particular. In it, there was a boy with the Z-mark of Russia's war on his arm, coloured in the red, white and blue of the Russian flag. He'd been taken from Kupyansk at the same time as Sasha. His name was Artem and he was Ukrainian.

The photographs were from the Perevalsk school website, which is packed full of patriotic Russian content. One post I found described special classes about Crimea, which the school described as 'historic Russian land'. The pictures in military uniform had been taken in February 2023, on Russia's Defenders of the Fatherland Day. A year after Russia declared war on their country, Ukrainian children were in Russian-controlled territory being taught 'gratitude and respect' for the invaders.

Scrolling on, I came across a photograph of the school director, Tatyana Semyonova. A formidable-looking woman, her hair was a stripe of brown with a layer of bleached blonde on top, like a helmet. I called her using a Russian mobile so she'd think I was local and might pick up. It worked. The director told me she had no problem with dressing Ukrainian children in the uniform of an invading army. 'So what? What can I do?' She certainly wasn't worried that the 'Z' symbolised a war against their own country. 'What kind of a question is that? No one is forcing them.' When I tried to ask more, the line cut out.

That day in Dinklage, I wondered what Sasha's mother made of the international arrest warrant issued for Russia's president. She replied without hesitating. 'Not only Putin, but all his main people, all the commanders, should be on trial for what they did to the children. What right did they have? How were we supposed to get them back? They just didn't care.'

The Undesirable Activist

ROSTOV-ON-DON, JANUARY–FEBRUARY 2019

Shortly after Anastasia Shevchenko was arrested as 'undesirable', her daughter fell seriously ill with bronchitis. Alina was seventeen and severely physically and mentally disabled. She lived in a specialist care home, but Anastasia visited several times a month and was always on hand whenever her daughter got sick. In hospital, Alina needed round-the-clock attention and specially prepared food, and the nurses were too stretched to cope with that. In January 2019 the teenager badly needed her mother. But when Anastasia asked a judge for permission to break her house arrest and travel to hospital, he refused.

The following day the opposition activist was questioned for hours by investigators. Anastasia had been charged under a law that banned dozens of groups with links abroad as 'undesirable organisations'. It was only when the interrogation was finally over that she was told her daughter had been rushed to intensive care. Alina's heart had stopped. The doctors had managed to revive her, but she was on a ventilator and desperately sick.

It was hours more before Anastasia was cleared to travel, rushing to her daughter's side through a blizzard and over black ice. By the time she reached the hospital it was late and the doctors wouldn't allow her into the intensive-care unit. The next morning, when she finally took Alina's hand, it already felt cold. Anastasia was allowed to sit and hold her daughter for just a few minutes before the doctors ushered her out. Alina died later that same day, among strangers.

It was a few days later that we travelled south to Rostov-on-Don for the next hearing in Anastasia's case. The activist arrived in a lilac puffer coat with an electronic tag strapped around her ankle. She wore a skirt on purpose that day, not to hide the monitor.

After the confines of her 45 m² flat, the short walk from the prison officer's car to the courthouse was a chance to stretch her legs and breathe in the outdoor air. At future hearings, as the officer got to know Anastasia better, he would park his car further away to extend the walk. Sometimes he'd allow her to wait in the fresh air a little longer than strictly necessary. But in early February it was snowy and cold and the pair headed straight into court.

The hearing was an appeal against the strict house arrest that had kept Anastasia from her dying daughter. She'd already handed in her passport and all her bank cards, so there was no way she could escape. In any case, the single mum was scared of giving the authorities any excuse to lock her up again and take her away from her remaining two children. After her arrest she'd spent two nights in a prison cell where the lights were always on, the toilet was a hole in the ground and cockroaches scuttled around the sink. The walls were covered in scrawled messages, mostly left by young prisoners on drugs charges. The activist was fed through a hole in the door 'like some kind of dog' and strip-searched by police, who made her spread her buttocks for a check.

Anastasia's story elicited a lot of sympathy. A few days after her daughter's death, several hundred women marched through the deep-frozen centre of Moscow. Many had pinned black love hearts to their chests and carried stuffed toys in memory of Alina. They called it the March of Mothers' Fury. I wondered whether the women were nervous about chanting 'Freedom to Anastasia Shevchenko' as they were followed through the streets by police. One told me the case proved you could now be arrested in Russia for nothing at all. 'We can't stay scared forever. We have to stop this. This system feeds on our fear.' Others I approached that day were still too nervous to speak on camera.

Russia had dozens of political prisoners by 2019, far too many to tell all their stories or attend all their trials. But for me, Anastasia always stood out. It was partly the personal tragedy she suffered while under arrest. But she was also the first person ever prosecuted under a law introduced in the wake of the Maidan revolution in Ukraine, as Putin grew paranoid about similar stirrings at home. He was convinced the protests in Kyiv had been engineered by the West to oust its then pro-Moscow president. In Russia, groups with foreign funding suddenly became objects of increased suspicion, viewed as subversive.

Once an organisation was added to the 'undesirable' list, deemed a threat to Russia's 'constitutional order', anyone linked to it or taking part in any of its activities could face prosecution. That might mean as little as reposting an article or tweeting about the banned group. The offender would usually be fined for the first and second administrative offences, but investigators could then open a criminal case with the threat of a significant prison sentence. In 2021 the law was tightened even further so you only needed to offend once to trigger a full criminal investigation. Anastasia's own first fine was for a debate with a local member of the ruling United Russia party. The second was for attending a political seminar.

The terms of her house arrest meant I couldn't speak to Anastasia about any of this directly at first. So, ahead of the court hearing, I met her mother, Tamara, instead in a café near their flat. Anastasia's son, Misha, came along to the interview: seven years old, and with his mother's tight blonde curls. He'd had trouble sleeping ever since police had raided their flat and spent five hours searching every corner. They'd even gone through the children's schoolbooks, tipping them on the floor and stepping all over them.

When Anastasia began to run into trouble, Tamara had asked her daughter to give up her activism for the sake of the children. Anastasia promised to be careful, but felt strongly that she needed to be able to look those children in the eye without shame when they asked in the future what she'd done in the face of so many arrests and persecution. 'She was too active,' Tamara told me, glumly. 'It seems she said too much.'

The evidence that police removed from their home amounted to a T-shirt with the slogan 'Fed up!', referring to Putin, some car stickers and a ballpoint pen marked 'Open Russia'. The group had been founded in the UK by Mikhail Khodorkovsky, the ex-oligarch, and banned in Russia in 2017. Now in exile, Khodorkovsky believed the only things 'undesirable' to the Kremlin were a free, flourishing Russia and losing power. He had vowed to go on helping anyone brave enough to keep pushing for those goals.

The night the police took their mother away, Anastasia's children sobbed themselves to sleep. Tamara herself still seemed stunned, especially by the idea her daughter was a security threat. 'In what way? By going to a demonstration? Holding a seminar?' Anastasia had been involved with all sorts of local-level activism before Open Russia, from complaining about potholes to pushing for repairs at local hospitals. She was once detained for placing 'Stop Putin!' stickers around town and she'd recently been taking parcels to the growing list of political detainees in Rostov. Anastasia's ex-husband was in the military and at some point he was told to get her to stop, but it was futile. In 2016 Anastasia founded the Rostov branch of Open Russia and soon made it the most active group in the country. 'I felt happy and useful,' she'd tell me later. 'We could have done so much good if they hadn't started the repressions.'

The following day in court I heard Anastasia speak for herself for the first time, appealing for release from house arrest as she awaited trial. She spoke quietly and simply about her daughter, Alina, and her own pain. First, she addressed the judge on his podium beneath the two-headed eagle that symbolised Russia. 'I know this hearing is hopeless, but I don't know how many more victims you need before you understand that you are taking the wrong path, the wrong decisions.' Anastasia then turned to the burly prosecutor opposite. 'I would ask you not to display pointless cruelty to my family. You deprived me of the chance of hugging my daughter. If I'd gone to hospital a day earlier, I could have done that.'

The court adjourned. When the judge swished back into the small wood-panelled room, he ordered Anastasia's strict house arrest left unchanged. The activist's supporters were still shouting

'Shame!' and 'Monsters!' from their benches as he swished back out again.

ROSTOV-ON-DON, DECEMBER 2019

While her mother was under house arrest, fifteen-year-old Vlada was often responsible for taking Misha to school, striding ahead as her little brother dragged his heels along the still-dark, frosty streets of Rostov. Every now and then she would pause to let him catch up, then pull his woolly hat down more firmly over his curls, chastising him for being slow.

Vlada had been forced to grow up fast. She was grieving for her big sister Alina, worrying about her mother, and chaperoning her brother, all on top of her school studies. She was also doing the shopping and walking the dog. There was no hint of the resentment you might expect from a teenager torn from her friends, and from fun. Vlada was proud of her mother and the two had grown close.

One afternoon, I met the children from school and we took Misha on his scooter to the park. Vlada was missing shopping with her mum, who shared her love of a bold fashion statement. The teenager had one startling green contact lens and one blue and liked to wear chunky trainers, even in the snow. Her coat had a giant hood trimmed with pale pink fake fur that sat on top of thick dyed-ginger curls. She made me laugh, talking about house arrest, when she explained how her mother treated a trip to court or to the investigators like a day out. It was a chance to choose an outfit and apply some make-up, Vlada told me. To dress up, after weeks stuck inside in a tracksuit.

At McDonald's she took a selfie with her brother and posted it to her Facebook blog. *Just taking my brother out for a walk. Nothing new.* She added her hashtag *#chroniclesofahousearrest.* Vlada used the platform to keep people informed of her mother's arrest, as Anastasia was banned from using the internet. She and her mother would joke that the teenager was her avatar. Vlada had been attending other activists' trials, like Anastasia used to, and in June 2019 she took her first trip abroad to accept a prize for her mum. The Boris Nemtsov Foundation in Germany was honouring Anastasia's courage in defending democratic values. In 2022 the prize would go to Volodymyr Zelensky.

Vlada is tough, but so was what she was going through. 'You see your mum being led in handcuffs to some court cage to be called a British agent and a "threat to the constitutional order". My mum wanted to tell people the truth: that it was time to change our leaders, that things aren't going well. So they arrested her. They're afraid.' At that point, Misha piped up to tell me that the two days when his mother was in custody had 'dragged on like a whole century'. Reunited, the children liked to bring Anastasia fragments of the outside world she was missing under house arrest. One night they told me they went out specially to take photos of a bright moon. 'She looked at it for a really long time.'

Vlada was spending so much time discussing court hearings, case files and investigations with her mother, she'd begun to feel a bit lost with her own age group. She struggled to relate to the teenage things that worried her friends, when what worried Vlada was that Anastasia would be found guilty and locked up. I asked whether she was ready for that. She was not.

She'd recently been invited to the Sakharov Centre in Moscow to address an event on political prisoners, in place of her mother. With her red curls and emerald-green dress, she stood out sharply from the mainly grey-haired audience of long-time opposition supporters and intellectuals. As they gathered, I recalled an evening there a couple of years earlier when we'd filmed people writing letters to political prisoners. Volunteers would select names at random from a long list and write to make sure their correspondents didn't feel forgotten. Even then, the number behind bars was growing.

Waiting for her turn to speak, Vlada paced the centre's exhibition on Soviet political repression, tapping at her phone. I wondered whether she'd heard of Andrei Sakharov, the Soviet dissident whose work is honoured and continued by the centre. She wasn't exactly sure what he did. The crowd was growing and so were Vlada's nerves. 'I wrote a speech, but it was too sad, so Mum and I added some jokes. I'm not sure they'll get them,'

Vlada worried. Then she was up: '*Privet!* My name is Vlada, my mum is Anastasia Shevchenko, and she's been under house arrest for nine months.'

Vlada told the audience her mother felt lucky: not to be arrested, but with all the support. The criminal charge labelled her an 'enemy of the state', but her door had not been daubed with graffiti and there'd been no abuse on her rare appearances in the streets. Instead, friends and supporters had been taking the children to the cinema or the swimming pool. They brought food and gifts, as Anastasia couldn't work and they had no income. On Anastasia's birthday, barred from entering her house, they'd strung a celebration banner outside.

'So many good people are being arrested that Mum jokes there'll soon be a pretty good community in Russian prisons. At least she'll have people to talk to,' Vlada quipped, and by now even the sleepy old men were sitting up and listening. She spoke slightly hesitantly, but from the heart, and pledged that her own generation wouldn't tolerate such treatment. 'I'm just fifteen. I want a normal childhood. I don't want all this, like some kind of Greta Thunberg. But this regime gives me no choice.'

The investigators had allowed Anastasia a phone for her daughter's trip, and as soon as Vlada got off stage, she called home with an update. 'It was a bit shaky. But the jokes went down okay.' I wondered whether she wished her mum had never got involved in politics and spared them all this. I wasn't surprised by her reply: 'I always thought my mum did everything right, and I still do. Things are bad. But she's not guilty of anything.'

As she got ready to leave, Vlada learned that there was a crew outside from NTV. Its staff were regularly deployed to harass opposition figures and then produce scandalous films about Russia's 'enemies' and 'friends of the junta'. It was a dramatic slide for a channel that once produced hard-hitting reports on the horrors of the first Chechen war. Even in Putin's Russia, I worked alongside an NTV team to get into Afghanistan through a Russian military base right after 9/11. We then travelled together on horseback to desert front lines as the Northern Alliance took on the Taliban. But the NTV of those years was long gone. Through the Sakharov Centre window, I counted seven people hovering near the door and Vlada was nervous about stepping out. But even NTV hadn't yet stooped so low as to target teenagers: the man they were waiting to ambush was the activist who had invited her to speak, Vladimir Kara-Murza.

'Few things still shock about political repression in Putin's Russia, but this case is one of them,' Kara-Murza told me, as he collected his coat. 'It's a purely political crime. In other words, it's not a crime at all.' He argued that Anastasia's only offence was to belong to an organisation that the government didn't like. 'It's important not to speak about political prisoners as statistics. They're real people with real lives which are being ruined arbitrarily by the repression of this government.'

A friend then pulled his car up close to the Sakharov Centre entrance and Kara-Murza headed out, past the television cameras. 'I'll try not to swear!' he shouted a laughing promise over his shoulder towards his lawyer and Vlada was able to slip out unnoticed in his wake.

ROSTOV-ON-DON, FEBRUARY 2020

It was the touch of the wind on her face that Anastasia missed most under house arrest. That and the smells, colours and crowds on the streets. After thirteen months of confinement, in February 2020 a judge suddenly permitted the activist a short daily walk. Anastasia was also freed to speak to everyone apart from witnesses in her case, so I joined her as she headed to collect Misha from school through the melting remains of a heavy snowfall.

Anastasia's very limited new freedoms still banned her from entering the school yard, so we waited outside by a *babushka* in a headscarf who was smashing the pavement ice with an axe. Misha soon came flying through the gate for a bear hug, a daily joy that Anastasia had dreamed of for over a year. Despite his chattiness as we walked home, with Bailey the terrier puppy splashing through the slush puddles, Misha had taken Anastasia's initial arrest particularly hard. He'd seen a psychologist for several months, even after she was released, because he would wake up screaming for his mum.

Anastasia had always known that opposition activity was risky, but the criminal charge had still come as a shock. 'It's a nightmare, but if you are a political activist in Russia today you have to be prepared, somehow, for prison.' In the run-up to her arrest she had often suspected that police were following her. She would see figures lurking in the shadows, then dismiss that as crazy. 'I thought I couldn't be important enough.' When she saw the notes and photographs in her case files, she discovered that she'd been under surveillance for months. The shadowy figures had even followed her on a date with a Dutch man she met on Tinder. 'I just can't understand when I suddenly became dangerous. There's absolutely no basis for that.' She found the idea of her undermining the constitutional order particularly ridiculous at the very moment that Putin was rewriting Russia's basic law purely to extend his stay in power. She was under no illusions about her case: 'They're showing others: if you're active, you'll end up suffering like her.'

Pushed to remember when her activism had begun, she thought it was probably in 2014 with the Ukraine war. 'I didn't think I was doing politics, really. I just thought if something was happening, I could go to a protest or a picket. It's in my character. I can't be silent. Even now, when I see something on the news I think I should go and demonstrate.' She paused then, and smiled. 'My investigators will see this [interview] and say it's a good job they arrested me!'

Apart from her daily walk, Anastasia couldn't stray more than five metres from the base unit for her electronic tag or the alarm would go off, bringing an inspector round to check up on her. She'd begun carrying the whole contraption with her around the house, even to the loo. She'd also concluded that the plastic bracelets were designed for men. It took her fifteen minutes to get her tights on, through the device, and the tag was so ugly that her children had customised the last one with stickers.

Anastasia tried to distract herself during the long hours at home by reading three books a day, cultivating vegetables on the window ledge and learning to moonwalk like Michael Jackson. Anything to suppress the wave of depression that would rise periodically. 'There are days when I just don't want to do anything. But I know my mum and the children are watching, and if I start to fall apart then that's it.'

For a long time, her investigators were the only people she could speak to outside her family and, over time, they'd become chattier, curious to hear about her trips abroad. They even worried that their role in her prosecution could get them barred from travelling themselves. Sergei, the young prison official with smiling eyes who walked her to court and to interrogations, let her watch Russia competing in the biathlon on his phone. Anastasia was genuinely saddened when he died of Covid before her trial.

But her case files contained one more disturbing discovery. For six months, she realised, her investigators had been spying on the family through a camera installed in the air-conditioning unit above Anastasia's bed. The video footage, which runs for many hours, showed Anastasia in her bra and the children partially dressed. There were screen shots in the files and detailed transcripts of the family's conversations. Anastasia called the intrusion perverse. Vlada was mortified. No evidence of subterfuge was ever captured, or produced in court, but the family were struggling to feel unwatched.

On a wall in Anastasia's living room there was a small, framed photograph of her as a smiling first-time mother, holding her baby. On a shelf just below was the white urn that held Alina's ashes. A little icon was propped against it. Anastasia took the urn down and cradled it, talking a little about the day when a doctor had told her and her then-husband that their daughter had brain damage. It was caused by the meningoencephalitis she'd caught as a newborn. The doctor strongly advised the couple to abandon the little girl and gave them an hour to decide while he went for lunch. Anastasia looked after Alina for as long as she could manage but when her daughter was five she needed medicines her mother could not get, and constant professional attention. Anastasia was persuaded to place her in care. The family would visit with homemade borscht, specially pureed, and sit chatting, holding the child's hand.

'I'll never forgive that judge that Alina died alone. I just wanted to be by her side,' Anastasia told me. She desperately wanted to scatter her daughter's ashes at sea to make up for a short life spent in closed rooms. 'I want to set her free, but that's impossible under house arrest.'

'What do you see as the main problem facing Russian society? The fact that most people think it will never happen to them.'

Anna Politkovskaya, questionnaire for the 'Territory of Glasnost' project

The Summer of Protest

MOSCOW, SUMMER 2019

In the summer of 2019, Moscow exploded in protests that now look like a last burst of freedom. They were sparked by an election that normally passes barely noticed. Opposition forces including Alexei Navalny's team had tried to field candidates for the Moscow city parliament, but election officials declared large numbers of their support signatures invalid. When the key figures were blocked from taking part, crowds began taking to the streets in protest.

On 27 July they refused to disperse. Article 31 of the constitution is clear: Russian citizens have the right 'to gather peacefully, without weapons, and to hold meetings, rallies, demonstrations, marches and pickets'. Those were the words a teenager called Olga Misik read out to riot police, sitting cross-legged before them. She also read the relevant articles about free elections and free speech. That day, more than a thousand protesters were arrested as the security forces moved in, batons raised, and dragged and shoved people into police vans. Olga Misik was detained later, on her way to the metro.

Images of protesters being battered went viral. Women's faces covered in blood, and young students kicked and beaten. The Moscow mayor claimed that the crowd had gone on the attack, 'compelling' officers to use 'perfectly appropriate' force. But the police violence, captured on mobile phones, propelled even more Muscovites onto the streets. Many I met there had never demonstrated before in their lives.

The rallies came during a dip in Putin's famously sky-high approval rating, with the economy under pressure from falling oil prices and Western sanctions. The patriotic boom times that followed 2014 had passed. Opposition figures were claiming that what they called the 'social contract' had been broken. They meant the idea that Russians had accepted a loss of basic rights and freedoms – free press, free speech, free elections – in return for a comfortable standard of living. It wasn't a conscious choice, more a gradual acquiescence. But that summer even the communists were protesting, calling for honest elections. Putin's own party, United Russia, had become so unpopular that it was fielding candidates for the Moscow election as if they were independents. Putin was not on the ropes, far from it, but his system did seem to be malfunctioning.

The president studiously ignored the tensions, riding around Crimea with his nationalist biker friends. In Moscow, officials then did what they know best, and tightened the screws. The Investigative Committee defined the protests as a riot, opened a criminal case and began to bring charges with hefty prison sentences attached.

It became known as the Moscow Case, and a student blogger named Egor Zhukov was one of the first to be charged. The 21-year-old shared a prison cell with armed robbers for a month while investigators scoured security footage for evidence of their claim that he had corralled the protest crowd. Finding nothing, they turned to old posts on Zhukov's YouTube channel, in which the young libertarian had called Putin a tyrant. For phrases like 'fight the system hard' and 'do all you are capable of', he was charged with calls to extremism and placed on a register alongside members of ISIS.

The prosecutions gave the protesters new cause and fresh momentum. The following weekend, tens of thousands stood in the pouring rain and chanted for political prisoners to be freed. *Otpuskai!* Let them go! Some brought cardboard cut-outs of the detainees. There was music on stage and famous rappers and actors in the crowd. As a rare exception, the protest had been authorised, perhaps in the hope that it would be small and the excitement would fizzle out.

For many I met in those weeks, mostly young, that summer of 2019 was a political awakening. They were the Putin generation, Russians who'd known almost no one else as president. Now, students were crushing into court to support their friends, their dyed hair and tattoos a sharp contrast to the prosecutors' stilettos and the protective vests of the bailiffs. One group set up a bot, an automated online consultant, to help other students learn their rights and locate lawyers if they were arrested. They were also crowdfunding to help pay protesters' fines and prepare parcels for prison. A student, held for eight days, appealed to the bot for John Locke's *Two Treatises of Government* to be sent to his detention centre. 'Kind people, respond if you have this book!'

When Egor Zhukov was finally brought to court, via video link at first, the blogger showed no sign of being cowed. 'I don't know whether I'll be free. But Russia definitely will be,' he declared, and dozens of students squashed into the corridors outside began sharing his speech on social media. A science undergraduate with bright-red headphones looped around his neck decided it wasn't all bad to be in prison. He pointed me to the surge in subscribers to Zhukov's blog. 'So many new people want to know you!' A politics student, Mstislav, said seeing friends livestreaming their arrest from the back of police vans was his 'new normal'. Another student thought his generation had more to fight for than older Russians. 'We will live in this country not for twenty years, but for one hundred. And we want to live that hundred years in a good country.'

In early September 2019 several of the Moscow Case prisoners were released, a move almost unheard of in Russia. They included a tall and quietly spoken student called Daniil Konon, who had been a volunteer for one of the opposition election candidates. He signed up to help out of curiosity, but when his man was blocked from the race, Daniil joined the protests, confronted for the first time with Russia's political reality. He told me the investigators had initially threatened him with a fifteen-year sentence. It seems the pressure of the streets had actually secured his freedom. 'I was scared,' Daniil admitted later, in a park near his home. 'Before, I looked at all that talk about political oppression like, it probably exists, but I don't see it,' and he held up his fingers in front of his eyes to illustrate. 'Now I see they can falsify whatever they want and just put people in prison.' The days of keeping the blinkers on and heads down were over.

As that summer turned towards autumn, the protests petered out. Navalny's team shifted its attention to the elections that had sparked it all, calling on people to cast a 'smart' vote. His team identified candidates with the best chance of defeating Putin's party. Other opposition figures argued for a total boycott of a sham election. At the end of September there was a large rally calling for the remaining Moscow Case prisoners to be freed, but October followed with a fresh wave of detentions.

When Putin finally commented on the summer protests, he suggested that young Russians would do better channelling their energy into improving the birth rate. But the summer of 2019 had touched people beyond the usual circles, and memories of the brutal crackdown, and the sense of injustice, would linger. When neighbouring Belarus erupted in giant protests the following year after a rigged presidential election, the authorities in Russia were on their guard.

Diary entry, Moscow, 28 September 2020

My visa expires on Wednesday and the Foreign Ministry is playing mind games, holding out to the last possible moment. If they don't give us the paperwork today or tomorrow morning at the latest, we're screwed. My rational mind tells me they're just trying to make us sweat, which I won't do. I love reporting on Russia, because it's a story that really matters. I guess it boils down to whether they want to spark a scandal with the UK, albeit a mini one. My guess at the moment is probably not. But you never quite know.

Blame the Russian Federation for my Death

NIZHNY NOVGOROD, OCTOBER 2020

On the day Irina Slavina decided to kill herself, she baked an apple charlotte for her mother's seventieth birthday. At 13:34 she was at the bank when her husband called for a quick chat. She then bought two bottles of kerosene and dropped in to the coffee shop where her daughter worked. She gave her a bank card, some money and a hug, and told her that she loved her. At 15:20, outside the Interior Ministry in Nizhny Novgorod, Irina Slavina poured fuel on her left arm and set herself on fire.

There is a video taken from a CCTV camera and it is terrible. It clearly shows Irina on a bench among three bronze figures that form a monument to Russian police through the ages. Almost immediately, flames appear on Irina's arm and rush up her sleeve. A passer-by darts towards her but she pushes the man away several times. He rips off his jacket and tries bravely to beat down the flames but the fire is already too intense. The man steps back, pacing helplessly, and Irina tumbles to the floor. In the coffee shop where Irina hugged her daughter, Margarita sees her mother's last post on Facebook. She had published it moments before lighting the match. It reads: 'I ask you to blame the Russian Federation for my death.'

***

When Irina died, there was an initial flurry of shocked reporting on social media and in the independent Russian press. But as it faded, I was left thinking about the horrific act I'd seen and the woman at the centre of it. Irina was my age, give or take a few months, and a journalist. Much of the commentary I'd read in Moscow had hinted at depression or despair, but that interpretation felt too easy. Irina hadn't hung herself or taken pills. Setting herself alight was a public act with a political message. She had chosen her spot deliberately, at the gates of the Interior Ministry. It emerged that she'd openly debated with herself whether or not to do it a year earlier, on Facebook.

Facebook post, 20 June 2019

> I wonder, if I carry out an act of self-immolation outside the entrance to the FSB (or the city prosecutor, I don't know yet), will that bring our country even a little bit more quickly to a bright future? Or will my sacrifice be pointless. I think it's better to die that way than like my grandmother did at fifty-two, from cancer.

Friends posted beneath. *Don't even try it, it won't work*. Irina wondered why not, when all it needed was *a bottle of petrol and some matches*. Alexander replied that it wouldn't bring the 'bright future' she wanted any closer. Others chastised her. *You have a mother, husband, kids, a dog! They love you. No regime is worth their tears*. Irina reasoned with them that such an act would be for the children. Her tone was earnest and her words disturbing. *I am not thinking about death, so much as whether my death could be useful*. Someone called Stas told her bluntly it would not. *There's no point hanging yourself in a deathcamp. The executioners will only thank you.*

At some point, Facebook itself intervened with an automated message: *Click here for information on what to do if you are thinking of harming yourself*. Then life moved on for everyone. Except Irina.

Irina and Alexei met in 1989 when they were walking their dogs. Alexei had spent half his life at sea in the navy and Irina was a

Russian teacher, until she felt stifled in that role and decided to become a journalist. The Nizhny region had blazed a reformist trail under the governorship of Boris Nemtsov in the 1990s. 'It was the dawn of liberalism, of freedom and democracy. We had strong, independent journalism then,' Irina's friend Mikhail Iosilevich recalled. But by the time she began reporting, things had changed. Irina worked initially at a local paper, *Nizhegorodskaya Pravda*, as part of the pool of reporters following the regional governor. But she soon tired of being told how to spin things. If bus fares went up, the pool had to report on the good news for bus drivers who could finally get a better wage. One day, in exasperation, she published the instructions she'd been sent for the upcoming elections. Reporters had been told to portray Alexei Navalny as an American project and a 'Lilliput' compared to the 'Gulliver', Vladimir Putin. Once Irina exposed that, her career in government-controlled media was over.

In 2015 she decided to create *Koza.Press*, or Goat Media, and began building a reputation as the only independent journalist in town. She was a woman with good contacts and a knack for asking awkward questions of those in positions of power. After starting on Facebook, she set up a website with help from her businessman friend, Iosilevich. He was known locally as the Flying Spaghetti Monster, the leader of a spoof religion who hosted weekly gatherings for activists at his 'church' to encourage debate and free thinking. For a long time, the police left him and his friends alone as oddballs.

For Irina, *Koza* became a passion but also a source of stress. She did almost all of the work herself, writing late into the night and at weekends because she couldn't afford to pay for help. As an old friend put it, Irina wasn't into rewriting press releases or publishing stories 'to order' or for cash, which was common practice. For her, journalism was supposed to change the world for the better. Everyone I met in Nizhny described Irina as a woman with both a passion for the truth and a powerful sense of justice.

At the Committee Against Torture, an independent group which was also based locally, staff told me she would bring them stories of human-rights violations to investigate and people to help, but was never so protective of herself. 'It didn't matter how powerful a person involved was, or how aggressive – if Irina thought something was important, she would write about it,' Olga, one of the group's activists, told me. She reminded me that Irina had been taking a real risk. 'In Moscow, there are a number of journalists writing about serious things, but Nizhny is small. There was just one. Irina attracted all the attention.' That's not entirely accurate: Olga also got her car tyres slashed regularly for her work exposing torture and abuse. Shortly after she gave birth, someone daubed graffiti on her fence damning her as an 'enemy of the people'.

The pressure on Irina had been growing over the year and a half or so before her death. 'Her writing was direct and honest. She wrote about excesses by the security forces and the authorities. Of course, some people didn't like that,' the journalist's lawyer, Evgeny Gubin, explained. We were speaking in his cluttered office in Nizhny, the desk strewn with copies of all the many cases in which he'd represented Irina. I spotted a little rubber duck on his filing cabinet, the symbol of opposition protests a couple of years earlier led by Navalny. Evgeny told me cases were constantly being brought against Irina that he never stood a chance of winning in court, even when there was no evidence against her. 'In political cases, it's impossible to win here.'

The most recent fine Irina had faced was for an article about the coronavirus pandemic. Investigators claimed she spread 'fake news' by reporting on an outbreak, even though it was later confirmed officially. Another charge was for an 'unauthorised protest' after she walked down the street with a portrait of Nemtsov on the anniversary of his murder. There was also a fine for insulting local communists by objecting, in colourful language, to a plan to commemorate Stalin with a plaque. Irina's daughter Margarita told me her mother was strong, 'like silicon', but she had felt her growing weary from the fight.

In public, Irina remained defiant. 'The police clearly have nothing more important to do than to read my posts on Facebook. I'm happy they're my regulars,' she wrote online. But the fines were high and *Koza.Press* made no money, as few companies wanted to advertise with her. She had to crowdfund to pay the penalties and it was getting harder to ask for help. Irina's husband would later describe the pressure on her as 'crushing'.

Things came to a head at 06:00 on 1 October 2020 when the doorbell rang. Outside were twelve people, including investigators and armed police. A policewoman stood over Irina as she got dressed, then the journalist and her husband were shut in a room with no phones so they couldn't call their lawyer. The police began searching for proof of links to the banned Open Russia pro-democracy group. They eventually left after four hours, taking the family's laptops and hard drives and even Irina's notepads from press conferences covered in doodles. She was told that she'd been designated a witness in a criminal case against her friend and financial backer Mikhail Iosilevich, who was accused of cooperating with Open Russia. Irina wasn't accused of anything herself, but the long search was intimidating and intrusive. She also knew that more often than not official witnesses end up as suspects.

On Facebook, and in messages, Irina reassured friends that she was fine. That evening, the last before her death, she wrote several news stories for *Koza.Press*, including a short account of the criminal investigation she was now caught up in. 'Politically motivated prosecution of businessman begins in Nizhny Novgorod.' The article described the case against Iosilevich, then mentioned the search of Irina's own flat and the homes of five others. They included the local Navalny co-ordinator, who told me later that the search squad had tried to break down his front door, then barged in in body armour and balaclavas. They'd turned the entire flat upside down 'like bandits'.

On 1 October at 23:29, Irina posted her last news story on *Koza.Press*, a piece about the poor-quality renovation of a city square. The next day, fully sober and without any medication, the journalist, wife and mother-of-two headed for the pavement outside the Interior Ministry and set herself alight.

I spoke to Irina's husband a few days later as he was heading out of town to 'get away from things'. He agreed to chat for a few minutes by phone. Alexei had known nothing about Irina's terrible plan and was clearly shattered by it, but he wanted me to know that his wife was not depressed. 'That's a long-term thing, it doesn't appear in a flash,' he said, and he'd seen no sign of such illness.

Alexei described Irina as energetic and active but revealed that she'd been extremely angry about the police search of their home. He called the experience 'another slap in the face by our country'. He could not explain what his wife had done. 'It was her decision, she did it and now we're left to accept that and try to protect our memories of her ... so that her death is not in vain; so that there are some changes in political life here.' I asked what changes he meant. 'You know what is happening in our country. What else can I say?'

When Irina discussed self-immolation on Facebook, long before she went through with it, she had wondered publicly whether it would make a difference. After her death, her friends tried to believe it would, 'Otherwise it was completely useless and that's so horrible I can't even think it,' as Olga put it at the Committee Against Torture. Evgeny, Irina's lawyer, was certain the suicide was an act of protest, not one of despair. 'She wanted to draw attention to the lawlessness of the security forces. It didn't mean they had broken her, it was her protest. That's how I understand it.'

Some time later, in Lithuania, I saw a display of posters outside the former KGB building in Vilnius in memory of Romas Kalanta, a young man who had doused himself in fuel and set himself on fire in 1972. Like the message Irina had left, his death note read: 'Blame only the regime for my death.' Kalanta's suicide brought thousands onto the streets in anti-Soviet protests and he became a hero of Lithuania's movement for independence. Reading Kalanta's last words, my mind rushed back to Irina and I wondered whether she had hoped for a similar impact.

But there were no mass protests when Irina died, just a carpet of flowers at the spot. Someone placed her photograph among them, long blonde hair flowing, hugging her dog. Handwritten signs made promises. *Ira! We won't forgive them!* and *Free*

Speech = Irina Slavina. When the shrine first appeared, city cleaners would sweep it away each morning, but each time people came back with replacements.

When I'd finished writing my story on Irina's death, I sent it to my editor in London with a morose note. *I fear I may not have done this justice.* At that moment, back in Moscow from Nizhny, I was struck more than ever by the huge gap between the price some were paying for standing up to the system and their chances of actually changing anything. Irina's act was so extreme, her sacrifice total, and I struggled with the idea that it would pass barely noticed. There would be no uprising against tyranny. Most people would see Irina as a disturbed soul, if they heard of her at all.

Email to editor, 11 October 2020

Irina's story has been bothering me. Everyone in opposition there has been harassed, persecuted. So she was not only objecting to what they did to her, specifically, but to the system that does that to people. What's so shit about it is that it will change nothing. 'Spaghetti Man' [Mikhail Iosilevich] was only accused of his 'crime' when Irina died. The investigator could have dropped the case. But instead, a week after her death, he pressed formal charges against Mikhail. That's what she changed by dying. Nothing.

Irina's daughter tried to continue *Koza.Press* with a family friend, but it was never the same. The promises made by fellow journalists to write for free and keep Irina's cause alive came to nothing and on 2 February 2021 the site published its final report. It was one sentence: an announcement that the Investigative Committee had refused to open a criminal case on Irina's suicide.

The official resolution posted by *Koza* stressed that the journalist had been placed under no undue pressure by the police search of her flat and was not 'incited' to commit suicide. Rather, it suggested she had a personality disorder that made her battle with the 'current political authorities' an obsession. After what the committee called a 'full, posthumous psychological-psychiatric analysis', it stated that Irina's 'demonstrative' death was entirely in character and cast her as an ideological warrior, driven by hatred and vengeance. It concluded that local law-enforcement agencies were not responsible.

The day after Irina died, her twenty-year-old daughter, Margarita, stood in the centre of Nizhny with a rebuke. Her poster read: 'While my mother was burning alive, you were silent.' It was a cry for Irina's awful act to jolt a city and its people out of apathy. But two years later Margarita had to take to the streets again. This time, her sign read: 'My mother would have said, *Putin, go to hell with your war*! But Putin had already killed her.'

For that silent protest, on the spot where her mother took her life, Margarita was charged with discrediting the armed forces and fined. She told me that was nothing compared to the horrors faced by her friends inside Ukraine and insisted that her country's leaders would one day be held to account. 'I don't know how, yet, but power will change in Russia. Because the war crimes Russian officials have committed cannot go unpunished. The world community will not allow it.'

Margarita was sure lots of people in Nizhny opposed the war, behind closed doors. She thought they were donating money to Ukraine to buy drones and weapons, rather than marching in Russia through the streets. But a few days after Margarita was detained for her protest, her own brother picked up the phone and called the local military recruitment office. Two years after Irina Slavina killed herself, the journalist's only son headed for Ukraine as a volunteer soldier for Russia.

Stay Human, Please

ROSTOV-ON-DON, 18 FEBRUARY 2021

Anastasia Shevchenko spent the week before verdict day preparing for a life behind bars. If she was sent to prison, her mother would look after the children. But the activist had been making audio recordings for Vlada and Misha to listen to when she was gone. There was a mixture of practical instructions, like how to read the electricity meter and switch on the oven, and goodnight wishes so the children would hear her voice before bed.

Vlada had scoured the shops for the items on her mother's prison list, from a notebook to keep a diary, to warm socks and cockroach traps for her cell. It was all there, packed up in a big bag, when we dropped in to see the family the night before the hearing. Anastasia told me she and the children had been curling up in the same bed to sleep that week, anxious to be as close as possible for what time they had left. 'I'm not afraid, but I do worry about my family. I explain to them that there is life after jail, but they cry anyway, especially Misha. I can't even explain to them why I'd go to jail, or what it is I did that we should be separated. I don't know where I committed a crime, because I really didn't. But I'm treated like a very dangerous person.'

Anastasia could now count on one hand the number of friends whose flats had not been searched, or who had not faced administrative charges or criminal prosecution. 'It's total political repression, and I'm ashamed of that. But we have to speak out or Russia will turn into some kind of North Korea and I don't want that future for my children.' She was also clear on why all this was happening. 'It's fear, because they are weak. They know young people won't vote for them in five to ten years, so they're trying to save their regime by making every opposition activist a criminal.'

Two weeks earlier, Anastasia had been just as forthright in public. She used her 'Last Word' in court to question whether the state hadn't 'sucked enough blood' from her family.

Rostov-on-Don courthouse, 5 February 2021

I believe in open dialogue between those in power and society … I stand for open cooperation with other countries, honest rules of business, open and honest media and open and real elections. For an open Russia. I want my children and yours to live in a clean and lovely city. In a country where the laws and the rights of people are observed. Where there is no political repression.

I've heard a lot of people say, 'You know, it's not down to us. It's Moscow.' No, I don't know that. Adults have to take responsibility for their decisions. I ask you not to participate in political repression. I am not asking for myself, but for you and for your children.

Stay human, please. That is my last word.

Anastasia arrived at court for her final hearing to the cheers of dozens of supporters queuing in the snow. By then around forty foreign-based organisations had been blacklisted and banned as 'undesirable' and the eccentric Spaghetti Monster from Nizhny Novgorod was the first 'undesirable' activist to be locked up ahead of a trial. 'I thought sending someone to prison was a big deal and you needed some actual reason for that,' Iosilevich told me later, still bemused. 'I was wrong. They put people away very easily.'

The prosecutor in Anastasia's case had asked the judge to sentence her to five years, which was close to the maximum possible. The courtroom for verdict day was tiny, but the press were allowed in, along with Anastasia's family, so we pushed through to secure a place. The nationalist activist whose complaint had launched the entire criminal case also made it into court, filming everything cheerfully for his blog.

Anastasia's story had made the front page of the independent *Novaya Gazeta* newspaper and someone passed her a copy with the word 'Undesirable' splashed across her photograph. Sitting up at the front, but not in a cage, Anastasia kept sending reassuring looks towards her children on the benches. But they could also see the big prison bag beside her. The public had to stand for the verdict, which included a summary of the entire case and all the evidence. It lasted over four hours, with the judge's mumble even harder than usual to make out through a face mask.

Young Misha endured the first part hopping valiantly from foot to foot until someone took pity and led him out to a café for ice cream. Behind me, a German reporter slid onto a seat where he fell asleep, mouth slightly open. There was a small stir as the socialite Ksenia Sobchak slipped in late to show her support. Back in 2018 she had run for president on an opposition platform and Anastasia had campaigned for her. But Sobchak's late father had been close to Putin and the previous night she had dropped by the activist's flat: her sources had reassured her that Anastasia would get a suspended sentence.

The sources were right. When the judge reached the last sheet of paper in her thick pile, she duly pronounced Anastasia's peaceful political activity a 'threat to state security' and found her guilty. But she ordered a four-year suspended sentence, which is about as lenient as Russian justice gets. Only Anastasia herself wasn't pleased, because she insists she's innocent. The sentence meant she was banned from all political activity and from travelling abroad, and was obliged to check in with the prison authorities every month. If she was charged with anything else at all, even failing to wear a face mask, her suspended sentence could be converted into prison time.

But the house arrest was over, the electronic tag she loathed was coming off, her prison bag could be unpacked. Anastasia could go home that night with Vlada and Misha. As soon as he realised that, the little boy buried himself in his mother's arms and declared it the best day of his life.

That evening Vlada posted her last 'chronicle' on Facebook next to a photograph of Anastasia smiling up at the camera, with a big basket of flowers.

Facebook post, 18 February 2021

Hi. Today my mum was given a four-year suspended sentence and probation. Lots of people came to court, half of them didn't make it inside and had to stand in the freezing cold for six hours. Huge thanks to everyone … our house is full of flowers … This day is not a victory, of course. But we are together and we will fight on … Tomorrow we can go shopping and to the cinema. My feelings about this sentence are mixed. We need to study all the restrictions and then decide how we live. Mum will be back online, but not today. She's forgotten how to use a phone. #chroniclesofahousearrest are over.

War Criminal

KYIV, MAY 2022

There was something almost pitiful about the suspected Russian war criminal being led into a Ukrainian court. Vadim Shishimarin was twenty-one, but the soldier's elfin features and baggy, hooded top gave him a teenage air. Locked into a glass cage for the hearing, just a couple of metres from me, he kept his shaven head bowed and shoulders hunched. The prison guards had removed the laces from his tall black boots so he couldn't harm himself. But asked directly by the judge whether he had murdered an unarmed pensioner, Shishimarin was clear. 'Yes, totally.'

Just three months since Russia's invasion, this was Ukraine's first war crimes trial. Those in charge in Kyiv knew they had to be seen to seek justice and not revenge, holding a trial so swiftly and in an active conflict zone. The start of the hearing was delayed as the world's TV crews fought to squeeze into the small courtroom and bickered over the best spots. I hid among the cameras, avoiding the spillover room with a video feed for reporters. I wanted to feel the mood in the courtroom itself, to see the faces and the details.

Just a few months into the war, Ukrainian prosecutors had already registered more than 11,000 alleged crimes against civilians by Russian forces. They hoped everyone identified could one day be brought to trial and this first case was all about showing there was no impunity. Most of the men suspected of crimes were back in Russia, but the files were being readied should they ever return to the battlefield and get captured. Ukraine was also preparing for a future international tribunal.

The politicians and the officers who had permitted Russian troops to kill and rape Ukrainian civilians, to loot and foul their homes, were safe behind the thick walls of the Kremlin or inside the giant Defence Ministry building not far from my old Moscow flat. Instead of Putin or his generals going on trial, it was a scrawny young tank commander who was first to face a life sentence. Shishimarin's lawyer, appointed by the Ukrainian court, told me that no Russian official had even been in touch with him.

The story of the crime that emerged in court that day was as tragically pointless as the war itself. Shishimarin was from Siberia, born more than 3,000 miles east of Moscow in Irkutsk. He'd joined the army two years before the invasion of Ukraine because he was poor and needed to support his mother and siblings and pay his debts. His war lasted just five days and ended in murder and chaos.

In court, Shishimarin and another captured Russian named Ivan Maltisov described how their elite tank unit from the 4th Kantemir Division had stopped for the night soon after crossing the border into Ukraine. The soldiers rigged trip wires around their camp to give them early warning of enemy attack, but someone from their own unit stepped on one in the dark. Four men were injured in the confusion. The following day, Shishimarin was ordered to escort a column of vehicles with the wounded soldiers back into Russia, but they were ambushed on the way by Ukrainian troops. Local villagers say at least ten of the Russians were killed. They buried them in a field by the road, marking the spot with a scrap-metal cross. Shishimarin survived and fled the scene with four other men, hijacking a getaway car at gunpoint and puncturing its front tyre in the process. It was as they limped in that stolen Volkswagen through the village of Chupakhivka that the soldiers spotted 62-year-old Oleksandr Shelipov.

Ivan Maltisov remembered the moment they saw the retired tractor driver in the street. 'He was either on his phone or getting it out.' A third soldier began yelling at Shishimarin to shoot the pensioner, to prevent him informing on their location to Ukrainian troops. They could have stopped and confiscated the man's phone. Even checked who he was calling. Instead, as Maltisov remembered it, 'Under pressure, Vadim fired … three or four shots.'

Shishimarin never spoke much above a whisper in court and his voice was muffled further by the glass that encased him. 'I didn't want to shoot. I fired to get him off my back.' Under questioning, he had to admit that the soldier screaming orders to shoot had no actual authority over him. Shishimarin could have refused.

The widow of the man he had killed sat opposite him in court. When it was her turn to give evidence, Kateryna Shelipova described spending the night before her husband's death sheltering with him in their cellar from the shelling all around. The next morning, Oleksandr took his bike and went to inspect the damage. As he headed home, his phone rang and he paused to speak to a friend, standing between two plum trees. Kateryna heard the shots. When she cracked open their gate to investigate, she saw Shishimarin at the back window of a passing car, rifle raised. 'Then I looked the other way and saw my husband. I ran up to him, but he was already dead. He'd been shot in the head. So I started to shout. A lot.' When the judge asked what her husband of forty years had meant to her, Kateryna broke down. 'He was my everything. My protector.'

At one point, she addressed the soldier directly. 'Tell me … what did you feel when you killed my husband? Tell me please … do you repent of the crime?' Shishimarin mumbled in reply. 'I understand you won't be able to forgive me.' But he asked for that nevertheless.

When Putin sent Shishimarin to war, he claimed that Russian speakers in Ukraine needed protecting from a murderous regime in Kyiv. Now Kateryna Shelipova turned to the man who had shattered her life, too, when he aimed his Kalashnikov at her husband. 'Tell me please, why did you come here? To protect us? Who from? Did you protect me from my husband, who you killed?'

The trial concluded in under a week. The first Russian war criminal was given a life sentence, later reduced to fifteen years.

Mugs

LONDON, MARCH 2022

When I got back to London from covering the first few weeks of war, I watched footage of Vladimir Putin addressing a vast crowd in a Moscow sports stadium. The Russians roared support for their president and his invasion. The whole event at Luzhniki had been carefully choreographed with an audience bussed in specially. Some people may well have supported the war; others probably worried they'd lose their jobs if they refused to turn out. At the gate they were all handed banners with 'Z' symbols and slogans. *Za Putina. Za pobedu.* For Putin. For victory. Four years earlier, I'd been at the same stadium when Russia hosted the World Cup. Now Luzhniki looked like it was hosting a fascist rally.

After I was expelled, I'd kept my plastic beer cups from the World Cup as a memento of happy, heady times. A precious few weeks when the police were under orders to be friendly, normal duties like battering protesters temporarily suspended. I stacked the pint pots in a kitchen cupboard next to the mugs I'd accumulated from all over Russia. There was one from Murmansk, where we spent days waiting for clear weather so the military could fly us to their Arctic base. One from Nizhny Novgorod was a gift from a friend of the journalist Irina Slavina. There was also a substantial selection of Putin mugs, now pushed right to the back. One portrayed a much younger man, posing topless and macho on horseback. The images were a throwback to the cult of personality I'd first reported on in his early years as president, when a hit pop song had cooed about wanting 'a man like Putin'. Those were the days when the world was intrigued by the ex-KGB man now in power. A shadowy figure, thrust into the spotlight. As journalists in Moscow, we searched for clues to what made Putin tick, and in 2022 people would do that again in an attempt to understand why he'd invaded Ukraine and how to stop him. I haven't spent much time lately, or on these pages, probing Putin's psychology. Wondering what moments in his youth, in the KGB, in history might have formed him. Or re-interpreting the cautionary tale he told interviewers in 2000 for his 'astonishingly frank self-portrait', *First Person*, about the dangers of confronting a cornered rat. Plenty of other people have done that over the years, and their books are all on my shelves. In the end, I think the man can be understood by his deeds. Putin is Mariupol. He is Bucha. He is what he has done to Ukraine.

I often think about Russians' response to this war: about those who support it, loudly, and those who probably don't, but who stay silent. I wonder how I would act, and people close to me, if we knew that speaking out against the war would get us arrested, perhaps a long prison sentence.

Way back in 1974, Alexander Solzhenitsyn published a text which he called *Live Not by Lies*. The author had been charged with treason and stripped of his citizenship for his *Gulag Archipelago*, a shattering portrayal of the Soviet prison camps where he'd been imprisoned. From enforced exile, his new text addressed Soviet citizens for whom change through elections was impossible and change through protest terrifying. But instead of objecting that 'nothing depends on me', or 'I can't change anything', Solzhenitsyn called on people to refuse to live by official lies. That meant not working as a journalist if you can't tell the truth, and not holding a banner or spouting a slogan in praise of a system you don't believe in.

Almost half a century later, that call might apply to the Russians who agree to be bussed to Luzhniki or other mass rallies for Putin, or the state media employees who go on working in his propaganda machine because they have family to feed and a mortgage to pay, or because they convince themselves that they are small and insignificant cogs. Solzhenitsyn condemned such compromise. 'We are not called upon to step out onto the square and shout out the truth, to say out loud what we think. That's scary, and we are not ready. But let us at least refuse to say what we do not think,' he urged. He believed such moderate, passive resistance would undermine the whole edifice of the Soviet regime. Solzhenitsyn would be barred from returning to Russia until that regime collapsed, seventeen years later.

When I got kicked out, people would tell me it was a 'badge of honour' and congratulate me for getting under the Kremlin's skin. At first that niggled, because I still felt the loss. The remnants of my many years in Russia as either student or reporter were all around me in London, as reminders of the enormous time and effort I'd invested. My bookshelves were loaded with Russian literature and history. I had crates full of notebooks from reporting trips across the country and a phone full of contacts and friends I'd probably never see. Even squeezing the last drop of shampoo from a bottle marked in Cyrillic script felt stupidly like the end of an era.

Six months later, the invasion of Ukraine killed that nostalgia dead. Reporting from the Donbas at first, and then places like Bucha, I was documenting what Russia was doing instead of being forced to hear its denials and distortions.

When I returned from Ukraine in March, I binned all the Putin mugs. For a long time, I couldn't bear to see any of the Russia stuff. I couldn't bear even to continue writing this book.

PART VIII

Last Days

MOSCOW, LATE AUGUST 2021

When I started to plan a leaving party, I realised how many people had already gone. A couple of weeks earlier, *Novaya Gazeta* had declared a 'Mass Exodus' from Russia, which the newspaper put down to the 'collapsing space' for civil and political rights. The pressure had increased significantly over the past year as the country moved towards elections for parliament in mid-September. The whole political process had been under tight control for years, but elections are always a potential flashpoint for protest. All over my Moscow neighbourhood there were official posters inviting Russians to turn out and 'vote for your future', as if they could actually change something.

The lists of 'foreign agents', 'undesirables' and 'extremists' had been growing fast. They were the three main labels applied to those judged hostile to the state, with penalties of escalating severity. Above all that was the label of traitor, now applied more frequently than ever. But the milder-sounding designation of 'undesirable' was serious enough, and shortly before I was expelled, it was applied to the media for the first time: the investigative website *Proekt* was banned in July 2021 as a supposed 'threat to the foundations of the constitutional order and the security of the Russian Federation'. That came shortly after a corruption investigation into the family of the interior minister, though

Proekt's previous reporting will have ensured it numerous other powerful enemies.

The BBC office had been ghostly empty since Covid, so in my last days in Moscow I was able to slip in quietly to collect my things. As I was clearing my desk, I overheard a Russian Service correspondent trying to get a comment on the US withdrawal from Afghanistan, but none of his usual contacts wanted to be quoted. 'We can't speak to the foreign press, in the circumstances.' The reporter saw me shredding papers and came over to dump a whole load of my rubbish into the recycling. 'Now, when they interrogate me, at least I can say I personally helped kick her out.' He gave me a hug. 'It's really messed up.' Another colleague who saw me among the scraps wrote later to say she was sorry I was going but distressed to be left behind 'in this Gulag'.

It took some time to go through all my files for the things I wanted to keep. There were my notes from when Nemtsov was murdered, right up to the attempted assassination of Navalny in August 2020. An archive of a dark time. I found the transcripts of a documentary we made back in 2016 about the shrinking space for public protest. One of the activists we followed would pull on a rubber Putin mask, walk onto Red Square and get arrested. Repeatedly. Another, Ildar Dadin, went to jail just for standing silently with a protest sign. I wrote to him in prison and when he got out, he told me about his brutal treatment behind bars. Much later, he would travel to Ukraine and join the fight there against Russia.

There were cuttings and transcripts from a huge range of old stories: ISIS brides in the southern republic of Dagestan, the Kremlin's troll farm spreading global disinformation, a scandal over state-sponsored doping in sport. Taped to the wall there was a picture of me chasing a government minister, who looked startled, clearly not used to being questioned. I found my files from the constitutional reform of the previous summer and remembered the referendum then that was a giant act of theatre. We'd filmed people voting in mobile polling stations, lured there by questions about preventing same-sex marriage and protecting pensions. They were a distraction from the only issue the Kremlin really cared about, which was keeping Putin in power. He was changing the constitution to serve another two terms as president. Just declaring himself dictator-for-life wouldn't work: Putin prefers to position himself as the people's choice. A true democrat.

As the carrier bags beside my desk filled up with files, there was a news flash on my phone. Each Friday the justice ministry would add new names to its blacklist of foreign agents, announcing more than a hundred in 2021. This time it was the turn of the independent TV channel Dozhd.

A few days later, I visited Dozhd headquarters in a converted factory district of Moscow, now filled with fashionable restaurants and coffee bars. The open-plan newsroom was an industrial space of metal beams and concrete blocks with a glass meeting room that had the word 'sex' in pink neon above the door. Inside, the daily news huddle was underway. In one corner, chief editor Tikhon Dzyadko lolled against a pink SMEG fridge, in the other was a seat made of giant ceramic feet. The TV team weren't surprised by their new status. Some were even quite proud of it as a mark of their quality. But being a 'foreign agent' brought trouble. For Dozhd it meant extra financial scrutiny and much more paperwork, forced to account for everything it spent. It would also have to publish a clunky disclaimer on all publications to highlight its 'hostile' status.

Out in the newsroom, journalists were already copy-pasting the health warning onto their stories. From now on, the twenty-four words in Russian were obligatory on every single broadcast or text, including social media. Trying to squeeze it all into a tweet was a challenge.

Foreign Agent Disclaimer

> This statement/material was created and/or distributed by a foreign mass-media organisation carrying out the function of a foreign agent and/or a Russian legal entity carrying out the function of a foreign agent

If the channel missed the warning just once, the fines were big and incremental. But Tikhon wasn't so much worried about the money as the message that this disclaimer sent. 'The status of "foreign agent" means that we, Dozhd, are enemies of the state. Agents of some foreign nation. It's not true. We are patriots. But no one wants to be associated with an enemy of the state.' The channel wasn't as heavily reliant on advertising as some other media because it had switched to donations after previous run-ins with the authorities. Losing ad income wouldn't be a killer blow. But this was such a blatantly political move that to Tikhon and his team, the future felt precarious. 'It's very bad. And it could become much worse, any time.'

I stood on the side of the set to watch a programme go out, presented that day by Ekaterina Kotrikadze. The bulletin began with a freeze-frame declaring the channel and all its contents the work of 'foreign agents'. Then came a headline about a woman under house arrest for tweeting about a protest against the imprisonment of Alexei Navalny. Each time Ekaterina referred to Navalny or his FBK anti-corruption foundation, she had to inform the audience that they were 'extremists' and 'foreign agents'. That made for a lot of hostile forces in one bulletin. I have no idea whether some official body was tasked with watching the channel to check what went out, or whether that was left to Russia's growing army of citizen snitches.

In its short life, Dozhd had been buffeted from one crisis to another. It launched on cable in 2010 and came to prominence during major protests against election fraud in 2011–12. It made its name and audience with a fresh, slightly chaotic style, and an attempt at balance. The channel was somewhere that opposition voices could go, long banned from the state-controlled airwaves. But Dozhd would try to interview a range of actors, including Russia's leadership, and ask the questions state media stopped posing years ago. Then, in early 2014, it got into hot water over history. The channel asked viewers whether Leningrad should have surrendered to the Nazis in the Second World War to avoid hundreds of thousands dying of starvation in a city under siege. The very notion was treated as blasphemy. The channel was promptly dumped by almost all its satellite and cable carriers and the advertisers quickly followed. Then Dozhd got evicted from its studios.

'It was like we were sitting in barracks for patients with the plague.' Tikhon remembered those times when not only did the money stop flowing, officials stopped giving them interviews. The 'foreign agent' status was the next phase, as if that plague had erupted in frightening spots. 'That's exactly what they wanted. To say, look, it's not safe to watch them. It's not safe to work with or talk to them. That's what they want.'

Tikhon saw the attack on independent media as part of a clear trend: the drop in Putin's political capital, after the Covid pandemic, was followed by a rise in repression. The same had happened in 2011–12, after the mass protests, and it was all about reasserting control. When he was asked about the repression at his annual press conference in December 2021, Putin talked about hostile external forces trying to 'tear Russia apart' from within. The man formed by the KGB only ever saw threats and plots. But Tikhon sensed that a line had been crossed. 'I think there's an understanding in the Kremlin that the pretence of being a democracy is over. It's like there's a new page now, and they're saying: *This is who we are*. And as for those independent organisations, human-rights activists and independent media: we don't need them here anymore.' In the same way, it would have been far harder to imagine Russia expelling a BBC correspondent a couple of years earlier. By 2021 the Kremlin really didn't care.

That day, chatting on set between broadcasts, I asked Tikhon why he stayed in Russia in such a climate. With so many others leaving, it was a question I had to ask almost everyone by then. Tikhon told me he belonged in Russia, his whole life was there, and so was his sense of purpose. The young team at Dozhd were still on board, ready to continue the fight, and they clearly had an audience. Just one weekend after the channel's listing as a 'foreign agent', it had acquired thousands more subscribers. Not everyone wanted to be spoon-fed propaganda.

That interview at Dozhd was part of my final report from Russia, a film about my expulsion and the context it was happening in. At one point, Matt, the cameraman, interviewed me in my flat and then filmed as I flicked through old photos at my dining table. It was something I'd asked others to do, multiple times, but becoming the story myself was an odd feeling. The photos went right back to my earliest days for the BBC in Moscow and I noticed how relaxed we all looked back then. We hadn't always been seen as the enemy. I had snapshots from the Russian far east, where we went in search of endangered tigers, and from a trip south with a Norwegian explorer on the trail of a Viking god. From one box, I dug out a photo of Boris Nemtsov standing in deep snow in his swimming trunks, just after an Epiphany dip. I don't remember taking it or why it was newsworthy. But there he was, young-looking and full of life a decade or so before he was killed.

Another day we were filming outside the Foreign Ministry when a group of young lads, high on something, briefly circled on skateboards. Drawn to our camera, they shouted obscenities about their government and declared loudly that they hated Putin before skating off. Behind the scenes, the BBC was still battling to get my expulsion reversed. But as we filmed near the ministry skyscraper that day, I got an email passing on a message from the Kremlin: there would be no last-minute reprieve.

The venue we'd found for my leaving party was a bar not far from the spot on Tverskaya where I'd bought Soviet *shampanskoye* in 1992 from old ladies lining the street. Now I would drink cocktails there and say my goodbyes. We gathered a good group of friends and colleagues and some of the remaining independent journalists who didn't mind being seen with us. Anastasia Shevchenko's lawyer came, and I wondered what it was like being a defence attorney in a country where political detainees are always found guilty. He reminded me that Anastasia wasn't in prison, and in Russia a suspended sentence is a big win. There were speeches and music and some tears. There were also nervous discussions about why this had happened and who might be next.

The DJ eventually switched from Kes's Cuban salsa requests to some party classics, and the bar girl burst through the crowd of dancers to body pop in the middle of the floor. Soon she was hugging everyone and crying that she'd miss me. I reminded her that we'd only just met. 'But I'm the bar girl!' she declared. 'We have to stop this shit. We have to overturn the government!' Then she moonwalked her way back to mix more drinks.

The Final Battle

MOSCOW AND ST PETERSBURG, 2021

When Alexei Navalny survived the attempt to kill him in 2020, the Russian authorities warned him to stay away from the country or be arrested. The charge was absurd: the politician and anti-corruption campaigner had supposedly failed to report to a probation officer under the terms of an old, suspended sentence. But he'd been unconscious in Germany at the time, where he'd been flown by his wife after being poisoned. When Navalny recovered, he publicly accused Putin of trying to have him assassinated. Putin retorted that if Russian agents had wanted him dead, they would have finished the job.

Life as a political émigré was not for Navalny. He spent five months receiving treatment in Germany where the chancellor, Angela Merkel, said laboratory tests confirmed 'unequivocally' that a Novichok nerve agent had been used to attack him. Then, as soon as he was fit enough to travel, he made an announcement. 'On Sunday 17 January I will return home on a Pobeda Airlines flight. Come and meet it.' *Pobeda* means victory and Navalny ended his Instagram post with a winking emoji.

He landed in Moscow accompanied by a horde of journalists who'd scrambled to buy seats on the same flight. They tailed him through the airport, cameras rolling, until he paused to utter a few words next to a wall poster of the Kremlin. 'Everyone's asking if

I'm scared. I'm not scared. I feel completely fine ... because all the charges against me are fabricated.' Navalny then made it as far as passport control, where he was arrested. His custody hearing was held inside a police station the very next day. He would never walk free.

For a while his supporters kicked back against his detention. On 23 January 2021 large crowds took to the streets in more than a hundred towns and cities across Russia. There was even a small rally in Yakutsk, eastern Siberia, where it was −40°C. In central Moscow, protesters filled Pushkin Square, shouting for Navalny to be freed and for a 'Russia without Putin'. They waved signs urging others not to be afraid, not to stay silent. Passing cars hooted their horns in support and some played Viktor Tsoi's 'Peremen' at high volume on their stereos, a Soviet-era song for change. It had been the anthem of the giant pro-democracy protests in Belarus in the summer of 2020, when a neighbouring dictator had suddenly looked weak. The summer when Navalny was poisoned.

When protesters filled streets and squares across Russia after his return, they weren't only driven by anger at his arrest, or the attempt to kill him. Navalny's team had just dropped another video bombshell, releasing a video investigation that took aim at the president himself. They called it *Putin's Palace* and it was watched on YouTube by millions. The film featured a 3D visualisation of a mega-residence on the Black Sea that Navalny said was being renovated for Putin, complete with pole-dancing stage and private vineyard. He declared it 'the most expensive palace in the world', built on corrupt cash. 'What was it all for? The twenty years in power, all the repressive laws, the dismantling of politics and the constitution?' he asked his audience. 'It was all for gold and marble ... and an aqua disco.' Recorded in Germany before his return to Russia, Navalny ended the video with a plea for action: 'We have to stop putting up with this ... Our future is in our own hands. Don't stay silent.' Among the crowds that followed his call and came out in protest, I spotted a fair few waving gold-sprayed toilet brushes. They were mocking the grotesquely expensive fixtures and fittings of Putin's palace.

The riot police followed their familiar drill. 'Robocops' in black body protection, helmets and tinted visors snatched protesters from the crowd and carried them off face-down. By the end of the day, Moscow's detention centres were overflowing. Ten of Navalny's close associates ended up on criminal charges, accused of inciting people to break the Covid restrictions by joining a mass protest. Pro-government rallies went ahead with no problem and no apparent risk to anyone's health.

A few days after the January protest, the offices of Navalny's Anti-Corruption Foundation, FBK, were raided by police who broke through the doors with a circular saw and crowbars. Someone at the top had decided enough was enough. On 16 April 2021 the Moscow prosecutor's office petitioned the courts to declare the entire Navalny network 'extremist'. That would mean an immediate and outright ban, with forty or so regional offices forced to close. Anyone then taking part in their activities could face a prison sentence of up to six years. 'Participation' might be as little as making a financial donation. The prosecutor who filed the petition had been the subject of an FBK corruption investigation a couple of years earlier that discovered he owned property abroad that no state salary could ever cover.

Team Navalny began disbanding immediately, for self-protection. The court's decision was never in doubt.

Irina Fatyanova ran Navalny's headquarters in St Petersburg up until the day it would have cost her freedom. When the office opened in 2017, I'd seen supporters there queuing round the block for the chance of meeting Navalny himself. Many were young, drawn by his personal charisma as well as his forensic YouTube investigations. The corruption-busting agenda was very popular and it was damaging to Russia's elite. But Navalny had higher ambitions. He was preparing to challenge Putin for the presidency in 2018 and needed a national network. The St Petersburg headquarters was to be the first. So many people crammed into the small office to hear him speak that the windows steamed up completely.

Four years later, Navalny was in custody and I found the headquarters locked and empty, apart from a printer and a coat rack gathering dust. Irina and her colleagues had gutted the place, deleted their social media accounts and purged laptops and phones of anything that tied them to the politician and might get them prosecuted for extremism. The last thing they'd removed from the office was a signed photograph of Navalny from the wall. It was an image captured with the crowd on opening day.

When Irina and I met not far from the office, in a park with a pond and a palace, she was nervous. She'd consulted a lawyer before agreeing to an interview, afraid that one wrong word, especially to a foreign journalist, could land her in serious trouble. Her fears were well-founded. In late 2023 Ksenia Fadeeva was sentenced to nine years in prison for 'creating an extremist organisation'. She was the former head of Navalny's headquarters in Tomsk, Siberia.

In St Petersburg, Irina told me that she and her team had felt the pressure rise after Navalny was poisoned. Things got worse when he flew home a few months later. 'As soon as Navalny said he was coming back, the authorities started coming for us.' Irina's house had been searched, she was sure that her phone was being tapped, and she was being followed by 'men in hoods'. 'I don't think there's been one calm day since then when I haven't worried about a knock on my door, or some criminal case.'

Navalny's team knew that an extremism designation would be a serious blow to their operations. The label had been applied to the Jehovah's Witnesses in 2017, since when almost 500 members of the religious organisation had faced criminal charges. Dozens were serving long sentences, mostly just for continuing to attend prayer meetings. In Surgut, a Siberian oil town, a group of Witnesses showed me the burn marks where they'd been tortured by interrogators using electric shockers. The men's injuries had been documented by doctors. I never fully understood why the Jehovah's Witnesses were treated so harshly, unless it was for their American roots. But if a religious organisation could face such persecution, then the risk to Navalny's allies was far higher.

'We don't know how hard they want to crack down,' Irina worried. 'But they'll be the ones who decide what is extremist activity, and what isn't, and that's frightening.' She saw the closure of Navalny's political network as a win for the Kremlin but as a sign of weakness, too, because it showed they feared him.

Having cut formal ties with the group, Irina was planning to stay in St Petersburg. She thought she might somehow carry on in politics, perhaps run for local election, restarting resistance from the bottom up. 'I want to change things,' she told me. 'I don't want to look the next generation in the eyes and be ashamed.' But Irina hadn't yet defined her own limits. 'Many are deciding to leave the country, and I respect that. I don't know what has to happen for me to go.'

Some members of Navalny's team who'd already left had set up a remote headquarters in Lithuania, fully equipped with TV studios. It meant they could continue their livestreams far from the surveillance and the searches and the threat of prison. They were still in the process of reinventing how they worked. Navalny's chief of staff Leonid Volkov told me they were trying to reach those who knew that what was happening in Russia was 'very far from normal'. He believed people were growing tired of Putin, especially the young. 'But we never promised a quick win. Unfortunately a dictator can be very persistent. It could last for years.'

In April 2021 Navalny appeared at a court hearing via video link with gaunt face and shaven skull. He'd been on a hunger strike for more than three weeks and his uniform hung from a shrunken frame. But from his prison he called on Russians not to give in. His team knew that once their organisation was labelled 'extremist' then joining a street demonstration for Navalny would be like coming out in public support of al Qaeda. So they called a protest before the court ruling was due, timing it to coincide with Putin's state of the nation address on 21 April. They pitched it as 'the final battle' for a free Russia.

That day, in the Manezh hall beside the Kremlin, Putin addressed the gathered elite of Russian politics. From a giant blue stage, flanked by tricolour flags, he preached of a powerful nation united against hostile forces in the West. With tens of thousands of troops already massed close to Ukraine's border, Putin warned the West not to cross Russia's 'red lines' or it would regret that 'more than anything in a long time'. Once he was done, Navalny's supporters took to the streets chanting for Putin to go.

The police deployment was massive. They'd closed off all the main squares in the city centre, using barriers, human chains and dustbin trucks. The protesters split up, roaming side streets and converging now and then to shout Navalny's name. Very unusually, the riot police stood back and let them march. Walking alongside the crowd, filming, I saw people's confusion: the protesters were used to being confronted with batons and violence. Without it, they were unsure how to act. There were perhaps 10,000 of them, fewer than in January, and not as many as Team Navalny had hoped for. Some said they were there because they supported him personally and were angry at his treatment. Many more had just come out to demand change, no longer prepared to settle for Putin's standard offering of stability.

But the 'final battle' wasn't fought for long. Within a couple of hours the crowd had thinned until the wandering groups of protesters were barely distinguishable from the late-night shoppers and bar-hoppers in central Moscow. The chants for Navalny's freedom and of 'Putin, Killer!' were fading away. The turnout was nowhere near enough to put Putin under pressure. But the pressure on the opposition would become even more intense.

Navalny's network was declared 'extremist' in June 2021. By the time I had to leave Russia, two months later, most of his key allies had already fled. Irina Fatyanova would follow in November 2021, calling it 'the hardest decision of my life'. Others who didn't make it in time were prosecuted. Navalny himself was still getting messages out from prison and his team were still working abroad. But the criminal convictions were stacking up: a two-and-a-half year sentence, then nine years, then another nineteen for running an 'extremist organisation'.

For years, journalists had asked Navalny how he was still free when he was so fiercely critical of the Kremlin. Some would wonder to his face how he was even alive, as he campaigned against Putin and his allies as 'crooks and thieves'. In August 2020 they got their answer. Navalny was supposed to be dead, but he survived. So the Kremlin had him locked up and it had no intention at all of ever releasing him.

Diary entry, Moscow, 20 August 2021

Went to the doctor for a check-up and the first thing he tells me when I open the door is that he's ashamed of his country. I don't know him well, I've only seen him a few times, but he's suddenly apologising. He tells me people bury their heads when bad things happen to others. They don't react until it affects them directly. Now he's rattled. Because it's the journalists for now, but who will be next? The clinic is foreign-funded, so he speculates that maybe staff there will be called traitors one day, too. If you need anything, you have our support, he insists as he accompanies me out. It still costs me sixty quid at reception for the consultation.

Goodbye to Anna

MOSCOW, 22 AUGUST 2021

A week before I left Russia, Anna cooked courgette fritters at her dacha and we reminisced about the earliest days of our friendship. It began with her six-week visit to the UK in 1991, arriving in my life at Worcester Shrub Hill Station in her bright-red cape. She told me now that she'd wanted to stand out. She was nineteen when we met, studying English to be a teacher and just married. At that point Russia was still part of the USSR and Anna was on her first trip beyond its borders, overwhelmed when my mother took her on the weekly shop to a supermarket piled high with choice.

    Like every Russian who's been to England, she remembers the cold inside our houses. Most Russian flats are so warm that even in mid-winter you have to open the little *fortochka* window to breathe. Worse than the cold, though, it turned out the girl from the USSR had been hungry. Her stay was split between my house and several other students in my Russian class. But one girl's mother was on a diet and made the whole family fast with her, including their guest. Anna ended up spending most of the tiny stipend she got for teaching us on food. 'I remember you saying we were going for tea at someone's house and it was just that. Tea. No snacks.' The following year in Moscow, where I was overfed in every home I visited, I realised how mean we must have seemed as hosts.

That last day at the dacha, I teased Anna about how long she used to take in our bathroom. Waiting for her to get ready in the mornings, I always feared we'd miss the school bus. I couldn't understand all her hair products and make-up and she could never understand my saggy leggings and jumpers with holes in them, when capitalist Britain had shops 'full of beautiful stuff'. She couldn't fathom why I liked sitting cross-legged on the floor, either. Whenever I tried that in Moscow, *babushki* would yell at me about getting piles until I was shamed up off the concrete.

We'd shared these memories before, over the years. But I'd never heard about the church sermon Anna now remembered. One Sunday, my mother had taken her to our local church and the priest talked about Soviet troops shooting protestors in Lithuania. 'He called for prayers for our Catholic brothers and sisters in Vilnius,' she recalled. In 1991 the crowd outside the TV tower in Vilnius were protecting Lithuania's independence from communists still loyal to Moscow. When the protesters linked arms, the Soviet tanks kept rolling forward. Fourteen people were crushed or shot on what became known as Bloody Sunday. Western journalists had seen the killings and been to the protesters' funerals, but an official was despatched from Moscow to tell them it hadn't happened. They were informed that a photograph of a man dying beneath a Soviet tank was an 'elaborate fake'. That was the last year of the USSR, but it might have been Putin's Russia.

Anna and I never discussed politics much over the years, although I'd tell her about my reporting trips and she sometimes used my articles for students to discuss in her English classes. We'd been through a lot together, good and bad, including personal tragedy and loss. We were close, but politics had never been part of it.

That day at the dacha, I told her I'd been looking back through my notebooks and found one of my early feature stories from Moscow in 2003. It was a TV report about how male moose couldn't cross a new motorway to mate, so the authorities had built a special tunnel to help. I'd filmed a 'piece to camera' hand-feeding a mini moose as I described its love life. *A concrete crash barrier and a fence are stopping the moose mingling at night ... two serious obstacles to moose romance.* 'Had you stuck to stories like that, your life would have been different,' Anna told me.

A few days later, we met up again in Gorky Park and wandered along the embankment we'd first visited together so many years earlier. Back then, the park keepers would flood all the paths in winter and leave them to freeze, creating the best ice-skating track I'd ever seen. Gorky Park in 2021 was all falafel food trucks and boules alleys, but it was still fun. That last evening was warm and the paths busy with couples out walking and teenagers on scooters. In one spot, a man with a guitar had drawn a big crowd who were singing along to a hit from a cult Soviet film. Behind them, across the Moskva River, the Russian Defence Ministry was all lit up like a Christmas tree.

At my leaving party, we slow-danced to ABBA, hugged and cried. I assumed we would meet again, though not soon and likely never in Russia. Anna had let all her visas expire, even the UK one, and she was always bad at writing, even in the early years. We danced together to the Stone Roses for old times' sake. 'I am the Resurrection', arms out wide.

Swan Lake

MOSCOW, 24 AUGUST 2021

As soon as her house arrest was lifted, Anastasia Shevchenko was free to travel inside Russia, though she had to inform the prison authorities whenever she left her home town. The 'undesirable' opposition activist was still a convicted criminal, albeit with a suspended sentence. When we met in Moscow during my last week in Russia, she told me she also needed a stamp of approval from her neighbours every three months. 'They have to write that I'm a good person, that I treat my children well. If they don't do that, it's a problem.'

Anastasia had travelled up from Rostov to promote her new book, based on a diary of her arrest. She handed me a copy when we met in a riverside park, but even in 'liberal' Moscow only one place would stock it. The book was so frank that her lawyer had warned it could bring new problems, a comment Anastasia laughed about as she shared it with me. She'd decided to publish anyway, in the hope that her family's story might make people care about the political repression Anastasia now saw all around. She thought it might show that anyone could be next. It could be them.

In Moscow that day, though, Misha, Vlada and their mum were free to wander among the skateboarders and strolling couples on the river bank, watching the boats and enjoying the sun. Their walk took them past the gargantuan Peter the Great statue that most Muscovites have loathed since it appeared in the 1990s. A giant-sized Peter on top of a toy-sized ship, it's horribly unavoidable. The statue is also oddly inappropriate, as he's the tsar who thought Moscow so backwards he founded a whole new capital to the north, on a swamp.

We sat on a bench, backs to Peter, as the children ate ice cream and chips and we talked. I'd wanted to say goodbye after all the trips to Rostov and all the months following Anastasia's fate. Even after her sentencing, she admitted she was still nervous. 'I don't feel safe in this country. I'm even afraid when I hear someone knocking at the door. I understand they can come at any moment. Every time you read the news you think, God, when will it end? When will this machine of repression stop?' By then, they weren't only coming for the activists. It was lawyers, comedians and musicians too. But Anastasia was determined not to let fear rule her life. 'I don't want to go to jail, of course. But at the same time, I'm ready. I know how to survive.' That's why she was off to talk about her diary-book on Ekho Moskvy later that day, the last editorially independent radio station still on air, and it's why she was confident enough to sit in public and talk to me. When I queried that, she shrugged. 'Yes, maybe it can make things worse.'

We filmed an interview, but we also chatted at length as usual. Anastasia wanted to know how I felt about being expelled. I told her I was sad that Russia was closing in on itself and that people like her were the real victims of that. But Anastasia didn't feel like a victim. She felt strengthened by her experience and certainly stronger than the prosecutors, police and judges who had pursued her. She'd discovered that the machine of repression was not powered by ideology or any sense of conviction. Repression was a job, with a good reward scheme. One investigator on Anastasia's case got promoted for securing her conviction and the whole office got new furniture and a fresh coat of paint. 'But yes, we are closing in, and they are sending the message that the last people fighting should now leave the country. If they stay, they will have to suffer in silence.'

Many of Anastasia's friends and fellow activists had already taken the hint and gone. They assured her that she'd leave, too, once her sentence was served and she could travel. But she couldn't imagine that. The court and prosecutors had painted her as an enemy of Russia, but she saw herself as a patriot. She wanted to stay in her country and help change it. That day, Anastasia told me her biggest ambition was to run in a free and fair election in Russia, and to win.

Six months later, Russia invaded Ukraine and Anastasia was shocked and angry. There were suddenly men in military uniform in Rostov and people taking selfies beside big 'Z' symbols in support of the invasion. Anastasia's city in the south is close to the occupied eastern Donbas region of Ukraine and had had a slightly edgy feel since the conflict began in 2014. In my early Russia years, I remember producing stories in the region about Cossack cultural revivals, feasting on crayfish and beer with men with big moustaches. More recent visits had involved unnerving encounters with other nationalists and 'patriots' mixed up in the fighting in Ukraine.

Like many Russians, Anastasia had close relatives across the border. In February 2022 that included a little girl who was trapped in Kharkiv under heavy shelling. Polina had cancer and the war had cut her off from the medicine she needed to keep it in remission. When I called Polina's mother for an interview, the little girl was playing in a bathtub lined with blankets and filled with her toys because her parents judged it the safest place in their building.

Anastasia felt powerless. One wrong word, one angry post about the war on social media, and her suspended sentence could be converted to jail time that would keep her from her children for years. But she saw everything that was happening and felt sick. She spent the first months of war staying home as much as possible, like a voluntary return to house arrest. Then she shoved her life into a couple of suitcases and fled Russia in the middle of the night with the children. It was a nervous journey in a borrowed car, taking a circuitous route, disguised in hats and dark glasses.

The next time I met Anastasia was in September 2022 in Lithuania. Safely outside Russia, her political commentary had become sharper. 'Day by day, I start to feel like a human at last, when I can finally say that it's a crime what our country is doing,' she told me, as we caught up by the side of a lake in Vilnius. She was at a gathering of Russian opposition members in exile that I'd gone to report on, curious to hear what they were thinking and what they had planned.

I've met Ukrainians who believe that even the most persecuted Russian activists are cowards, arguing that the risk they face for standing up to Putin pales compared to being attacked by his military. They often point to the lack of protests abroad, even when Russians are safe there. Anastasia puts such harsh judgement into context. 'What is going on in Russia now is like total fear ... because we know the authorities can do anything. It's not only prison, or fines. You can be poisoned or killed. It's like a huge prison, all the country.' Now she was free of that captivity, Anastasia did feel a duty to speak up. 'I think all we can do now as Russians is say sorry, and protest against Putin. Because he is the reason for what's going on. He is why so many people are dying.'

A British documentary maker had picked up on the activist's story after her trial and began following her once she was freed from house arrest. The film captured Anastasia's journey to the Black Sea to scatter her eldest daughter's ashes, the child who had died alone because of the political prosecution of her mother and a cruel system that had concealed how sick Alina was, until it was too late.

Now Anastasia had fled Russia, she was a 'wanted' woman for violating the terms of her sentence. She'd be arrested if she returned. But her mother, Tamara, was still there. Even though Anastasia had been punished for her politics, even though they had family in Ukraine who were suffering, Tamara did not want to leave Rostov. After years of state TV programmes, day and night, she'd ended up more convinced by the propaganda than by her own closest relatives. It took Anastasia significant effort to persuade her mother to join her.

Her own decision had been sealed the day her son's primary-school class were told to write letters to Russian soldiers in Ukraine, wishing them victory. Instead, Misha wrote that they had no right to fight their neighbours. Anastasia sounded proud when she told me that, but she knew the risks. In February 2023 a man in Tula would be arrested when his daughter drew an anti-war poster in a school art class. The internet was full of flash mobs of schoolchildren lined up like a letter Z or performing songs for 'Uncle Vova', short for Vladimir, in which they pledged to follow Putin into 'the final battle'.

Much later, living in Warsaw, I clicked on one of Anastasia's Instagram posts to discover that Misha had starred in the latest video clip by Pussy Riot. The punk protest group called their new song 'Swan Lake', after the ballet that was played on a loop as the 1991 coup played out on the streets. In the clip, phrases from state propaganda spew from the mouth of a Pussy Riot TV presenter. *They're bombing themselves. Discrediting the army. Traditional values. Import substitution. Partial mobilisation. Denazification. There's no panic.* Underneath a freeze-frame of her son from the video, Anastasia had typed: 'We're all waiting for Swan Lake.'

When the Crab Whistles on the Hill

MOSCOW, 31 AUGUST 2021

On my last night in Moscow, I sat awake into the early hours writing a final despatch. At the kitchen table, looking over towards the dim red stars and golden domes of the Kremlin as I had many times before, I thought about the man who'd ruled from there for so many years. The lights opposite were burning late like mine, but Putin had been running the country from his bunker for a long time.

When the Covid pandemic hit, the man who constantly asserts Russia's might had been so terrified of infection that he retreated into extreme isolation. Visitors had to quarantine for up to three weeks before getting close, even the World War II veterans who would share a podium with him on Victory Day. Putin's long tables for meetings with world leaders who wouldn't take a Kremlin coronavirus test spawned endless memes. But it was during Covid that Putin wrote the essay that argued Ukraine had no right to exist as a nation. It was in isolation that he must have dreamed up his plan to invade, without anyone to tell him it was crazy.

In August 2021 all that still lay ahead. The skies above Moscow, and Ukraine, were still calm. Out in the corridor our cases stood packed and ready to go, alongside the travelling crate and papers for the dog. All orderly now, after a chaotic scramble. The one advantage to leaving in a rush was avoiding our landlady's face when she spotted the large missing chunk of wall in the hall. The owner of our flat was a synchronised swimmer with a taste for all that glitters, including wallpaper, and the apartment had been a gift 'from Putin' for winning an Olympic medal. Smudge had taken a liking to the plaster when she was teething and we never got round to filling the hole.

We were flying out via Brussels, which meant we needed a negative Covid test because the Sputnik vaccine we'd been given wasn't recognised in Europe. I suspect the clinic we went to for a test just typed up the certificates and binned our blood samples. The pandemic had revealed a lot about Putin's Russia. There was the lockdown, introduced far too late, then tightly enforced using facial-recognition technology. There was the time I went to a village called Sputnik to report on attitudes to the Sputnik vaccine and people were so nervous of Russian-speaking foreigners with microphones they almost ran us out of town. But most damning was the doctor who told me how much of the vaccine had been wasted. Her colleagues would sign certificates to confirm that patients had been given their mandatory jab, then tip the dose of vaccine down the sink. Sputnik had been hyped heavily on state TV as the wonder jab and totally safe. But this wasn't some distant war the propagandists were selling. It was an issue that affected people immediately, personally and directly. When it came to their own health, it turned out many Russians just didn't trust the state.

It was close to midnight when Kes and I slipped out of the flat to say goodbye to our neighbours. Yura brought a bottle of Venezuelan rum and his mother had a little bag of apples to chase it down with. The dogs ran rings round us in the yard as we toasted our friendship and the future under a light drizzle. When war broke out a few months later, Yura would leave Russia, too, for America.

Vladimir Putin was going nowhere. He'd just got the constitution changed so he could rule until 2036 if he wanted, late into his eighties. But so many of the people I'd met and interviewed over the years had now left the country. Others still there admitted they had an escape plan, somewhere to flee when the moment came. I'd never thought for a moment that I would be joining them on the outside, or that I'd be going with the labels 'anti-Russian' and 'security threat' ringing in my ears.

I tried to drown out the noise. Ever since my expulsion had become public, near strangers had been stopping to commiserate and tell me they hoped things would change soon. It was those Russians' kindness that I thought of that final night, looking out over the city that I'd grown so attached to. The country I'd called home.

Interview for BBC film, Moscow, 26 August 2021

Who is it you're angry at? Ultimately, at Putin. I blame Putin for changing this country from one of opportunity to one without freedom. One where political activists, opponents, journalists are not free. I don't know where this will end. But where it's going is not good.

At least you can leave … Yes, some of my [Russian] friends have joked that I'm lucky. They wish they could be expelled. But I do worry about what's happening to the country I'm leaving behind. To the journalists, and just to the people who would like to live differently.

Will you ever come back? I learned a new phrase in Russian yesterday. *When the crab whistles on the hill.* I don't think it will be soon.

It was still dark when we left for the airport, the damp streets of Moscow nearly empty. We drove north, past the Lenin Library and up Tverskaya Street, leaving the Kremlin behind. Back there, too, was the spot beneath St Basil's where Boris Nemtsov had been shot and where volunteers still guarded a shrine six years on. They stood on that bridge around the clock, in rain, snow or sun, protecting photographs and flowers from occasional nationalist saboteurs and the more regular threat of street sweepers.

At check-in at Sheremetyevo, I took a photo of Smudge on top of her crate and sent it to Anna. 'We all love you madly and will miss you.' Soon we were settling into our business-class seats: we would never fly Aeroflot again and I'd accumulated lots of air miles. My foreign editor called to say he was sorry and wouldn't give up on getting me back, but we both knew it was a lost cause. As the take-off announcement came over the tannoy, I tweeted the picture my team had presented me with as a leaving gift. It was a cartoon of me being sent packing by a boggle-eyed Putin in his Kremlin tower, Lukashenko lurking beneath and Kadyrov, bushy-bearded, skiing manically towards me down a mountain. Only a cute, floppy-eared Cheburashka was clinging to my leg. The cartoonist was Sergei Elkin. He would be declared a 'foreign agent' the following year.

One flight, several hours and a train under the Channel later, we emerged into England, a country that hadn't been home for twenty-one years. We'd booked a 'pet taxi' for us and the dog, and as we pulled away from the tunnel, I asked the driver to switch on the radio. The *PM* programme was on air and the words of my final despatch from Moscow filled the car. I sat with Smudge on my lap and the boot stuffed full of our belongings, as the car moved north. 'By the time you hear this I'll be on my way to England, expelled as a "national security threat" after more than twenty years of reporting on Russia. I still can't really believe it.'

PART IX

Truth on Trial

UKRAINE AND RUSSIA, 2022

A few months into the Russian invasion, I was standing among the ruins of somebody's home while the village head listed thirteen names of dead civilians. He knew them all, and he knew they'd all been shot by Russian soldiers. Like Bucha, and many other towns and villages, the Russians had occupied Andriivka as their advance on Kyiv stalled. They'd branded walls and doors all around with their 'V' and 'Z' signs.

Before the war, the village had been a few dozen houses by the side of a road. Now many of those homes were heaps of fire-blackened bricks, with the occasional iron bedstead or oven poking through. Any garden gates still standing were painted with a series of symbols marking which plots had been checked and cleared of mines and which still had unexploded shells. Houses that seemed more or less intact on the outside had been ransacked inside.

I met Alina clearing up her driveway as her son attempted to patch up the damage to the roof from shelling. The pensioner pointed to the bullet holes around her door where soldiers had shot their way into her home. They'd then trashed it and looted everything valuable, leaving only the small display of Orthodox icons she showed me still untouched on the living-room shelf. The Russians must have spent hours there watching films because

Alina had filled two sacks with the pirate DVDs they'd left behind, compilations of thrillers and action films, mostly from America.

The whole time the soldiers had been making themselves comfy in her home, Alina had been cowering with her family in their vegetable cellar. I asked what she'd felt, stuck in the damp below ground and she repeated the words several times. 'Horror and fear.' Then she looked up at me, in anger. 'Let the Russian people come here and see what they did to us!'

But the Russian people were not seeing it. They were seeing reports about precision strikes and high-tech missiles and Russian troops rescuing grateful Ukrainian civilians. They were watching a 'Special Military Operation', so much more clinical and contained than the actual war. By then, the rights group OVD-Info had recorded dozens of prosecutions under Article 207.3, the 'fake news' law. More than 3,000 people had been charged with the separate administrative offence of 'discrediting' the armed forces. Russians who wanted independent news about their country would have to seek it out surreptitiously, like back in the USSR, only via VPN rather than shortwave radio. Putin's war on free speech was almost won, more than twenty years after the first battle for control of the state media.

Ilya Yashin ignored the official censorship. In Moscow, the opposition politician hosted a YouTube channel, and when the war began, his subscriber count shot up. In April 2022 he talked there in detail about the killing of civilians in Bucha. He showed BBC footage filmed soon after the occupying Russian troops had fled, leaving bodies lining the streets. Another stream described Ukraine as 'a sea of blood, a sea of tears and no end to this war in sight'. He was charged with 'discrediting the armed forces' and fined four times, but he refused to stop or to leave the country. He said that the only guilty people were those who had unleashed a 'criminal massacre' in Ukraine.

By then, Yashin was one of very few prominent opposition figures inside Russia still speaking out. Two years after he lost the regional election in Kostroma, he'd been elected to a municipal district of Moscow, where he focused on bread-and-butter housing and social problems rather than urging the removal of Putin. In 2021 he resigned from that post, as his presence was bringing extra pressure, with endless inspections and intimidation. After the all-out invasion of Ukraine, a former colleague, Alexei Gorinov, was imprisoned for seven years for 'spreading false information' about Russia's military. His crime was to question how appropriate it was to hold a children's drawing competition when children were dying in Ukraine every day.

Yashin knew he would be arrested, eventually. 'As soon as the first missiles flew at Ukraine, I went to the dentist and got my whole jaw sorted out. I got all the holes and cavities filled because in prison, no one will treat you,' he told a journalist ten days before he was detained. He was picked up on 27 June 2022 while out walking in a city park and initially sentenced to fifteen days in custody for 'resisting a police officer', though he had done no such thing. Just as he was due for release, he was charged under the 'fake news' law for his discussion on YouTube of the war and alleged Russian crimes. The charge sheet asserted that in Ukraine the Russian military was engaged in 'defending the interests of the Russian Federation and its citizens and supporting international peace and security'.

When Yashin's trial got under way in late 2022, I was back in Ukraine witnessing Russia's 'support for international peace' directly. Russian forces were struggling to advance on the ground, so they'd begun launching cruise missiles and drones at Ukraine's civilian infrastructure. In the midst of a freezing winter, in a country where temperatures can easily drop to -15°C, Russia was trying to knock out the power, the heating and even the water supply to millions of people. Putin had decided to break the nation's spirit, to freeze it into surrender. The various hotels we stayed in all had generators, so we were never in the cold or dark for long, but I met elderly people who lived high up in apartment blocks, unable to use the lift even to reach the basement in an air raid. There were care-home workers managing sudden blackouts that left no water to wash elderly residents or even flush the loo. It was between reporting on those persistent, morale-sapping air raids and their consequences that I kept an eye on Yashin's trial in Moscow.

The verdict was a foregone conclusion. There was no way a well-known opposition figure would be acquitted when the whole point of arresting him was to scare others and stop them speaking out. But Russian courts still maintain the pretence of dispensing real justice, even as they rubber-stamp decisions made somewhere on high. Trials can last for days, lawyers openly challenge the prosecutors, and those in the cage get to question their accusers and speak out in their own defence. At times, you can even convince yourself that the accused has a chance: the judge seems reasonable, the defence shows quite clearly that the charge is false. Then comes verdict day and you're brought back to Russian earth with a bump.

Acquittals are so rare in political trials that a suspended sentence is greeted like victory: the judge knew the person was innocent, Russians reason, but couldn't let them off with nothing. If a case is particularly sensitive or high profile, a judge can close the hearings to both public and press. That didn't happen for Yashin, and dozens of his friends crammed into court alongside the reporters and TV cameras. At key moments, his supporters burst into applause, prompting the judge to threaten to kick them out.

Yashin's trial was the first serious opportunity to publicly challenge the Kremlin's lies about its actions in Ukraine, but in reality the chances were limited. When the defence lawyers asked the prosecution whether they had questioned the military about the killing of civilians in Bucha, or indeed investigated for themselves what had happened there in order to determine whether the accused was telling the truth, the judge struck out the questions as inadmissible. Yashin then took over and addressed Prosecutor Belov from the 'aquarium', the glass cage he was locked inside for each hearing. The defence ministry spokesman had described Russian forces 'withdrawing' from Bucha, the politician pointed out, but the ministry itself claimed they were merely 'regrouping'. So was the spokesman spreading false information, Yashin wanted to know? 'The cell next to me is free.'

The 'fake news law' had been drawn up and approved at high speed as the authorities moved to quash any criticism of the 'Special Military Operation'. But its application was highly selective.

Pro-Putin figures had also begun openly criticising Russia's military, although they steered clear of Putin himself. The Chechen leader, Ramzan Kadyrov, whose forces were fighting in Ukraine, publicly accused Russian generals of incompetence as their troops ceded territory. So did Yevgeny Prigozhin, the thuggish ex-convict who ran the Wagner mercenary group that would later revolt and march on Moscow.

At a custody hearing five months after his own arrest, Yashin had accused the court of hypocrisy. He wanted the judge to explain why Kadyrov and Prigozhin were not in the dock beside him. 'What is it? Are your knees shaking? ... My only weapon is the word ... You are not afraid of words, but Kadyrov's throat-slitters and Prigozhin's bandits scare you.' He accused the court of acting as political servants of the Kremlin and allowing Russia's rulers to believe themselves all-powerful. 'That is what brought our country to this war, with its tens of thousands of victims.'

The prosecution's case against the young politician was built almost entirely on the blunt attestations of the Russian defence ministry. The argument went something like this: the ministry says its soldiers didn't kill civilians in Bucha and any photos or videos suggesting otherwise are fake. In any case, Russia abides by international humanitarian law, which does not allow the targeting of civilians. Ilya Yashin knows this and is therefore lying. And by the way, he's a tool of the West and he's working against us. Part of the charge was that Yashin's decision to contradict the official line was motivated by 'political hatred'.

The prosecution presented no actual proof of anything other than that Yashin was the author of the YouTube video in question. At one point, the prosecutor described him as having 'anti-Soviet' views, before quickly correcting himself to say Russian. He also accused the politician of taking the media of 'unfriendly' countries as his source, the same countries that were supplying weapons to Ukraine. 'Yashin is helping the enemy.' But because of Russia's insistence on maintaining the pretence of justice, the facade of a free trial, the charge sheet against Yashin included a word-by-word transcript of his YouTube stream on the civilian killings in Bucha. That meant detailed descriptions of the crimes that

Russian troops were accused of committing. At the final hearing, in her summing-up, the judge read all 3,281 of Yashin's words out loud. In rapid monotone she quoted him describing 'post-apocalyptic' scenes in Bucha. 'Dead bodies with open eyes, their hands tied behind their backs.' Then she read out his description of the basements where more dead were found with their hands bound, signs of torture and 'bullet holes to the back of the head'.

In his YouTube stream, Yashin had explained how Russia denied everything in Bucha. But it used to deny sending troops to seize Crimea, too; it still denies downing a Malaysia Airlines flight over eastern Ukraine in 2014 and trying to kill Alexei Navalny in 2020 with a nerve agent. The judge read all that out loud, too, followed by a premonition of Yashin's own fate. These were his own words from back in April 2022, before he was detained: 'I think we will soon hear of the arrest of people who speak out about the tragedy in the Kyiv region, in order to scare everyone else. They didn't pass those military censorship laws for nothing.'

Yashin's final speech was delivered in a chunky cream polo neck from inside the courtroom cage. 'I feel physically sick when I think how many people have died in this war. That is impossible to accept, so I don't regret a thing … It's better to spend ten years in prison than die of shame in silence for the blood your government is spilling.' From that court he addressed Putin directly, holding him responsible for the 'slaughter' in Ukraine. 'The words "death" and "destruction" are forever associated with your name.'

Yashin then blamed Putin for waging a parallel war on the Russian people, sending soldiers to their deaths, forcing hundreds of thousands of people into exile and destroying the economy. 'Stop this madness immediately,' he told Putin. 'Pull out the troops.'

His final words were saved for his supporters. He quoted Alexei Navalny, who had told those attending his own trial a year earlier that Russia would one day be free and happy. That was before the war, when tough times were measured on a different scale. Hearing Yashin urging his allies to smile and 'enjoy life' in defiance of the Kremlin struck an odd note. After all, beyond those in the courtroom, many Russians were having no trouble carrying on more or less as normal despite the invasion.

But it was because the situation was so dire that Yashin was appealing to his allies not to despair. 'I know how you feel tormented by a sense of powerlessness and helplessness, but you must not give up,' he told those there to witness first hand what their country did to dissenters. 'Be brave, don't give in to evil. Resist … There are more of us than it seems.'

As they were bundled out, leaving Yashin alone in his cage surrounded by bailiffs, the little crowd chanted his name in solidarity and defiance.

On 9 December 2022, Judge Oksana Goryunova sentenced Ilya Yashin to eight and a half years. The activist greeted the news with 'V' signs for victory, a reassuring smile and shout towards his friends. 'Don't worry, everything will be okay!' There was more in a note he passed on to them later, via his lawyers. 'Only the weak try to shut everyone's mouths and squeeze out all forms of dissent. I'm not afraid. Don't you be.'

That day, Vladimir Putin was attending a regional summit in Bishkek, and at the end, the pool of loyal reporters who cover the Kremlin were allowed to approach. One asked the president for his reaction to Yashin's sentence and Putin at first pretended not to know who he was talking about. It's his standard game with opposition figures. 'He's a blogger,' the journalist replied, diminishing Yashin himself to play along. Putin sighed, then reminded his audience that he once studied law at university. 'I consider meddling in the work of the courts absolutely unacceptable.'

Liquidating Memory

LONDON, DECEMBER 2021

The Foreign Ministry man who kicked me out of Russia told me blithely that I was making a fuss about nothing. He suggested I should carry on covering Russia from London, writing up reports from the news wires. My idea of journalism hell sounded like the Kremlin's ideal: neutered correspondents, far from the scene, unable to witness anything or challenge anyone. Since I'd left, I'd largely resisted reporting on Russia for that very reason. But in late 2021, the attempt to close down Russia's most respected human rights group, Memorial, was an exception.

I had to follow the Supreme Court hearings by live tweets at my attic desk in south London. As the sides began their closing statements, I was scouring pictures posted online of Memorial's supporters, lined up outside the courthouse in the bitter cold. I flicked from one social media feed to another, spotting familiar faces among those being detained by police the minute they unfurled protest banners. Then the judge announced a recess and I sat poised for the ruling to be announced.

Memorial has been recovering Russia's history for decades, scouring state archives and seeking out survivors to document Soviet-era repressions and create a database of the victims. One project that began in 2014 involved fixing metal plaques onto hundreds of houses and apartment blocks to mark the last known addresses of innocent people arrested and executed under Stalin's rule. There were several opposite our block of flats, little signs no bigger than a couple of credit cards. Each one was engraved with a name, date of birth and execution date. The idea was to jolt people into remembering or researching those people's stories and then to reflect on them each time they passed. Some residents would complain that their buildings were 'being turned into a cemetery'. Some plaques were even removed.

From 2013, when Memorial had been listed as a 'foreign agent', the harassment of the group itself came in various forms. In 2020 the head of its branch in Karelia, Yury Dmitriev, was charged with sexual abuse in a case Memorial is adamant was concocted to punish him. In 2021, OVD-Info, a spin-off organisation that gives legal advice and support to protesters, was also listed as a foreign agent. That same year, after I'd left, a nationalist mob stormed Memorial's headquarters in Moscow, where a crowd had gathered to watch *Mr Jones*, a film about the Holodomor, the terrible famine in 1930s Ukraine caused by Stalin's policies. With a TV crew in tow, those who'd broken in rushed on stage calling the audience fascists and yelling, 'Hands off our history.' They disappeared long before the police arrived to lock the office doors with handcuffs, detaining everyone inside until they had made statements.

The campaign against Memorial reached its climax that December. In court the prosecution argued that the historical memory and human-rights group was a 'public threat' and called for both its branches to be shut for good. The basis for such a severe penalty was Memorial's occasional failure to stamp its material with a 'foreign agent' health warning, including its vast database of the victims of political repression. Prosecutor Alexei Zhafyarov made the case for closure: 'International Memorial … is almost entirely focused on distorting historic memory, first and foremost about the Great Fatherland War. Why should we, the descendants of the victors, be ashamed and repent, rather than take pride in our glorious past? Memorial is probably paid by someone for that.' To the mind of a Russian state official, exposing uncomfortable truths was only conceivable as a hostile act, backed by an enemy power. The group's own lawyers argued that its work was actually good for the health of the nation. They called the case for liquidation 'Orwellian', but their efforts did no good. There were shouts of 'Shame!' as the decision to close Memorial was read out in court.

Under Vladimir Putin, Russia has looked to its history for affirmative stories. Tales of greatness to bolster its new assertiveness on the global stage. The Soviet victory over the Nazis in the Second World War is infinitely more suitable for that purpose than the other truth of secret courts, prison camps and firing squads. 'We talk about the difficult pages of the past and that annoys them,' Oleg Orlov, the veteran human rights defender told me by phone. In 2023 he would be arrested himself and charged with repeatedly 'discrediting' the Russian army.

As I waited for the verdict on Memorial, I called Alexei Nesterenko, the pensioner I'd come to know in Moscow through his own personal history of Stalin's purges. The group had helped Alexei track down the KGB file that confirmed his father's execution. Now the guardians of that history were under attack, and Alexei found it disgraceful. 'This is our shame. But the authorities prefer to talk only about the good things in the past, and Memorial prevents that. It won't allow Russia just to move on.'

Phone call with Alexei Nesterenko, son of a Soviet-era 'enemy of the people', 22 December 2021

ALEXEI: I heard you are not allowed back to Moscow. What a nightmare. Maybe it will all collapse at once? They'll stop persecuting Memorial and let you back in and that will make me happy!
SARAH: That's if there's no war ... [in Ukraine]
ALEXEI: Don't say that! It would be a catastrophe. But it would destroy those in power, and I think they probably still have the instinct for self-preservation. But of course, it's horrible.

The work of Memorial isn't pleasant for anyone: not for the researchers who uncover crimes against the innocent, or the families who finally learn what happened to their ancestors. It's certainly not welcomed by the FSB, whose predecessor agencies carried out those repressions and which now wants the names of those responsible to be made secret again. But Memorial's work for education and enlightenment, begun in the earliest days of glasnost, was about defending democracy itself. For many, its closure represented the end of an era of hope.

It was two months after Memorial was officially liquidated that the first Russian tanks rolled into Ukraine.

Diary entry, London, 7 October 2022

Called into the office in case Navalny or Svetlana Tikhanovskaya won the Nobel Peace Prize. Country predictions were right but not the recipients. It went to human-rights defenders and groups from Russia, Belarus and Ukraine. Russia's Memorial, Ales Bialiatski of Viasna in Belarus, in prison, and the Centre for Civil Liberties in Ukraine. Harsh backlash from Kyiv.

Tweet by Mihailo Podolyak, adviser to Zelensky: *Nobel Committee has an interesting understanding of word 'peace' if representatives of two countries that attacked a third one receive @NobelPrize together. Neither Russian nor Belarusian organizations were able to organize resistance to the war. This year's Nobel is 'awesome'.*

It reminds me of that evening in a Kyiv kitchen before the invasion: the man who'd insisted Russians were just playing at dissent, that they'd done nothing.

This afternoon I spent hours with Evgenia Kara-Murza, whose husband is facing twenty-four years in prison in Russia for his activism. 'Didn't we do enough? Didn't we try? Didn't we suffer?'

Maybe it's symbolic that the three countries are together for this prize, some hope for the future. The people are not their leader, after all, though it sometimes feels that way. In Russia and Belarus, Memorial and Viasna shine a light on repression. Ukraine is where that leads. We should have paid more attention.

Diary entry, London, early January 2023

New Year's Eve is the biggest holiday in both Russia and Ukraine. Moscow celebrated this one by launching dozens of cruise missiles across the border as a parade of sequined singers performed on Russian TV before celebrities and men in military uniform sipping champagne. A few days later we discovered that Ukrainian missiles had destroyed a college in the town of Makiivka that night, killing a large number of newly mobilised Russian soldiers.

For his New Year Address, Putin stood before a backdrop of military figures in khaki and claimed Russia was fighting to secure its 'true independence'. He blamed the West for provoking the war by trying to 'divide and weaken' Russia. It was a bingo card of his favourite claims and complaints.

On social media my Russian contacts split into two. On the one hand were people posting New Year wishes and photos of tables piled high with food. On the other were those now outside Russia, describing 2022 as the worst time of their lives because it was the year their country attacked their neighbour.

On Facebook, an opposition activist described greeting 2023 with neighbours in her yard in Moscow, drinking champagne 'for peace' before returning home to a banquet of goose and chocolate tart. An 'excellent celebration'. She and a few others had published an alternative New Year's address. One woman filmed herself outside and the wind drowned out every word. A man was just a talking head at the bottom of his screen. There were references to a 'difficult' year and the need for freedom, but no one mentioned the war directly. The clip ended with cheery tunes. Happy 2023. It was a sad showcase of what was left of the opposition inside Russia, still free. Had they gone much further, they might have been arrested.

Hostages

I have seen many innocent people locked in cages in Russian courts, but this time the man with all the TV cameras pointing at him through the bars was one of us. In March 2023 Evan Gershkovich was the first Western reporter to be charged with spying since the Cold War, and it was a frightening new turn. His newspaper, the *Wall Street Journal,* and the US government are clear that the accusation is false. But as I write this in Warsaw, many months after Evan's detention, the young American is still in the FSB's Lefortovo prison, awaiting trial.

I was working in Ukraine when Evan was arrested. The image of him being bundled into a car with a coat pulled over his head was chilling. He had been detained doing his work, reporting a story. I don't know Evan personally, but many of my friends and colleagues do, and I do know his work. When the Covid pandemic hit in 2020, Evan was writing for the local English-language newspaper, the *Moscow Times*, and he and his friend Pjotr Sauer kept the rest of our Moscow press pack on its toes. Both in their thirties, and in their first big jobs, they produced stories about the exhausted volunteer student doctors on the front line and the giant temporary hospitals running out of beds, and they picked apart the dubious death statistics. I was impressed.

Evan wasn't in Moscow when Putin launched all-out war. He'd recently got a new job at the *Wall Street Journal* and left the country to wait for his replacement accreditation from the foreign ministry. Then came the invasion and the immediate censorship that made independent journalism potentially dangerous. The BBC has maintained its presence in Moscow, but in early 2022 many foreign reporters left to assess the risk. Some then started to return, cautiously, on assignment. That summer Evan was one of them.

By phone from the Netherlands, where he's currently based, Pjotr told me his friend had wanted to report out of Russia for as long as he could. 'He understood he had this chance, this privilege. Russian journalists were scared to be there, because they were being prosecuted and arrested. But he said as long as he was protected by his accreditation, he needed to be there and telling the story.' Given my own expulsion as a 'security threat', I wondered about that confidence in the power of the little green card issued to foreign correspondents, but Pjotr thought Evan's assumption was still reasonable. 'That was our rationale. Journalists had been harassed, followed, kicked out – like you. But the worst we thought was that he would be stripped of his accreditation and told to leave the country. These absurd charges were unheard of.'

On the day he was detained, Evan was outside Moscow gathering material for a story about the Russian defence industry. Pjotr doesn't think his friend was particularly nervous. Like others in the press pack, he'd talked about being followed and felt 'a bit more watched' by the security services. It didn't seem overly sinister, given the circumstances. Then Evan failed to check in with his newspaper and his family. Pjotr got a call from his friend's father, to break the news. 'When you realise he's been arrested for espionage, your heart just sinks. You know this is very serious.'

Evan was in the most 'complicated story' of his life, to use the language of the espionage lawyer Ivan Pavlov. The FSB claimed that the reporter had been spying 'in the interests of the American government', gathering information about Russia's 'military defence complex'. It released no evidence and no details. It's quite possible someone didn't like the focus of Evan's reporting. The goal could have been to intimidate the whole foreign press pack, which was certainly the result: reporters who had returned to

Russia left again quickly, led by the Americans. But many people suspected that Russia simply wanted to grab another American prisoner like Paul Whelan, and negotiate a swap with its own high-profile detainees abroad.

Like other friends of Evan I've chatted to, Pjotr thinks there's little point speculating on why the journalist was taken. 'It's only guesswork why they targeted him, because it's obviously not because he was spying. The charge is too ridiculous to even contemplate or discuss.'

Evan wasn't only in Russia as an ambitious journalist, drawn as we all were to a land of often important and always fascinating stories. His parents are Jewish émigrés from Odesa and Leningrad who left the USSR in the late 1970s, and his job in Moscow was also a chance to explore his roots. 'He felt something click in Russia,' is how Pjotr put it, who also grew up there. 'But he didn't fetishise it. He had no illusions.' Like me, both reporters had questioned their relationship to the country as soon as the war started. Pjotr describes that as like having an identity crisis. 'If the country you identify with does something so horrible, of course you start questioning the friendships you've had, those who support the war. There's a lot of reassessing and thinking.' He says when Evan went back to Moscow they would discuss whether it was right for him even to go out for a beer in the evening anymore. 'These are questions you ask yourself when you live in a country that commits war crimes. Many Russians have the same questions.'

The only sign Pjotr and Evan's other friends now get of him is via video from a Moscow court. Every couple of months he's brought in by the FSB for a custody hearing. His captors have to ask permission to keep him in prison even longer. Evan doesn't speak, just smiles weakly at the cameras from his cage, presumably wary of antagonising his captors.

I'm not sure whether it's better or worse that he knows how these stories go. As a Moscow correspondent, he reported on the deal done in December 2022 to swap a US basketball star arrested in Moscow with cannabis vape cartridges for a notorious Russian arms dealer serving time in the US. That athlete, Brittney

Griner, had pleaded guilty and spent ten months in prison. Evan has already been locked up for longer. He also knows that Paul Whelan, charged like him with espionage, is serving a sixteen-year sentence in a Russian prison camp.

On the fifth anniversary of his arrest, Whelan called me from there and all the optimism I used to hear in his voice had gone. He told me he was doing his best to keep his spirits up, still singing all his four national anthems in the morning, but it was getting harder. As we spoke for over an hour, the one time his voice broke was when he talked about his dog, Flora, a beautiful golden retriever who died while he was locked up. He'd always thought he'd get home in time to see her again. After five years in a cold, overcrowded prison barrack, sewing clothes five days a week in a sweatshop and, recently, getting assaulted, Whelan had had enough.

Washington and Moscow had managed two prisoner exchanges in the past year, and both times Whelan was left behind. He told me he felt abandoned and called the swaps 'a serious betrayal'. The US State Department has talked of 'multiple proposals' to get him and Evan out, but so far they've failed. Now Whelan had a nagging fear that, even if there was another swap, he wouldn't be part of it. 'I'm extremely concerned that I'll get left behind again. I'm told that I'm top priority, but obviously I haven't been. They've just left me in the dust.'

Evan's friends have all mobilised to help him as negotiations continue. Mostly journalists, too, they know the grim drill: how to send parcels, get books to him, campaign in his support. A team collects letters for Evan from all over the world, which they then translate into Russian to get past the prison censors. One friend has a pile of books on a shelf in her Berlin living room that she and Evan are reading and discussing together.

Even as they fight for Evan's freedom, they are grappling with their dilemma as reporters. The pull of Russia, both country and story, is still strong. Reporting from afar is no substitute, especially now. But by locking up a Western journalist on such a serious charge, Russia has made it quite clear that no one is protected. It looks like it's collecting hostages.

Freedom Costs Dearly

APRIL 2022–APRIL 2023

'Here are my responses to your six questions … I hope we get to discuss them in more detail over a glass of wine ☺.' I smiled at the line from Vladimir Kara-Murza, writing to me from his prison cell. It was November 2022 and the opposition activist who had been poisoned twice had just been charged with treason for speaking out against the Ukraine war. He knew he was facing twenty-five years behind bars, but he still managed to sound cheerful. He signed off, in neatly written script: 'Thanks again and hope to see you soon! Vladimir.'

Nine months earlier, when Putin launched his war, Kara-Murza had been in the US for his daughter's birthday. He had a home there with his wife Evgenia and their three children. He also held a British passport, although that wasn't a fact he liked to stress with talk of external plots and enemies so rife. He could have stayed abroad. In Russia, opposition supporters were already fleeing the country but Kara-Murza was adamant about heading in the opposite direction. He had insisted on returning before, both after the poisoning that nearly killed him in 2015 and after a second attack in 2017. As a Russian politician, he believed he had to be in Moscow, not 'sitting safely somewhere else'. His wife had accepted that because to try to change it would be to change

Vladimir himself. Unable to stop him, her one act of protest was always to refuse to help pack his bags.

In April 2022, Evgenia decided to accompany her husband as far as France. She booked them a 'nest-like' apartment looking out towards the Eiffel Tower 'like a picture from a movie' and the pair spent a couple of days wandering the streets hand in hand, taking the Bateaux Mouches, visiting museums and talking non-stop. She was recalling all this some months later in a quiet London courtyard, during several hours spent over tea and cake. Petite, and with dark cropped hair, Evgenia had arrived to meet me listening to Russian opposition rap, which she said was like therapy. Her husband, she agreed, was more of a classical music type. As she spoke of their trip to Paris, their last hours together, her voice cracked a couple of times. 'When I thought back, I realised how I'd tried to make that trip beautiful at every step, because deep inside I think I knew what was coming.'

Evgenia had been scared for her husband ever since he first collapsed in Moscow in 2015 and fell into a coma. 'There is a horror that comes into your life and it doesn't leave,' is how she explained the feeling. 'I'm always afraid of getting that call from him. Or from someone else, because he's not able to talk anymore.' In 2022 the call had come from her husband's lawyer, Vadim Prokhorov, who had been keeping an eye on his friend since his return, tracking his phone around Moscow. On 11 April the signal led to a police station and then stopped. The lawyer had to call to tell Evgenia her husband had been arrested. The next day Kara-Murza was permitted to phone her himself. 'He just said, "Don't worry," and that was that.'

Since then, Evgenia had been thrust into the role of her husband's full-time champion. She would travel the world, speaking out about his arrest and about the 'murderous regime' of Putin, and calling for support for Ukraine to fight the 'hideous war' her country had started. She wanted to do it, felt she had to, but it was draining. 'Vladimir had to be in Russia to show that you should not be afraid in the face of that evil. And I deeply respect and admire him for that. But I could kill him.'

Kara-Murza was initially detained for fifteen days for the minor offence of disobeying police orders. Then the serious charges began raining down, as if the investigators had locked him up while they looked for something to pin on him. First they found a recording on YouTube from a speech to US lawmakers in Arizona in which Kara-Murza accused Russia of war crimes in Ukraine. He cited the use of cluster bombs in residential areas and the 'bombing of maternity hospitals and schools'. For telling the truth, he was charged under the 'fake news' law which carried a long prison sentence.

The indictment itself was full of 'fake news'. The investigators deemed Kara-Murza's statements about civilian targets and cluster bombs in Ukraine to be false because Russia's Defence Ministry does not permit 'the use of banned means ... of conducting war'. Contrary to all the evidence, they stated that Ukraine's civilian population was 'not a target'.

The investigators then added a second offence of co-operating with a banned, 'undesirable organisation' by speaking at an event in support of political prisoners. The indictment highlighted a reference Kara-Murza had made to Russia's repressive policies.

The treason charge was the last, and the worst.

Vladimir Kara-Murza and I began exchanging letters a couple of months after his arrest. His first reply came on a single, neatly handwritten sheet, sent from a pre-trial detention centre in Moscow. Written in Russian to pass the prison censors, it was photographed by them and then forwarded to my email inbox.

Letter from Vladimir Kara-Murza (extract), 16 June 2022

Hello Sarah!

I'm fine, or as fine as possible in my circumstances. I can't say I was surprised by my arrest. We all understand the risk of opposition activity in Russia. I have had it worse, twice. You know about that. But I couldn't stay silent in the face of what's happening. Silence is a form of complicity. And I considered it unacceptable to leave Russia. I didn't leave after the two poisonings, either. A politician must be in his own country. I didn't think I had the right to continue my political activity, to call other people to action, if I was sitting safely somewhere else. Yes, the price of not staying silent is high. As Boris Nemtsov said, 'Freedom costs dearly.' But the price of silence is unacceptable.

I'd known Kara-Murza by then for several years, often bumping into him at opposition events or human-rights gatherings and during election campaigns that I was covering. I could never keep up with who he was working for at any one time, but they included Khodorkovsky's Open Russia and the Boris Nemtsov Foundation. Highly intelligent and with impeccable English, Kara-Murza had always stood out from the usual Moscow opposition crowd. He wore a tweed jacket that added to his faintly old-fashioned, gentlemanly air, was softly spoken and extremely polite. In one of his prison letters, he told me a favourite way of relaxing before his arrest had been to sit in his yard at home and smoke an English briar pipe from his collection. 'I hope I get to add another one before too long.'

He was no Navalny, highly visible, with a crowd of young, tech-savvy acolytes around him. Kara-Murza was better known abroad than at home and made slightly clunky documentaries about dissidents, not TikTok videos. But he was a deep thinker, a powerful orator and he was passionate about fighting the authoritarian rule of Putin. At the end of that first letter, Kara-Murza had drawn a smiley face and added an appeal. *Pishite eshe!* Write again. So I did, and I gradually learned more about the modern-day Russian dissident and the kind of Russia he believed in.

Vladimir Putin saw the 1990s as a time of crime and chaos but for Vladimir Kara-Murza it was an era of hope and potential. 'These were the best and freest days in the modern history of Russia, when a people's dignity prevailed over the state machine. I will never forget them.'

After graduating from Cambridge, he returned to Russia hoping to launch a political career. But the 'grey man' from the security services was already tightening his grip on power. As Western academics and journalists, me included, pondered 'who is Mr Putin?', Kara-Murza says he had no doubts. 'When he reinstalled the memorial plaque to [ex-KGB boss] Yury Andropov on Lubyanka Square and returned the Stalin-era Soviet anthem, everything was clear.' Putin's moves against the free press, free elections and independent justice system then followed, 'dismantling everything that was created during our brief period of democracy'. History should have been Russia's best defence against tyranny. Had the 1990s brought a proper reckoning with Russia's totalitarian past, including official condemnation and full lustration, Kara-Murza believed it would have been unthinkable for a KGB man to make it to the presidency in the first place.

In one letter, the activist argued that a 'large part' of Russian society had enabled Putin at the start, settling for the economic improvements that came with a high oil price and ignoring their shrinking freedoms. Now many had fixed their blinkers and kept their heads down, telling themselves they were powerless to change anything, in any case. But Kara-Murza did not accept for a moment that Russia was doomed to autocracy. Nor did he believe its people were all brainwashed Putin devotees and pro-war, pointing to all the letters of support he was receiving from all over the country. Many openly opposed the invasion of Ukraine, even though they knew their details could be logged by the prison authorities.

As Ukraine came under attack, I sensed more support for the war among Russians than the optimistic Kara-Murza would allow. At one point, I found myself in the Kyiv-controlled part of the Donbas region texting with a friend in Moscow. His messages were so packed with propaganda I thought his account might have been hacked. He'd never been pro-Putin, never watched state TV, and I'd always thought him pretty indifferent to politics. Reading lines straight from Kremlin Central was hard as I sheltered in a hotel bathroom during an air raid. Perhaps this friend's talk of NATO and Nazis was the only way he could justify the unjustifiable, because I also sensed his confusion and shock.

Kara-Murza believed that many people didn't know about the war crimes their troops were committing because of the fierce censorship from the earliest days of the war. Those who did were mostly too scared to speak out. Occasionally, after a particularly awful missile strike, people would leave flowers at statues in Moscow of Ukrainian figures like the poet Taras Shevchenko. Kara-Murza argued that his own imprisonment, and the treatment of other dissenters, was an effective deterrent to more radical action. 'I don't know if there is one country on the face of this earth where many people would be willing to risk years in prison for speaking out. I don't think this would be a fair or realistic expectation.' It was a point I thought about often. In that sense, Kara-Murza countered that the number of Russians who had protested was remarkable. 'Each one makes me proud and each one gives hope for a better and freer future for our country.'

Since the invasion, some countries had been denying visas to Russians, closing borders and cancelling cultural events. Kara-Murza didn't agree with such collective punishment. His own close friend had been murdered for opposing Putin's regime, dozens of friends and colleagues were in jail, and he himself had been poisoned twice. Was he to blame for what Putin did, too? Or should Western politicians examine their own role, in continuing to do business with Putin long after his authoritarian ways were exposed? 'They ignored a fundamental maxim of Russian history, that internal repression is always accompanied by external aggression.'

Above all, Kara-Murza wanted to highlight those who did step up, the thousands detained after February 2022, mostly in the immediate aftermath of the invasion. 'I hope that the world hears these people. This is Russia too.' He would often cite the example of 1968, when seven dissidents were arrested and beaten for protesting on Red Square against the Soviet invasion of Czechoslovakia. Those people were seven reasons not to hate the entire Russian nation, Kara-Murza argued. 'Today, the world has thousands of reasons for that.'

For Kara-Murza, silence was not an option. Like his hero figures of 1968, he wanted a clean conscience. Those dissidents had believed their goal of freedom was impossible. But history gave Vladimir his source of hope. 'As we know now, their cause wasn't so hopeless after all.'

Kara-Murza had been in prison more than six months when prosecutors added the treason charge. Even for an optimist like him, the news was a severe blow. His lawyer told me the activist wasn't up to speaking for a while. 'He still needs to absorb things.' It was a grave step up from being labelled 'undesirable' or an enemy 'agent'. But Kara-Murza hadn't passed secrets to foreign powers: he was being prosecuted for his political views, voiced publicly at home and abroad. The only remotely similar case had been in the 1970s, when Alexander Solzhenitsyn was convicted of treason for exposing the horror of the Stalinist Gulag and forced into exile.

It's far easier to be found a traitor these days. The law was changed in 2012 when Putin returned to the presidency. It's now enough to offer 'consultancy' or 'assistance' to any foreign organisation that's considered a security threat. No secrets have to be divulged and the definitions are deliberately vague. Few made a fuss when the amendment was passed. In Kara-Murza's case, investigators maintained that he was working for the US-based Free Russia Foundation, which it classed as a security threat, and cited three speeches he'd given abroad. One of the speeches Kara-Murza was to be tried for described the persecution of political opponents. According to the charge sheet, his words risked damaging Russia's global reputation 'by presenting the country internationally as a state in which human rights are violated'.

When Kara-Murza made contact by letter again a short while later, he told me he was 'honoured' to be in the company of Solzhenitsyn, pointing out that the Nobel Laureate had eventually been exonerated. 'The real traitors are those who are destroying the wellbeing, reputation, and the future of our country for the sake of their personal power. Not those who are speaking out against it.' Kara-Murza the historian assured me that time would put everything in its place.

As he waited for trial, filling his own time with books, prayer and exercise, he admitted that 'some days are better than others'.

His investigators refused to let him speak to his wife or even his children by phone and the censors could hold up his letters for weeks. For a long time even his priest was denied visits. It was vindictive treatment and the source of much pain for a man who thought about his family 'every minute of every day'.

His lawyer, Vadim Prokhorov, was his one remaining connection with the outside world. The two had been friends for two decades since they'd joined Nemtsov's opposition party. But by phone from Moscow, Prokhorov was blunt with me about his friend's prospects. 'They tried to kill him twice but the *chekisty* were so cack-handed, they failed,' he said, referring to the security services. 'Now they're trying another way: locking him up for years for open public criticism of the actions of the regime, which is something we all have every right to, according to the constitution.'

For himself, he told me things were 'very turbulent', but for now the lawyers were being left alone. Then he paused. 'Mind you, Nemtsov wasn't getting any threats before they murdered him.' In September 2022 hundreds of thousands of Russians had fled the country after Putin announced a partial mobilisation for the war. Young men, including some perhaps who had supported the invasion as an abstract thing, now voted with their feet against actually fighting in it. Had those Russians stayed and protested instead, Prokhorov reflected, then perhaps things might have changed. For the lawyer himself, leaving wasn't an option then. Abandoning his clients ahead of their trials would be 'like a surgeon leaving an operating theatre'. Besides, as friends, he had to defend them however hopeless their cause. Kara-Murza described his lawyer as one of the strongest, most principled people he knew.

Prokhorov admitted it was increasingly lonely work, his friends all in prison or exile. 'The darkness is off the scale. The Soviet dissidents used to say that it's darkest before the dawn, but I want to know whether things will get even darker, or if this is the worst it will get.'

In April 2023 Vladimir Kara-Murza was convicted on all three charges and sentenced to twenty-five years in prison. When

I spoke to his wife, Evgenia, she was numb. She had no idea when she would see the love of her life again and couldn't travel to Russia to visit in case she was detained herself. She'd told me once that the only way to get her husband out of jail was for Putin's regime to collapse. 'So I have to do what I can to make this day happen sooner. To rescue Vladimir so he can continue his work.' She also had to stay strong for their children.

The trial was held behind closed doors, so that when Kara-Murza made his final address from a cage of bullet proof glass, his only audience in court were the prosecutors, investigators and judges. Their job was to punish Kara-Murza for his courage in speaking out, and to silence him. But they failed. The activist's supporters got hold of his speech and published the text online. More than a denunciation of one man's rule, it also conveyed Kara-Murza's dream of another Russia. The Russia of Boris Nemtsov, not of Putin. 'There is a different, freer and more hopeful vision. That of a modern, democratic country that would respect both the rights of its own people and the norms of civilised behaviour in the world.'

That vision is what had carried Vladimir Kara-Murza so far. It would be the faith he now had to cling to in the solitude of his prison cell.

Epilogue: The Ruins

JANUARY–MARCH 2024

Two years after I first heard bombs exploding in Ukraine, the sense of shock has receded into a kind of numbness. In Kyiv, where life seems normal until the air-raid siren sounds and another missile strikes, shops sell war-branded merchandise: khaki sweatshirts and even camo raincoats for dogs, printed with patriotic slogans. *Be brave like Ukrainians.* This country is now famous worldwide for its resilience, but the mood these days is overwhelmingly sombre. The gains on the battlefield are shrinking, there's retreat in some parts, and the rows of fresh graves are growing at the cemeteries. You see them as you drive through Ukraine: clusters of blue-and-yellow flags in every town and village, one for the grave of each soldier. A coffee shop called 'Idealist' has its own slogan printed on the window. *All we need is love – and victory.* I watch a man hobble by in military trousers and wonder whether he has a prosthetic leg. There are now so many amputees.

Outside Ukraine there's talk of fatigue with this war, as though it's actually costing something to those who utter the words. Hints that Zelensky should negotiate with Moscow have begun creeping into conversations and newspaper op-eds, as if Putin is somehow unbeatable. Pope Francis, who once suggested Russia had been 'provoked' into invading, has caused uproar by saying

Kyiv should consider raising the 'white flag'. He didn't call on Russia to pull back its troops. It's like people beyond Ukraine's borders – or at least beyond its neighbourhood – have forgotten the sheer horror they felt on 24 February 2022. That was partly a fear of what might follow the invasion of Ukraine; where Putin might go next. Over time the spectre of an expanded war, even possible nuclear attack, has faded. Instead, many people feel the fighting is far away from them, grinding on somewhere in eastern Ukraine. Not nice for those caught up in it, but nothing for the rest of us to worry about.

Ukrainians don't see it that way. In February 2024, after another Russian strike on Kharkiv, I found a family wandering among the ruins of their home. They'd escaped death by two minutes and about a hundred metres because they'd just stepped out of the building when the missile hit. Maryna saw the dark shape slam into her block of flats before she was thrown off her feet by the blast wave. Maybe the Russian soldiers who'd fired at the teenager's home told themselves they were fighting Ukrainian 'Nazis', like Putin had claimed. Perhaps they accepted another of his justifications for war, that NATO forces were an imminent threat on Russia's border. But in real-life Kharkiv they killed seven people in their beds that day, including a child. Most will have been Russian speakers like them. All lived in a five-storey *Khrushchevka* block of flats, identical to blocks all over the former USSR. The kind the soldiers' own families probably live in.

That's where Maryna and her mother Anastasia had returned to search for scraps of their lives before the big diggers scooped everything up with the crushed furniture and concrete. They'd already found a suitcase that survived intact with Anastasia's best evening dress inside and were joking about the advert they could write. *Made to withstand a Russian missile*. They'd also recovered Maryna's birth certificate, dirty and crumpled. Somehow her mother was still smiling. When I asked how she managed it, she hugged her daughter close. 'It's because we're here. We're alive!'

Anastasia wanted the world to see the destruction of her home and understand her country's suffering. She hoped people would realise that Ukrainians were not only protecting their own independence: she told me they were standing up to Russia so that no other country had to endure the pain of sending men to the front line, seeing their homes destroyed or fleeing their country as refugees. But Anastasia said Ukraine couldn't do it alone. 'We need the weapons to shoot down the missiles that attack our lovely, cosy homes.' Kharkiv, in north-eastern Ukraine, is so close to the Russian border that a missile aimed at the city will hit within seconds, usually before any warning can sound. But stuttering Western support, especially a freeze on military aid from the US, has left Ukraine dangerously short of air-defence systems, as well as forcing soldiers to ration their ammunition in the trenches.

The backdrop of diminishing aid, with fears of worse if Donald Trump returns to the White House, added to the grim mood in the run-up to an anniversary nobody wanted to mark. Two years earlier, I'd filmed men rushing to fight at the front as volunteers, and women making Molotov cocktails in the park. Now I was filming conscription officers out hunting for unwilling recruits as social media channels alerted local men on how to avoid the patrols. We followed a soldier who'd had his arm blown off near Bakhmut but had chosen to go on serving in the military as a recruitment officer. Pavlo told me the draft-dodgers made him angry, that they weren't patriots. But when I asked about his own friends at the front, he admitted that his entire company were either dead or had life-changing injuries like his. No wonder a friend in Kyiv told me her partner barely left their flat anymore, in case he was rounded up.

The slump in morale is one reason Zelensky decided to shake up his military command structure and sack the general who'd been in charge from the start. He wanted someone who would project positivity, not talk of 'stalemate' as General Zaluzhny had done. The day that news broke, I visited the presidential palace. Threading through the yards of nearby houses, past checkpoints and piles of sandbags, I emerged from a dark corridor into a room full of gold leaf and chandeliers. It was the first time I'd seen Zelensky up close since we'd taken a helicopter trip with him across Ukraine, visiting the front lines just before the full-scale invasion. He had been friendly and open then; now the man across the table was tetchy. Zelensky was struggling with the military's demands for more soldiers and the increasing reluctance of civilians to fight. The suggestion that he'd removed his top general because he was a potential political rival annoyed him intensely. His face lit up briefly when a team member passed a note to tell him a group of war prisoners had just been exchanged successfully, then slid back into a frown. Zelensky was as determined to fight as ever, still committed to the cause. But like Ukraine, he seemed exhausted.

Up in Kharkiv a woman wondered aloud how many more soldiers would give their lives battling for territory occupied since 2014. How many would die fighting for people who've long held Russian passports and consumed nothing but Russian propaganda from their televisions. Maybe Ukraine should just let them go, she ventured. Another woman told me she was forever being asked when she'd 'settle down'. But who was she supposed to marry, she wanted to know, when Ukraine's best men were being injured or killed. Such comments signalled a shifting mood, but there were others to counter them. A woman who'd just left the occupied south-east told me people there were still desperate to be liberated, still waiting for the Ukrainian military. And a mother I spoke to next to her son's grave was sure the soldiers had to go on fighting. She saw no choice. 'We're all afraid. But isn't it better to fight, than to give in and live enslaved by Russia?'

They call Kharkiv the unbreakable city, but large parts of it are in tatters. Even the hotel we used to stay at has a giant hole blown out of its side. The windows of a Nordic café opposite are boarded up, although inside it's as busy as ever. A waiter who was on shift the day of the attack admits he had trouble sleeping afterwards because whenever he closed his eyes he would hear the missile careering towards him. But he was struggling on. Adapting. Like Kharkiv itself, where children have begun going to school underground in classrooms built on the metro. Down there, they can safely ignore the wail of the air-raid sirens. Up above, old red-and-white trams still criss-cross the city with passengers in big hats and coats pressed against steamy windows. Many of the shop fronts they pass are covered with wooden sheets for protection, decorated with defiant poetry or paintings.

Just twenty-five miles from the border, Kharkiv was always a Russian-speaking city, but I've never heard more Ukrainian on its streets. One friend, who has family in Russia, told me everything changed on 24 February 2022. 'All I feel now is anger and hatred,' Natalia remembers. 'Now, when my relatives write, I just reply *Glory to Ukraine!* and that's it.' After a recent barrage of missiles killed eleven people, the mayor announced that Pushkin Street would be renamed after the Ukrainian philosopher Skovoroda. All over town, people take their Russian literature for recycling and send the money they raise from the paper to buy pick-up trucks for the army. By trying to destroy Ukraine's national identity, Putin has given it an enormous boost.

One night, I met Natalia in a packed bar. There was a karaoke side room, a band on stage at the back and a man wandering round in a wolf's head with flashing lights. Everyone was doing their best to ignore the war beyond those walls. Before long the air-raid alarm on my phone vibrated. Ballistic missile threat. I looked around. No one was moving from the dance floor or from their seats.

On 16 February 2024, the Russian opposition activist Alexei Navalny died suddenly in prison. In a stark statement, the Prison Service said that 'convict Navalny' had 'felt unwell' and collapsed after a walk in his Arctic penal colony. Doctors had been unable to revive him. For those Russians who wanted political change, it felt like the death of hope. They were desolate.

In Warsaw, as I took in the news, my own mind jumped back nine years to the moment in Moscow when I'd heard that Boris Nemtsov had been shot beside the Kremlin. That killing had caught me utterly off-guard. I felt it like a punch. Now my biggest realisation was that Navalny's death was not a shock. Russia had grown so much darker since Nemtsov's murder that nothing seemed impossible any longer.

Navalny had known the risks. He returned to Moscow after a near-fatal poisoning, fully aware that he'd be arrested.

That seemed foolhardy to some, but to Navalny it was an act of conscience. 'If your beliefs are worth something, you have to be ready to stand up for them and to make some sacrifices,' he explained later, adding that he refused to give Putin 'the gift' of staying away. Just a day before his death in custody was announced, Navalny had appeared via video link from prison for a court hearing, joking as usual. His persistent cheerfulness was itself an act of resistance.

On the day Navalny died, the veteran activist from Memorial human rights group, Oleg Orlov, went on trial in Moscow accused of 'discrediting the military'. The charge was based on an article in which he described Putin's Russia as a fascist regime. If Putin were to win in Ukraine, Orlov argued, a fascist Russia would be a serious threat to all Europe. The activist had already been convicted for expressing those views, and fined, but the prosecutor deemed the sentence too soft and the case was sent for a retrial.

In his final speech in court, Orlov underlined the link between the death of Navalny, the stifling of dissent and the invasion of Ukraine. Putin's aggression abroad was the logical culmination of his repression at home, the activist told the court, before addressing the judge and prosecutors directly with a warning. 'Do you not see the obvious truth? Sooner or later, the repressive machine will roll over those who launched it and who drive it on.' He told them their descendants would be ashamed of them. 'The same will go for those now committing crimes in Ukraine under orders.' It was a damning indictment from a man who'd devoted his life to documenting Soviet-era political persecution. Orlov was sentenced to two and a half years.

Navalny himself had refused to be silenced, even behind bars. He managed to get regular messages out via his lawyer, which his team then shared online. He would also make formal complaints about his harsh treatment so that he was granted a court hearing, and then use that as a political platform. As a result, his team calculated that he'd spent at least a third of his time in a punishment cell, held in isolation in a tiny space where he was deprived even of paper, books or family photographs.

Russia's external intelligence chief has said the activist died of natural causes and the same is written on his death certificate. But it took nine days before the authorities would release Navalny's body to his mother for burial and there was no chance of an independent autopsy. His allies are convinced that he was killed. As I write this, we have no evidence of that. But we do know that Navalny was persecuted for years because of his opposition politics. We know that in 2020 a Novichok nerve agent was smeared on his underpants, to poison him. When he survived, he was convicted of 'extremism' to stop his peaceful campaign for democratic change. Ultimately, Navalny died in prison because he wanted what his supporters always chanted. *Rossiya bez Putina*. A Russia without Putin.

On the day his death was announced, top international politicians and experts were in Munich for the annual security conference. In 2007 Vladimir Putin had made a charged speech at the same event, which questioned a world of 'one master, one sovereign' imposing its will on the rest. He was angry at the US-led invasion of Iraq, at NATO expansion to the east and what he saw as political meddling in Moscow's back yard. That day, a slim-faced, youthful Putin set down his challenge to US dominance. He made clear that Russia was reasserting itself.

In 2024 Putin wasn't invited to Munich: his 'reassertion' had led to the invasion of Ukraine. But Navalny's wife, Yulia, was at the conference. A few hours after learning of her husband's death, she stepped out onto the platform where Putin had once stood and demanded that he be held personally responsible 'for what he has done to my country, my family and my husband'. Yulia Navalnaya had always been her husband's rock and his muse, at his side and in the shadows. Now she was forced to take centre stage, alone. Her raw grief made her short speech desperately painful to watch. Holding back tears, her lower lip shaking, Navalnaya said she didn't know yet whether to believe the 'terrible news' from Russia. But if it was true, she appealed to the world via Munich, then 'we have to come together and defeat this evil'.

Inside Russia, crowds began laying flowers in her husband's memory. Navalny was not universally liked among the liberal opposition: some couldn't get past his early dalliance with Russian nationalism, others criticised his initial equivocation on the status of Crimea, which got him forever damned as a Russian imperialist by Ukrainians. But Navalny's politics evolved over time, and what he represented above all was the possibility of change. The right for Russians to choose who leads them, in a truly open democratic race.

That's what they were mourning as they brought flowers, laying them at monuments to the victims of political repression in Soviet times. In Moscow, the Solovetsky stone became one focal point, installed by Memorial in the early 1990s when there was hope that the days of people being imprisoned and killed for their politics had passed. The symbolism of the crowd's choice of shrine was powerful. There was no outburst of angry protest, just this quiet act of defiance. Even so, hundreds were arrested and each evening, men with their hoods raised to hide their faces moved in to clear away the flowers, the notes and the photographs. Such open opposition to Putin, just weeks before his re-election in March, was intolerable.

Soon after Navalny's death, his team revealed that there had been negotiations under way for a prisoner swap. After the full-scale invasion of Ukraine, their fears for his life behind bars had soared. They said the deal would have meant exchanging Navalny together with two Americans, believed to be Evan Gershkovich and Paul Whelan. In return, Russia was to get back a convicted FSB hitman from Germany who Putin had described as a 'patriot'. Now that Navalny is dead, Whelan's family tell me there has been 'no forward movement towards Paul's freedom'. As I write, Evan has already spent more than a year in custody.

Vladimir Kara-Murza also remains a prisoner, though I am not sure my letters are reaching him anymore. He's spending much of his time in punishment conditions, but from what I can tell, his resolve is as strong as ever. A few days after Navalny's death, Kara-Murza appeared on a video link to a Moscow court for an appeal hearing and used the chance to urge Russians not to fall into despair. His voice firm, he insisted that change in Russia was inevitable. 'No one can stop the future.' Kara-Murza's wife, Evgenia, told me she had watched that short video of him in prison uniform 'a thousand times' and remains proud of him 'for staying true to himself despite this hell'. But she is deeply worried. Her husband's health is deteriorating as the nerve damage caused by his poisoning spreads to his right side. 'It's a serious condition that could lead to paralysis.'

When I asked Evgenia where she found her own faith in the future, in the dismal conditions of today, she talked of the final years of the USSR and the protests that erupted then, seemingly from nowhere. But if Navalny's death hadn't done it, I wasn't sure what might trigger such protest. In the early months of the Ukraine war, I saw a refrigerated train carriage full of dead Russian soldiers and wondered then whether the growing number of casualties might one day destroy any popular support for the war, perhaps even for Putin. I wondered whether grief and anger might overcome fear, and the men's wives and mothers become a political force. It had happened before, during the Chechen wars, but this time there's been little sign of that. The rows of Russian soldiers' graves are growing, though, and so is the number of draft-dodgers and deserters. 'We need to do everything possible to be ready for the moment when the regime shows cracks. For when we get that chance,' Evgenia Kara-Murza told me.

Alexei Navalny's chance of leading such change has gone forever. Two weeks after his death, his team couldn't find a hall that would agree to host his coffin and allow people to file past the body as is Russian tradition. They struggled even to persuade a funeral company to provide a hearse. But they eventually got a church in the suburb where Navalny had lived and I found myself watching images of the politician, always so vibrant, now pale and still in an open coffin. For almost the first time I could recall, his wife was not beside him. Yulia Navalnaya was forced to watch her husband's last rites from abroad with their children, unable to travel to her own country for fear of being arrested as an 'extremist'.

Three weeks later, real extremists would carry out a terror attack on a Moscow concert hall, killing more than 130 people. The so-called Islamic State group said it was behind the mass shooting, the worst act of terrorism in Russia since the school siege in Beslan. But Putin claimed the real masterminds were in Ukraine and the suspects, clearly tortured, eventually said the same. The truth made him look weak and Russia vulnerable. Instead, he used the attack as a pretext to hurl more missiles at Ukraine.

But if there is a glimmer of hope for a free Russia – a hope for Ukraine, for Russia's neighbours and all beyond – perhaps it is in the images from Moscow of Navalny's funeral. Many thousands of mourners battled their own fear of the police to say a final goodbye. Not hundreds of thousands, not even tens of thousands, but they came. Outside the church, they chanted Navalny's name, 'No to war' and 'Russia will be free'. That day, and over the days that followed, the pile of flowers heaped on Navalny's grave grew so high that it covered the Orthodox cross marking the plot.

Since I was expelled, I've often been asked about my feelings for Russia. Someone will remind me of my tears in the airport deportation zone and assume that I'm yearning to return, if only the authorities would allow me in. Journalistically, the lure of the story will always be strong, of course. That's why some Moscow correspondents who left of their own accord have begun to trickle back. For now, the Kremlin seems confident enough to have them, as it makes gains in Ukraine and the economy holds up against international sanctions. No doubt the journalists tell themselves comforting stories about why they should be safe, but there are no guarantees. The rules of the game were made clear when Evan Gershkovich was arrested and they haven't changed.

But reporting the story is only one aspect of my relationship with Russia, which began years before I ever picked up a microphone. I used to feel at home in Moscow. In February 2022 that changed abruptly. Despite all the years I spent there, and all I've invested in the place, I no longer feel any nostalgia. I've said goodbye to Russia, for now. At least to Putin's Russia. Because after almost a quarter of a century with him in charge, there is little left that does not seem tainted.

I do hope there will be another Russia one day. A country that is comfortable enough in its own skin to leave others in peace. One in which the likes of Vladimir Kara-Murza, Ilya Yashin and Anastasia Shevchenko can all play a meaningful role. Where the journalists of Dozhd and other media can report freely and where Memorial might examine not only the crimes of the Stalin era, but those being committed today by Russia in Ukraine and against the Russian people. I would like to return one day to the country that Anna Politkovskaya, Boris Nemtsov and Alexei Navalny all dreamed of. But that is a Russia they will never get to see and one that I now find harder than ever to imagine.

Bibliography

Applebaum, Anne, *Twilight of Democracy: The Failure of Politics and the Parting of Friends* (London: Penguin, 2021 edn)

Ash, Timothy Garton, *Homelands: A Personal History of Europe* (London: Vintage, 2024 edn)

Belton, Catherine, *Putin's People: How the KGB Took Back Russia and Then Took on the West* (London: William Collins, 2021 edn)

Colton, Timothy J., *Moscow: Governing the Socialist Metropolis* (Cambridge, Massachusetts: Belknap Harvard, 1995)

Gessen, Masha, *The Man Without a Face: The Unlikely Rise of Vladimir Putin* (London: Granta, 2023 edn)

Harding, Andrew, *A Small, Stubborn Town: Life, Death and Defiance in Ukraine* (London: Ithaka, 2023)

Harding, Luke, *A Very Expensive Poison: The Definitive Story of the Murder of Litvinenko and Russia's War with the West* (London: Guardian Books, 2017 edn)

Kurkov, Andrey, *Diary of an Invasion* (London and Sydney: Mountain Leopard Press, 2022)

Miller, Christopher, *The War Came to Us: Life and Death in Ukraine* (London: Bloomsbury, 2023)

Nemtsov, Boris, *Ispoved' Buntarya [Confessions of a Rebel]* (Moscow: Partizan, 2007)

Nemtsova, Zhanna, *Doch' Svoego Otsa [Her Father's Daughter]*, (Moscow: Bombora, 2022)

Ostrovsky, Arkady, *The Invention of Russia: The Journey from Gorbachev's Freedom to Putin's War* (London: Atlantic, 2018 edn)

Plokhy, Serhii, *The Russo-Ukrainian War* (London: Allen Lane, 2023)

Politkovskaya, Anna, *Putin's Russia* (London: The Harvill Press, 2004)
—*A Russian Diary* (London: Harvill Secker, 2007)
Pomerantsev, Peter, *Nothing is True and Everything is Possible: Adventures in Modern Russia* (London: Faber & Faber, 2015)
Putin, Vladimir, *First Person* (London: Hutchinson, 2000)
Shuster, Simon, *The Showman: The Inside Story of the Invasion that Shook the World and Made a Leader of Volodymyr Zelensky* (London: William Collins, 2024)
Snyder, Timothy, *The Road to Unfreedom: Russia, Europe, America* (London: Vintage, 2019 edn)
Walker, Shaun, *The Long Hangover: Putin's New Russia and the Ghosts of the Past* (New York: Oxford University Press, 2018)
Yaffa, Joshua, *Between Two Fires: Truth, Ambition and Compromise in Putin's Russia* (London: Granta, 2020)
Zelensky, Volodymyr, *A Message from Ukraine* (London: Hutchinson Heinemann, 2022)
Zygar, Mikhail, *All the Kremlin's Men: Inside the Court of Vladimir Putin* (New York: Public Affairs, 2016)

Acknowledgements

I have many people to thank for making this book possible. Journalism is always a team effort and every story I have told on these pages is the combined work of so many people that it will be difficult to mention them all, but I will do my best.

Firstly I want to thank all those who have shared their stories over the years. Being a journalist can sometimes feel intrusive, but even in the most difficult moments of their lives, I meet people who trust us to listen to them and want us to make sure they are heard. I hope they feel I have represented them fairly and I am grateful to them all.

In Russia, I would like to thank everyone in the Moscow bureau over the years, starting with Sara Beck and Kevin Bishop, who gave me my first break. I am especially grateful to my friend and first producer Dasha Merkusheva who I worked with side by side all over Russia and the ex-USSR, most memorably in Beslan; to Liza Shuvalova for her wisdom and guidance, to Liza Vereykina for her creativity, and to Emma Wells, whose calm, charm and chocolate brownies are legendary. Thanks to Will, especially for his help as I was expelled, dealing with all the practicalities of a hasty departure mid-pandemic and with a dog.

In Ukraine, I want to make special mention of my team in those first, uncertain and frightening days of the full-scale invasion we so hoped would never happen. Tony Brown, Jon Hughes and Daria Tsipigna are all brilliant, and I couldn't have been with better people at such a time. Thank you, too, to our support teams in Ukraine for getting us to stories and helping to keep us safe. Sasha, in particular, is a rock. I later worked alongside many fabulous Ukrainian journalists, especially Mariana Matveichuk, Hanna Chornous and Kyiv bureau producers Anastasia and Hanna. I am particularly thankful to Matthew Goddard, whose beautiful pictures in Ukraine, Russia – and now across central and Eastern Europe – bring to life the stories I try to tell. A few months after the start of the full-scale invasion, he was also refused re-entry to Russia, labelled a 'security threat'.

This book is largely based on my on-the-ground reporting, combined with interviews recorded specially for these pages. However, for the chapters about Vladimir Kara-Murza I am grateful to the archivist at Trinity Hall, Cambridge, Alexandra Browne, to Sheila Hunter and to Vladimir's former teachers and fellow students for their memories, including Dr Clare Jackson, Professor Peter Clarke and Hubertus Jahn.

For the section on Russian studies in the UK I would like to thank Genny Silvanus, archivist at Christ's College, Cambridge.

I am grateful to Mr Criddle's brother, John, who was so generous with his memories of Jem, as he knew him, and told me many more amusing stories than I could ultimately include here. I am sorry that John died before this was published and I hope he would have enjoyed it. I would also like to thank Anthony Criddle, Mr Criddle's friends and former colleagues at Worcester Sixth Form College and Lisa Conner at Merchant Taylors' for digging out Jeremy Criddle's alumnus record and finally revealing the mystery of where my teacher learned his Russian. Sadly, Mr Criddle himself died when I was still living in Moscow, so I was unable to grill him in person about his past. I owe him a lot.

I would also like to thank fellow former students of Mr Criddle, especially Eleanor. I regret that our deep research into Bon Jovi hits of the late 1980s was cut from the final edit.

For the section on my later Russian studies, I thank the Fitzwilliam College archive for digging out the application form where I boldly declared that my future career plans were UNKNOWN. I also thank Professor Anthony Cross, who not only gave me a place at Cambridge despite my patent ignorance but has been a source of support and kindness ever since. His memories of Russian study were a great help.

I would like to thank Martin, my old boss at the Shamrock, both for the job then and the memories now. The other chapters covering my time in Russia in the early 1990s and travels around the former USSR are partly based on my own diaries and letters. But I couldn't have written these sections without the infinitely more eloquent diary of my then roommate, Mishal Husain. I also consulted the letters, photographs and memories of fellow Russian student Lucy Brown, and the photographic memory and personal archive of Christophe Peters, who was writing to his own parents about Russian politics when I was busy asking mine for cheese sauce mix and chocolate. I would also like to thank Christophe for proofreading my manuscript with a microscopic eye for detail. Thanks, too, to Dan and Dominika, for their huge hearts and their help for Ukrainians since the start of this war, and to Sandy and Jon for their generosity in supporting Nika, who I hope can return to Kharkiv one day soon. She and Natalia have infected me with their enthusiasm for a great city.

Over the years I have had many conversations with Paul Whelan. I never thought he would still be locked up, and still calling, so long after his arrest one cold New Year in Moscow, and I am grateful for his time and his thoughts. I would also like to thank Paul's brother, David, and sister, Elizabeth, who both shared so much, especially when Paul was first arrested. For all the family, I hope this ordeal is over very soon.

For my writing about Vladimir Kara-Murza, I am indebted to Evgenia for her time, her memories and her thoughts. She is no less impressive than her husband, and I am in awe of her strength as she fights to remind people not only of what has happened to him, but of what Russia under Vladimir Putin is doing to Ukraine. Many Russian activists are so focused on their own battle to change their country, they forget the suffering in Ukraine. Vladimir and Evgenia never have.

She once asked me when this book would be published, so that she could put a copy in Vladimir's office for him to read when he is free and back home. I would love to think that will happen soon and can only hope that I have done justice to an extraordinary man on these pages.

I would like to thank my agent, Matthew Hamilton, and my editor Ian Marshall for believing in this story from the start and encouraging me that I could write it. Thanks to all the team at Bloomsbury for getting me this far. At the BBC, I thank Kevin Silverton for his proofreading and I am grateful to Andrew Roy, Paul Danahar, Jonathan Munro and Tim Davie for their solidarity and support when I was expelled, and their vision for my new role, based in Warsaw.

As the strain of writing a book on top of my day job and the stress of reporting on a ruinous war sometimes felt impossible, Smudge's hugs have helped enormously. I must also thank my family: Ellie and Chris, my brothers Jonathan and Daniel for all their help and friendship. Thanks to Triona and especially to my Mum and Dad for their love and encouragement over the years. Mum died suddenly before I even graduated, but I hope she approves of what I did next.

I couldn't have done any of it without Kes. I want to thank him most of all for being there for me. For listening, for distracting, for advising. For allowing me to disappear off to Russia in the first place and then for abandoning everything he knew to join me. More recently, for letting me leave him and travel to Ukraine. He cares deeply about the topic of this book, too. A great writer, thinker and brilliant editor, and my best friend. Thank you.

Index

Afghanistan 46, 166, 196–7, 241, 276
Amelina, Victoria 149
Andriivka, Ukraine 307–8
Andropov, Yury 99, 329
Androshchuk, Yulia 76–7
'Anna' 291–303
Archangelsk: stranded seals 164

Baulina, Oksana 184
BBC 36, 164, 172, 201
  and the author 5, 84, 116, 129, 153, 163, 196, 197–8, 202, 223, 279–80, 303
  and Beslan school siege (2004) 170–71, 174
  and expulsions of journalists from Russia 63, 137, 279
  after invasion of Ukraine 188, 308, 322
  Monitoring 187
  Moscow bureau 162–3, 276–7, 280
  Russian Service 153, 201
  and World Cup (2018) 199–202
Belarus 2, 28, 35–6, 37, 40, 65, 319
  protests (2020) 250, 284
  Viasna (human rights organization) 319
Bellingcat (investigative collective) 90
Belov, Prosecutor Alexander 310
Berg, Frode 216
Beslan, North Ossetia 170, 171
  siege of School No. 1 (2004) 84, 169–71, 172–7
Bialiatski, Ales 319
Biden, President Joe 1, 216–17
Blokhin, Vasily 95
Bolvinov, Serhiy 146–7
Bonner, Elena 89, 203
Britannia, HMS 131, 132
Bucha, Ukraine 7, 27–32, 188, 271, 307, 308, 310, 311–12
Bush, President George W. 164

Cheburashka 210, 304
Chechnya/Chechens 166–7
  and Beslan school siege (2004) 84, 169–71, 172–6
  first war (1994) 16, 161–2, 167, 185, 241
  human rights abuses 36
  and Boris Nemtsov's murder 20–21, 22–4
  and *Nord-Ost* theatre siege (2002) 171–2
  and Putin (2003–4) 161, 167, 170, 185
  second war (1999) 161, 166–8
  see also Kadyrov, Ramzan
Clinton, President Bill 156
Committee Against Torture 255–6, 258
Covid epidemic 65, 114, 208, 224, 244, 276, 279, 285, 301, 302, 321
Criddle, Jeremy 47, 48
Crimea 37, 44, 49, 166, 181, 212, 234, 248, 342
  annexation of (2014) 6, 7, 13, 17, 18, 30, 133, 312
Cross, Professor Anthony 121–2

Dadayev, Zaur 20, 21, 22, 24
Dadin, Ildar 276
Defender, HMS 37
Dmitriev, Yury 316
Dnipro, Ukraine 71, 107–9, 179–80, 182
Donbas region, Ukraine 3, 6, 8, 13, 148, 180, 182, 271, 297, 329
Donetsk 'republic' (DNR) 2, 3–4, 7, 148
Dorenko, Sergei 158, 185
Dozhd TV 277–9, 345
Durytska, Anna 13, 14, 19, 20
Dzerzhinsky, Felix 80
  statues 80, 81, 85
Dzyadko, Tikhon 277–8, 279

Ekho Moskvy radio 13, 15, 221–2, 296
Elizabeth II 131, 132
Elkin, Sergei 304
European Court of Human Rights (ECHR) 176

Fadeeva, Ksenia 286
Fatyanova, Irina 285, 286–7, 288

FBK (Anti-Corruption Foundation) 278, 285
Federal Security Service (FSB) 128, 318
    and author's expulsion from Russia (2021)
        38–9, 116, 117, 138, 221–2
    arrest of Evan Gershkovich 321, 322, 323
    doping scheme at Sochi Olympics
        (2014) 223
    headquarters 79, 81, 95, 210
    and Vladimir Kara-Murza 90
    Lefortovo prison 206, 215, 321
    and Alexei Navalny 90
    and Boris Nemtsov 90
    and Putin 5, 129
    and Ivan Safronov 219–20
    and Paul Whelan 205–9, 210, 211, 212–14,
        215–16, 217–18
Fitzwilliam College, Cambridge
    University 121–2
Francis, Pope 335–6
FSB *see* Federal Security Service

Gaidar, Yegor 55
Geremeev, Ruslan 22, 23–4
Gershkovich, Evan 6, 321–4, 342, 344
Goddard, Matthew 189, 200, 279–80
Golubeva, Vera 97–8
Gorbachev, Mikhail 44, 47, 49, 55, 80, 85,
    135, 203
Gorinov, Alexei 309
Gorky *see* Nizhny Novgorod
Goryunova, Judge Oksana 313
Griner, Brittney 323–4
Grozny, Chechnya 166–7
GRU (military intelligence agency) 115
Gubashev, Anzor 20–21, 22
Gubashev, Shahid 20–21
Gubasheva, Zulay 20–21, 22
Gubin, Evgeny 256
Gudkov, Dmitry 25

Harding, Luke 195–6
Hasselhoff, David 123
Healy, Martin 126, 128–9, 130
Hill, Elizabeth 122
Hitler, Adolf 95
Holodomor, the 316
Hurd, Douglas 132
Husain, Mishal 49, 54, 55, 197–8

ICC *see* International Criminal Court
Ihnatenko, Olena 149
IK-17 prison, Mordovia region, Russia 209,
    210, 214, 215–17
Ingushetia, republic of 20, 166
International Criminal Court
    (ICC) 229–30, 233
Investigative Committee 248, 259–60
Iosilevich, Mikhail ('Flying Spaghetti
    Monster') 255, 257, 259, 262
Iraq 166, 209, 214
    invasion of (2003) 341

Islamic State group/ISIS 248, 276, 343–4
Izyum, Ukraine 145, 146, 147–8, 149

Jehovah's Witnesses 286
Joint Services School for Linguists (JSSL)
    47–8, 122, 133
Jones, Tom 6
JSSL *see* Joint Services School for Linguists

Kadyrov, Ahmad 167, 189
Kadyrov, Ramzan 20, 22, 23, 88, 167, 189–90,
    304, 311
Kalanta, Romas 258
Kara-Murza, Evgenia 83, 84–5, 86, 88, 89,
    319, 325–6, 332, 333, 342–3
Kara-Murza, Vladimir (father) 83–4, 85
Kara-Murza, Vladimir (son) x, 8, 19, 83–91,
    242, 325–33, 342–3, 345
Karelia 163, 316
Kasyanov, Mikhail 88, 89, 201, 202
Kazbek (Beslan parent) 170–71, 176–7
    and his children Alain and Jaqueline
        170, 177
KGB 93, 94, 99, 203, 210, 317
    headquarters 44, 80, 85
    and Putin 16, 222, 270, 279, 329
    in Vilnius 258
Kharkiv (and region), Ukraine 143, 146, 147,
    297, 336–7, 338–9
    the dead of Izyum 145–6, 147–9
    forensics laboratory 148
    Forest Motel 105
Khodorkovsky, Mikhail 57–8, 87–8,
    238, 328
Khrushchev, Nikita 7
Kolesnikov, Captain Dmitry 154, 155
Konon, Daniil 249–50
Kostroma, Russia: election (2015) 99–103
Kostroma Gay Pravda 100
Koza.Press 255, 257, 259
Kramatorsk, Ukraine 1, 3, 4, 149
Krasovsky, Anton 186
Kraynyuk, Sasha 229, 230–34
Kraynyuk, Tetyana 229, 230–34
Kupyansk, Ukraine 233–4
    Special School 229, 230–31, 234
Kursk nuclear submarine 153, 154–9, 185
Kyiv, Ukraine 28, 32, 71, 73, 75, 77, 184, 226,
    307, 337
    pre-invasion (2022) 1, 2, 3, 8, 71, 187,
        319, 335
    protests (2013-2014; the Maidan) 185–6,
        237
    war crimes trial (2022) 265–7

Lavrov, Sergei 114, 197
Lefortovo prison, Moscow 206, 215, 321
Lenin, V. I. 50, 53
    statues 61, 80, 81, 202
LGBT rights 199, 200
Lineker, Gary 199

INDEX

Lithuania
  Navalny's team headquarters 287
  see also Vilnius
Luhansk 'republic' (LNR) 2, 3–4, 7, 148,
  232, 233
Lukashenko, Alexander 35–6, 65, 138, 304
Lvova-Belova, Maria 233

Magnitsky, Sergei 18
Magnitsky Act (2012) 17–18, 87, 89, 90
Major, John 25
Malaysia Airlines Flight MH17 (2014) 312
Maltisov, Ivan 266–7
Mariupol, Ukraine 2, 182, 233
Maskhadov, Aslan 173
Matveichuk, Mariana 73
Medvedev, Dmitry 17
Memorial (organisation) 79–80, 81–2, 93, 95,
  96, 315–18, 319, 342, 345
Merkel, Angela 283
Merkusheva, Dariya 166–7, 174
Milashina, Elena 190
Moscow 43–6, 48–50, 90, 121, 122, 127, 153,
  163, 166, 198, 275, 291–2, 295–7, 301,
  303, 344
  BBC bureau 162–3, 276–7, 280, 322
  British Embassy 131–2
  Central House of Artists 80
  Christ the Saviour Cathedral 61, 62, 166
  Crocus City Hall attack (2024) 343–4
  Defence Ministry 28, 76, 219, 266,
    293, 327
  Donskoy Monastery 95–6
  Dozhd (TV channel) 277–9, 345
  Elizabeth II's visit (1994) 131, 132
  Foreign Ministry 35, 37, 64, 65, 67, 113–17,
    137, 139, 195, 221, 251, 280, 315
  Gorky Park 49, 293
  Gorky Street 45
  GUM shopping arcade 14, 19, 20, 205
  Guria (restaurant) 47
  Irish citizens 127
  Komsomolsky Prospekt 46
  Lefortovo prison 206, 215, 321
  McDonald's 47
  and Memorial 95, 316–17
  Metropol Hotel 205, 213
  Moskva (swimming pool) 61–2
  Muzeon 81
  Alexei Navalny's return and
    funeral 283–4, 285, 339–40, 344
  Boris Nemtsov's murder and
    funeral 13–15, 18–19, 22, 25–6,
    303, 339
  Nord-Ost theatre siege (2002) 171–2
  organized crime 57–60
  Pizza Huts 47
  protests: 1991 85;
  1992 53, 54–5;
  2011 17;
  2014 15–16;
  2015 24–5;
  2019 236, 247–50;
  2021 284–5, 288
  Putin's Luzhniki Stadium address (2022)
    269, 271
  St Basil's Cathedral 14, 49, 303
  Sakharov Human Rights Centre 25, 180,
    240, 242
  Solovetsky stone, Lubyanka Square 79,
    80, 342
  statues 80–81, 296, 330
  suicide bombings 167, 170
  and Wagner group 311
  Paul Whelan's trial 206–9
  Ilya Yashin's trial 309–10
'Moscow Case', the 248, 249–50
Murakhtaev, Alexei 254, 257--8
Muratov, Dmitry 190–91
Murmansk, Russia 154, 269

NATO 6, 132, 155, 329, 336, 341
Navalnaya, Ludmilla 341
Navalnaya, Yulia 341, 343
Navalny, Alexei 8, 278, 285, 319, 328,
  341–2, 345
  arrests and imprisonment 13 (2015), 283–5,
    287, 339–40 (2021)
  poisoning (2020) 7, 84, 90, 276, 283, 289,
    312, 341
  death and funeral 7, 339, 340–42, 343, 344
  and Irina Slavina 255, 256
  his team 202, 247, 250, 257, 285–7, 288,
    340, 342
Nebytov, Andriy 77
Nemtsov, Boris 12, 16–17, 255, 280, 345
  Confessions of a Rebel 23
  denounces annexation of Crimea 18
  and Sergei Dorenko 158
  and Vladimir Kara-Murza 83, 85–6, 87, 328,
    332, 333
  lobbies US for Magnitsky Act 17–18, 87
  on march against invasion of
    Ukraine 15–16
  murder (2015) 7, 8, 13–15, 18–20, 24–6, 49,
    90, 101, 189, 201, 256, 276, 339
  trial of suspected murderers 20–24
Nemtsov (Boris) Foundation 328
Nemtsova, Zhanna 17, 18, 24, 50
Nesterenko, Alexei 93–5, 96, 317
Nesterenko, Georgy Yakovlevich 93, 94, 96
Nicholas II, Tsar 132
Nizhny Novgorod, Russia 16, 269
  death of Irina Slavina (2020) 253–5, 256,
    258–9, 260
  Gagarin Street 203
  World Cup (2018) 200–3
Nobel Prizes 191, 319, 331
Novaya Gazeta 161, 162, 172, 187, 190, 191,
  263, 275
Novichok (nerve agent) 115, 283, 341
NTV 185, 241–2

Open Russia (pro-democracy group) 238, 257, 328
Orlov, Oleg 317, 340
Orlova, Karina 25–6
OVD-Info (rights group) 308, 316
Ozerlag labour camp, Russia 97

Parnas (People's Freedom Party) 100, 102–3
Pasko, Grigory 220
Pavlov, Ivan 218, 219–20, 322
Perevalsk, Ukraine: school 231, 232, 233, 234
Peter the Great, Tsar 122, 123
  statue 296
Peter the Great (ship) 154, 155
Pliats, Leonid 73–7
Podlevskyi, Vasyl 74, 75
Podorozhny, Oleh 145
Poitier, Sidney 135
Poland 133, 182, 232
  Gazeta Wyborcza 196
Politkovskaya, Anna 84, 161–2, 166, 167–8, 172–3, 187, 189, 190, 246, 345
Popov, Admiral Vyacheslav 154, 155, 159
Prigozhin, Yevgeny 311
Proekt (investigative website) 219, 275–6
Prokhorov, Vadim 22–3, 326, 332
Pushkin, Alexander: *The Bronze Horseman* 48
Pussy Riot (punk protest group) 195, 299
Putin, Vladimir 17, 62, 95, 153, 269–70, 303, 317, 344
  and Yuri Andropov 99
  annexation of Crimea (2014) 6, 7, 13, 18, 133
  annexes Ukrainian regions (2022) 2, 232
  and the author 125, 128, 130, 160, 185, 188–9
  his autobiography, *First Person* 270
  and Beslan school siege (2004) 174–5, 176
  his Black Sea residence ('Putin's Palace') 284
  control of independent and state media 185–6, 279, 308
  and Covid epidemic 301, 302
  indicted by International Criminal Court (2023) 229–30, 234
  and invasion of Ukraine (2022) 1, 2, 3, 4–5, 6, 7, 8–9, 31, 71, 129–30, 183, 185, 188, 267, 269, 270, 298, 299, 301, 320, 336, 339
  and Islamic terrorism 344
  and Evgenia Kara-Murza 326, 333, 343
  and Vladimir Kara-Murza 325, 328–9, 330, 331
  and KGB 16, 222, 270, 279, 329
  and Mikhail Khodorkovsky 57–8, 87–8
  and *Kursk* disaster 154, 155, 156, 157–8, 159, 185
  and Alexander Lukashenko 35
  his Luzhniki Stadium speech 269, 271
  meets George W. Bush 164
  meets Elizabeth II 131
  and Memorial 81–2
  and Munich annual security conferences (2007, 2024) 341
  and Alexei Navalny 255, 283, 284, 285, 287, 288–9, 340, 341, 342
  and Boris Nemtsov 12, 13–14, 16, 17, 18, 22, 23
  New Year Address (2023) 320
  and Anna Politkovskaya's death (2006) 190
  and protests (2019) 237, 248–9, 250
  relations with Biden (2021) 217
  rewrites Russian constitution (2020) 243, 276–7, 302
  state of the nation address (2021) 287–8
  unpopularity 248, 280
  at war with Chechnya 161, 167, 170, 185
  and World Cup (2018) 202
  and Ilya Yashin's campaign 100, 101, 102, 309, 311, 312, 313
  and Boris Yeltsin 16, 130

Raab, Dominic 196–7
Rostov-on-Don, Russia 238, 239, 295, 296, 297

Safronov, Ivan 219–20
St Petersburg 51, 100, 122, 123, 125, 128, 130, 133, 166
  Elizabeth II's visit (1994) 131–2
  Kunstkamera (museum) 123
  Mariinsky Theatre 123, 125, 126, 128
  Alexei Navalny's headquarters 285–6
  Nevsky Prospekt 125, 132
  The Shamrock 123–4, 125, 126, 127–30, 132
  Shipbuilders' Institute 122–3
Sakharov, Andrei 79, 89, 203, 240
Salisbury poisoning (2018) 115, 199, 207
Saransk, Russia 199, 200
Sauer, Pjotr 321, 322, 323
Sebastian, Tim 63
Semyonova, Tatyana 234
Sergiev Posad, Russia 212, 213
Shelipov, Oleksandr 266–7
Shelipova, Kateryna 267
Shevchenko, Alina 235–6, 239, 244–5, 298
Shevchenko, Anastasia 235–9, 240, 241, 242–5, 261–4, 280, 295–9, 345
Shevchenko, Misha 237, 238, 239, 240, 242–3, 261, 263, 264, 295–6, 297, 298–9
Shevchenko, Taras 76
Shevchenko, Vlada 238, 239–42, 244, 261, 264, 295–6, 297
Shishimarin, Vadim 265–7
Siemieikina, Svitlana 40
Skovoroda, Hryhorii 339
Skripal, Sergei 115
Slavina, Irina 253–60, 269

Slavina, Margarita 253, 256, 259, 260
Smudge (dog) 63, 65, 81, 223, 302, 303, 304
Sochi, Russia 155, 156
    Olympic Games (2014) 223
Solzhenitsyn, Alexander 331
    Gulag Archipelago 50, 270
    Live Not by Lies 270–71
Spitsyna, Kristina 40
Sputnik, Russia 302
Stalin, Joseph 53, 61, 82, 94, 95, 97, 113,
    135, 256;
    and famine 316
    Great Terror 201
    purges 93, 94, 95, 97, 316, 317
    statue 80–81
Stavropol, Russia: riot (1992) 53
Sturgess, Dawn 115
Sullivan, John, US Ambassador to Moscow
    (2019–22) 218
Surgut, Russia 286

Tarusa, Russia 196, 223–4
TASS 114–16, 137, 221
Thatcher, Margaret 16, 86, 135
Tikhanovskaya, Svetlana 319
Tolstoy, Leo 46, 76
    Anna Karenina 126
Trump, Donald 216, 337
Tsvetaeva, Marina 196
TVS (television station) 87
Tylik, Nadezhda 156–7

Ukraine 49, 187–8
    Budapest Memorandum 132–3
    Russian invasion (2022) 1–6, 7–9, 27–31,
    71, 73–7, 104, 105, 107–9, 143, 145–9,
    161, 179–83, 184, 185, 188, 227, 229–34,
    260, 265–7, 270, 298–9, 307–8, 309,
    321–2, 335–9

United Russia (political party) 248
United States
    military aid for Ukraine 337
    Magnitsky Act 17–18, 87, 89, 90
    prisoner exchanges 217, 324, 342

Vakulenko, Volodymyr 149
Viasna (human rights organisation),
    Belarus 319
Vidyaevo, Russia 156–7, 158
Vilnius, Lithuania 258, 292, 297–8
Vizchenko, Lt Colonel 38
Volkov, Leonid 101, 287

Wagner group 311
Wells, Emma 16
Whelan, Paul 205–18, 222, 323, 324, 342
Willis, Bruce 135
Worcester Sixth Form College 47
World Cup (2018) 199–203, 269
Wyatt, Caroline 165

Yaroslavl, Russia 17, 18
Yashin, Ilya 18–19, 23, 25, 308–13, 345
    and Kostroma election (2015) 99–103
Yatsenko, Ilya 205, 208, 212–14, 217, 218
Yeltsin, Boris 44–5, 50, 53–4, 55, 62,
    128, 130
    and Chechnya 161, 185
    and Elizabeth II's visit to Russia 131, 132
    and Boris Nemtsov 16

Zakharova, Maria 113–14, 221–2
Zaluzhny, General Valerii 337
Zaporizhzhia, Ukraine: airstrike 40
Zelensky, President Volodymyr 1–2, 4, 240,
    319, 335, 337–8
Zhafyarov, Prosecutor Alexei 316
Zhukov, Egor 248, 249

A Note on the Author

Sarah Rainsford is an author and BBC foreign correspondent whose reporting career in Russia has spanned Vladimir Putin's two decades in power. After stints as BBC correspondent in Istanbul, Madrid and Havana, she returned to Russia in 2014 and was based in Moscow from then until her expulsion as a 'security threat' on 31 August 2021. She is now the BBC's Eastern Europe correspondent.